For My Boys

MIRROR BOOKS

All of the events in this story are true, but some names and details have been changed to protect the identities of individuals. This book contains graphic descriptions of child abuse, self-harm and suicide.

© Claire Throssell

The rights of Claire Throssell to be identified as the author of this book have been asserted, in accordance with the Copyright, Designs and Patents Act 1988.

All rights reserved. No part of this publication may be reproduced, stored in a retrieval system, or transmitted, in any form or by any means without the prior written permission of the publisher, nor be otherwise circulated in any form of binding or cover other than that in which it is published and without a similar condition being imposed on the subsequent purchaser.

Published in Great Britain and Ireland in 2025 by Mirror Books, a Reach PLC business.

www.mirrorbooks.co.uk
@TheMirrorBooks

Print ISBN 9781917439329
eBook ISBN 9781917439336

Production: Christine Costello
Cover Design: Chris Collins

Printed and bound in Great Britain by
CPI Group (UK) Ltd, Croydon, CR0 4YY

For My Boys

CLAIRE THROSSELL
with Michelle Rawlins

mB
MIRROR BOOKS

I am Invisible
By Claire Throssell

I'm invisible because the person that you see
Well, the person that you see is the one that I want to be
But instead I'm the one too afraid to look in a piece of glass
As all I can see is the wounds and the scars of times long past
I'm broken so deep inside it's invisible to everybody's eyes
Nobody can see in my heart and my mind, a smile is a perfect disguise
People cannot see what's hidden, bruised bodies, hearts and minds
Or comprehend how, in the name of love, too many are cruel and unkind
I don't know exactly when, my life became full of fear, criticism and stress
Stalked, harassed and bullied. Even told how I should dress
It took everything away that I needed to survive
And in the cruellest way possible he took my precious sons' lives
Here I am now, still standing but oh so incomplete
Forever now invisible, to everyone I meet

To Jack & Paul,
a love that will last to infinity and beyond

Foreword

BY MELANIE BROWN, PATRON OF WOMEN'S AID

I AM so honoured to write this foreword for Claire.

Claire is a Survivor Ambassador for Women's Aid, where I am a proud patron. I have always been so impressed by Claire's bravery and determination to change things for other women and children, despite the fact she has gone through – and is still going through – a living hell. Losing your children is a parent's worst nightmare, and to lose your children to your abusive husband who planned to kill them is beyond most people's darkest fears.

Leading the Child First campaign for Women's Aid, Claire has gone above and beyond for survivors of domestic abuse in her campaigning. She has spoken so incredibly at events, in front of politicians and has given interviews to raise awareness of the dangerous decisions that can be made in the family courts. I know how scary that can be and how much courage and strength it takes on a daily basis.

I will say this. Don't just read this book. Buy it for a friend, recommend it to others and pass it on to anyone you feel should read it – friends and family, anyone you know who can make a difference – if you know someone in the police, in the courts or in politics, ask them to read it.

To me, Claire is a heroine. She gets up every single day to raise awareness and to help others despite the fact she's living with overwhelming grief. I know she will not stop until women and children are safe from the hell she has endured.

Prologue

IT WAS almost seven o'clock on the evening of October 22. I was sitting in my mum's living room when the doorbell rang, swiftly followed by an assertive knock on the door. I froze. Call it an instinct or a sixth sense but I didn't want to walk to that door and open it.

'It will be the boys,' my mum, Pamela, said. 'Back early because the visit hasn't gone well.'

I flinched. Something inside me told me it wasn't my two precious sons, Jack and Paul. I knew it wasn't them because whenever they came back from visits with their dad, they would run through the door, pushing and shoving each other to get to me first to sit with me. They wanted to hug things out because they were scared, hurting, and just glad to be home - and away from him. In the lead up to that knock on the door, I was in the initial stage of looking for a small property for the three of us after finally leaving my abusive husband. Whenever I talked about it, Jack and Paul would say 'Wherever you are Mum, is home.' Even as I write this, just thinking about those words, another piece of my already shattered heart breaks a little bit more.

That morning, I had dropped both Jack and Paul off at school as usual. Jack was first. I hugged him goodbye.

'I love you,' I smiled.

'To infinity and beyond,' came my eldest son's instinctive response. Sitting in the car, I watched as Jack made his way into school. Unusually, he turned back twice, something he had never done before, and I gave him a reassuring wave.

Next, I drove Paul to his primary school. Before he jumped out of the car, he hugged me tightly. As he dashed through the playground, I called: 'I love you.'

Just like his big brother, Paul looked back and said: 'To infinity and beyond.' Now, as that loud knock reverberated through the house, I instinctively knew something was terribly wrong. Call it mother's instinct. I had to stand up. I walked to the door, my body trembling. When I opened it, a local policeman stepped into the light. I could see him clearly. It's a small town and I recognised him straight away. We had often smiled and said hello to each other, dropping and picking our children up from school. I saw the recognition in his eyes too. That was when his expression changed, and I simply asked: 'What has he done?'

The reply was quick and to the point. 'There's been an incident at the house. A fire. You need to come with me now to Sheffield Children's Hospital, where your sons have been taken. Jack has been able to talk but Paul's a little bit poorly.'

A fire, at what had been our family home… where Jack and Paul were seeing their dad. My mind swam but I knew, I knew he had finally done it, something so terrible, so evil, nothing would or could ever be the same again.

He had harmed my boys.

Within a minute we were in the car, my mum was next to me. As we hurtled around every corner, overtaking everything on the road, and being driven through red lights, four thoughts occurred to me. Why did I say to the officers to inform the central police control room when we went through speed cameras? Why didn't I do what my brain was telling me to do and that was to scream every time my mum said, 'It doesn't sound good for our Paul does it?' I couldn't bear to even consider what 'poorly' could really mean. And Jack was talking, but did that mean he was ok? Nobody knew, or at least, nobody was telling me.

In the back of the police car, whether it was fear or maybe it was how I was being thrown around the passenger seat, or maybe a bit of both, it was becoming harder and harder to hold down the jacket potato I had eaten for my dinner. But my main thought was, how has it come to this? How had my life gone so horribly wrong?

But to make sense of it all, I have to take you back to the beginning.

1

IN ORDER to go back to the beginning, I have to take you back to October 19, 1996. It's funny how life, or fate if you believe in it, transpires. A moment in time that changes the direction of your life. In many ways, life is like a coin, there are always two sides to it. It can be cruel and ironic, but on the flip side, kind and fortuitous. I think the coin of life for many of us is intermittently flipped or tossed, and with it comes unimaginable consequences.

My flip of the coin began during a family holiday to Kent when I was 24. I stumbled and hurt my left hand and when I got home to Thurlstone, on the outskirts of Sheffield, where I lived with my parents, it was still hurting. I couldn't pull the handbrake while I was driving, let alone grip or hold anything, without a searing pain coursing through me. Mum insisted I get it checked out at the hospital. I finally relented and drove myself to Barnsley Hospital. X-rays revealed I had broken a small bone at the top of my thumb that resulted in me being in a plaster cast that stretched halfway up my arm.

At the time, I was working at Carpet World in Sheffield. Preparations were being made for a new store opening in Wakefield, about 15 miles from where I lived. Whenever there was a new opening, staff from other stores were asked to go and help out at the opening event. My area manager asked if I could go and support on the day. I agreed if my plaster cast was taken off, I would go and help. If it wasn't, I would stay at the Sheffield branch.

My pot came off and the coin was tossed. So, on October 19, 1996 I arrived at the Wakefield store, ready for the opening, and that's when I met Darren Sykes for the very first time. This is the only time I will write his name. Even writing it now makes me feel physically sick. From this point onwards, I will only refer to him as he, him or my ex-husband.

My first impression of him was not great to be honest. He was roughly my height but without much hair. The only thing that struck me was how blue his eyes were and the length and thickness of his eyelashes. When he introduced himself, he simply told me he intended to be the top salesman of the weekend. He aimed to walk off with the prize of a mini-TV and champagne, as well as earn a lot of money in commission.

'Nothing is guaranteed in life,' I said, unimpressed by his arrogance.

'Some things are,' he replied, with a cocky smile that spread across his face.

As the day went on salesmen kept coming over to me at the cash till. 'He's asking if you're single,' one of them said. 'He wants to know what you're like,' another told me.

Some women might have been flattered, but I was annoyed and started to feel uncomfortable. Every time I went into the staff room, he seemed to be there, and constantly commented on my shiny, black shoes that weren't particularly unusual.

By the end of the weekend, all I could think about was going home and putting my feet up. I handed over the sales figures to my area manager, and just as he had so confidently predicted, he had earned the most, the Champagne and mini-TV were his. The area manager gathered us round for a debrief. As I looked for somewhere to sit, the cocky, self-assured salesman winked at me, nodding that there was a spare seat next to him. I ignored him, not in the least bit interested, and sat down on the other side of the room. But he was persistent, and as I was getting ready to go home, he approached.

'It's customary for the top salesman to take the cashier out for a drink,' he said, cockily, as he victoriously held his prize.

'Maybe it is, but not with this cashier,' I retorted, not in the least bit impressed. 'Goodnight.'

I thought that would be the last I saw or heard of him, but the next day a single red rose was delivered to the branch I was based at. The message read: 'I will send a rose to you every day until you say yes.'

And in one single gesture, the stalking or love bombing, as we now know it, had begun. Every single day for three weeks, I received a red rose. Despite the persistent nagging doubt about how he had discovered which store I worked at, against my better judgement I couldn't help but feel flattered by his determination. I began to question whether I'd been too harsh in my initial assessment and wondered if he was more interesting than I had originally thought. I even began to feel guilty for how offhand I had been. He was clearly trying to make an effort, after all.

2

AFTER FINALLY succumbing to his insistent pleas for a date, I suggested we meet at a quaint pub in Stocksbridge, about five miles from where I lived. I remember thinking if it didn't go well, I could make a run for it and drive home. But my plans fell to pieces when he insisted on picking me up.

'I can say hello and introduce myself to your mum and dad that way,' he said. I was slightly taken aback. It seemed a bit soon.

He also asked what the dress code was, which I thought was a little odd, considering we were just going to a local pub for a drink, but I decided he was trying to make a good impression.

Despite how keen he had been for me to go on a date, he arrived late, then blamed me for giving him such poor directions. It was in the days before sat nav or Google Maps. For years afterwards he told anyone who was interested enough to ask that it was his hormones, and not my directions, that led him to me. As first dates go, it wasn't anything special. I had two glasses of wine, and we took part in the pub quiz. After a couple of hours, we split the bill and he drove me home.

Despite how unremarkable our first date was, the following day at work, a huge bouquet of flowers arrived, with a note saying, 'Thanks for last night'. Hindsight is a wonderful thing. At the time, I remember being slightly taken aback, but not enough for me to put an end to it. It's only with the passage of time, I have questioned the excessive and very public gestures. I suppose I thought it was romantic. Only now do I realise that he was creating an image. A grand gesture for everyone to see. If only I had rebuffed him at the time, I would be a very different woman to the one I am today.

Instead, we carried on dating and three weeks after our first date, my sister and her husband invited us to their annual bonfire party. The plan was he would meet me at my house after work and we would go over together, but I got stuck in traffic and was almost two hours late. When I got home, he was sitting on his motorbike on the drive, freezing cold.

'Why on earth didn't you just go home?' I asked.

'I didn't want to,' he replied. 'I wanted you safe because I love you.'

I was stunned. We still barely knew each other. Unsure what to say in return, I quickly invited him into the house out of the cold, because I sure as hell wasn't ready to reciprocate the sentiment.

But if I thought this over-enthusiastic sign of affection was a one-off, I was sadly mistaken. Two months after we started dating, we were shopping for our mums' birthday presents when we walked past a jewellery shop. I innocently mentioned how pretty one of the rings in the window was. It wasn't meant to be anything more than an observation, an off-the-cuff remark. There was certainly no deeper meaning, but within seconds, and certainly before I could object, he was pressing the buzzer on the door, which required an assistant to open it before being allowed in.

'What is it you are interested in?' the assistant asked, as she opened the door.

'We would like to try on a ring,' he said.

I was stunned. This wasn't something we had ever discussed. We still barely knew one another, but on hearing those words the shop assistant went into full sales mode. The effusive welcomes were quickly followed by us being invited to sit down in comfy chairs. In less than a minute, the amethyst and diamond ring I had innocently commented on was brought over on a velvet display cushion. Suddenly, the conversation had evolved to the best seasons to get married and questions about our plans. I was enthusiastically encouraged to try on the ring, as the assistant explained how rare oval cut amethysts were. Of course it came with an eye-watering price tag.

I quickly thanked the assistant for her help and left. Once we were back outside, and I could catch my breath, I turned to him. 'It's too soon,' was all I could manage.

But he wasn't in the least bit deterred. On another shopping trip, he nipped into a shop and bought me an enormous teddy bear. Again, I was slightly overwhelmed. I wasn't even the type of person who collected cuddly toys.

By December 1996, he was heavily hinting about the possibility of moving into my parents' house with me and suggesting I should buy him a 'commitment' ring. I didn't do either. It was still too soon, and I didn't buy into the fact I needed to get him a piece of jewellery to show how I felt. But I did stay with him and my feelings for him began to develop. We spent Christmas Day at my parents' house after he had persistently nagged me to ask them. I had thought about what to buy him and settled on a rally driving experience with an instructor. He was over the moon and even cried saying how touched he was. In return, he bought me underwear and clothes. I remember looking at them and thinking they weren't my style at all and the reality was they weren't actually for me; they were for him. The silky underwear was very risqué and the clothes were clingy and very low cut. I immediately regretted opening them in front of my parents and remembered thinking, not only will he enjoy his own present, but also the ones he had bought for me. I didn't have the heart to say anything, though. It was Christmas Day, and the last thing I wanted was to cause any upset or offend him.

After the festive season was over, we talked about going on our first holiday together. He suggested we should be away for Valentine's Day.

'It will be nice to spend some time alone with you,' he said.

We were still in that early honeymoon period, and I was swept away in the moment. We opted for Gran Canaria. His mum suggested we should go for two weeks, but I said no. I had already booked two weeks off for the summer and wanted to keep some spare time for myself. But he felt differently.

'Why?' he quizzed suspiciously. 'I want to spend all my free time with you.'

I felt suffocated. We had only been together a couple of months, and I had already invited him on our summer holiday to Cornwall. I didn't think it was unreasonable to want to keep a few days back to spend how I wished, but he was moody about it. I refused to back down and let him sulk. A couple of days later, another huge bouquet of flowers arrived at work.

'I love you,' the message read. My heart softened and naively I instantly forgave him and on our next day off we booked the holiday to Gran Canaria.

I hadn't told anyone at work we were a couple, preferring to keep my private life just that. But five days before we were due to go away, I was working at a different store, in York, preparing for a new opening. Part way through my shift, I saw a woman walking through the store holding a giant Cupid-shaped balloon. She could barely keep hold of it; it was that big. I assumed it must have been a decoration for the store. But then the area manager for Manchester, Paul, pointed the woman towards me and suddenly everyone in the store started looking at me. My cheeks reddened as I realised this ridiculous monstrosity of a balloon, with a red rose attached to it, was for me.

'Guess who?' Paul grinned, coming up behind the florist.

When I didn't respond, he said, 'Don't worry. We gave him permission.'

Despite his previous, very public, grand gestures, I was still taken aback. We hadn't discussed telling colleagues about our relationship, but now the decision had been made for me.

I quickly called him and didn't hide how horrified I was.

But he just laughed. 'A princess deserves an audience,' came his reply.

I know some women would love the attention, but I was struggling with how all-consuming it was. I tried to reason with myself and to remember we were in those early stages – that was supposed to be when you wanted to spend every single minute of every day with one another wasn't it? I wondered if I was being a bit grumpy. After all, I had agreed to the holiday, and I hadn't called the relationship off, so I decided to just forget about it and look forward to our first trip away together.

It was good to escape the damp drizzle of Yorkshire and lap up hours of glorious sunshine. But we did have different ideas of what the holiday was for. I was keen to explore, go swimming, and relax. Whereas what he wanted was to have sex twice a day, and when he wasn't dragging me off to bed, his hands were all over me. He was constantly touching me, with no regard to who could see. Naturally, I protested, embarrassed by his overly physical affection, but he brushed off my objections.

'We're on holiday,' was his response. 'Don't be such a prude.'

After we got home, he spent more and more time at my parents' home of a weekend. On Easter Sunday, we had the house to ourselves and shared a bath. He had started calling me Lou, a shortened version of my middle name, Louise. He said he liked having his own private name for me, that no one else called me. He even saved my number in his phone as 'Baby Lou'. That Easter afternoon, not long after we had got into the bath, he suddenly announced, 'I want to marry you.'

I quickly changed the subject. Yet again, it was far too soon.

'Lou, I'm being serious,' he insisted.

'I'm not,' I retorted, firmly.

But he wasn't deterred and started asking more often about moving into my parents' house. I knew they wouldn't be keen. They didn't know him that well, and didn't like the idea of change, but he kept saying how it would mean we could spend more time together, especially as we both worked long hours. It would also be like a trial run before we bought our own place together. When I put off asking my parents, the narrative changed to *'Why aren't you asking your parents?'* This swiftly moved to accusations. *'You don't want me to move in, do you? You don't love me. If you loved me, you would speak to your mum and dad.'*

Worn out by his constant nagging, I spoke to my parents.

'Is this what you want?' my dad asked.

I didn't give them a definitive answer, but did explain it would mean he wouldn't have to do as much travelling, and it was hard trying to maintain a relationship when we didn't get to see a lot of one another.

Hesitantly, my parents agreed. I think more for my sake, as they could see how much pressure I was under. So, in June 1997, eight months after our first date, he moved into our family home.

It was nice to feel like our relationship was developing. We had trips away to the coast and turned the day he took part in the rally experience I'd bought him for Christmas, into a family occasion with his parents. But there were things that niggled away at me. When he was given a bonus at work, he asked me how he should spend the money.

'It's your money. You should choose how to spend it,' I replied. I think I was trying to find out what his priorities were. I soon found out. He had always loved motorbikes and he spent every penny on a custom-designed and hand-painted motorbike. It was exclusive, expensive and guaranteed to be the centre of attention.

'You need to get that microchipped and probably go back to Leeds,' I said, trying to hide the disappointment I felt and make him realise that I'd hoped better of him. I'd been hoping he would show his commitment to me by putting some of the money towards the deposit for a house.

Needless to say, he ignored everything I said, and two months later the bike was stolen.

'You should have told me what to do with the money,' he said.

I was flummoxed. I told myself he was just upset about the bike, but his assertions didn't end there.

'I bet you arranged for the bike to be stolen,' he accused.

'What,' I quizzed, horrified by how ludicrous he was being.

But my protestations didn't count for anything.

'You're a liar and a thief,' he snapped.

I was hurt, upset, confused. He had chosen to spend his money on himself, as opposed to us and our future together. I hadn't objected, aware it was his money and not mine to have any influence over. But even then, he had ignored my advice then blamed me when it all went wrong. I should have challenged his behaviour there and then or ended our relationship. I did neither. I'd never been someone to just give up. I had already invested so much time and emotional energy into us and persuaded my parents to accept him into their home. They had even allowed him to share my room, something they never granted my sister and her partner. They had made huge allowances, welcoming him into our family, so I felt like I couldn't just give up after the first hurdle.

He never apologised for calling me a liar and a thief. Instead, after wrangling with the insurance company for weeks on end and managing to secure the full value of the motorbike, he simply moved on, as though nothing had happened. I questioned myself, wondering whether I should have been more assertive and told him how to spend the money. If I had done that, maybe none of it would have happened. He certainly didn't say anything to convince me otherwise.

He did put more hours in at work, promising to put his extra wages towards our future. It wasn't an apology, but I read it as his way of making amends.

That summer we went to Cornwall on holiday with both sets of parents, my sister and her husband. I was happy to have a break and told myself the break would be good for us. And in many ways, it was. The weather was good, and we had some great days at the beach. But one night while we were out for dinner, Jon, a man I had dated very briefly walked into the pub with his partner. Instinctively, I felt nervous of a reaction from beside me. I knew how possessive he was and the last thing I wanted was for him to cause a scene. Then my mum spotted Jon too.

'I'm sure that's…' she started, unaware of how I was desperately trying to avoid a difficult situation. 'Aren't you going to…'

I cut her off. 'No, I'm not,' I said quickly.

I'd hoped he hadn't heard, but then Dad noticed Jon too.

'Isn't that who our Claire went out with?' he merrily chirped up, oblivious to my apprehension.

'Shit,' I silently thought, and knew I had no choice now but to acknowledge Jon.

So, as he approached our table with his new partner and family, I stood up and said hello. After a few polite exchanges, Jon and his party moved on. My parents were laughing about the chances of bumping into someone we knew on holiday. I hoped the event had passed without any aggravation. No such luck. Later that night when we got back to the tent, he asked question after question about my previous relationship, demanding to hear every detail. He only stopped when, exhausted, I stepped outside the tent to get some fresh air.

A couple of days later we were all on the beach, when one of the beach bowls we were using to have a game with, rolled in some bird droppings.

'It couldn't have happened to a better person,' he laughed at me. 'It's a good job it's on your ball and not mine.'

I tried to ignore his stupid comments but, the centre of attention, he was on a roll.

'Look at her standing there like a moron. Hurry up. We are waiting to play. Find a rockpool or something to wash it.'

Biting my tongue, I did exactly that. But I couldn't clean it all off.

'Come on,' he shouted. 'It's only a bit of poo.'

Made furious by his hurtful insults, my patience snapped. I walked straight over to him and put a tiny blob of the poo on his prized Tasmanian Devil T-shirt.

'Never mind. It's only a bit of poo,' I retorted, returning his taunts.

Instantly his mood changed. Instead of making me the butt of his jokes, he was furious.

'You dirty bitch,' he yelled, quickly pulling off his T-shirt and throwing it onto the sand, making retching noises.

'Pick it up,' he yelled at me. 'You can wash it, and it better come out or you are buying me a new one.'

How the tide had turned. For the rest of the afternoon our families tried to make light of the situation, embarrassed by his reaction, but it did nothing to sedate his anger. Even when they told him to drop it, he refused. I lost count of how many times he called me a 'silly bitch' or reminded me I would be forking out for a new T-shirt. As we walked back to the tent, you could have cut the atmosphere with a knife.

'Don't think you're sleeping next to me after what you have done,' he snarled.

I didn't argue. I was furious, but also deeply upset by how horrible he had been towards me. He refused to let me back into the tent we shared until I had been to the launderette to wash and dry his T-shirt. Dinner was a sombre affair. I didn't trust myself to say anything, knowing I would burst into tears, humiliated and hurt. That night I unzipped our sleeping bags that we had joined so we could sleep together and slept on the ground sheet alone. The following morning, I woke up and he was leaning up on his elbows, staring at me. I turned around to avoid his gaze, but then he started talking.

'I was watching you sleep and thinking about what my life would be like without you in it,' he said.

I wasn't prepared to just give in. 'You would get on with life, find someone better than me, and be happier.' My self-worth was at rock bottom.

'I love you too much, I would die,' came his reply.

It was the last thing I had been expecting. I had been expecting another rebuke, another insult, or another snide remark.

Instead, I got what I inferred as a long-awaited realisation that he really did love me, despite how vile he had been towards me. I told myself he'd realised he had gone one step too far this time. Yes, he'd been embarrassed by his T-shirt getting mucky, but had overreacted. He had apologised, he really did love me. He was sorry. That's what I wanted to believe and I forgave him, but no matter how hard I tried, I didn't and couldn't forget.

As we approached the one-year anniversary of our first date, things had settled down. The incident in Cornwall and the issues around the motorbike had been resigned to the past. He bought a car instead, and the rest of the insurance money was put into a savings account for 'our future' – a phrase which became embedded into his conversations, especially when he took on extra hours at work. His constant reminders that he wanted to get married were there too, but I did my best to divert the conversation whenever it came up, still feeling it was too soon.

For our anniversary, he had booked my favourite restaurant. We had been several times in the year we had been together, and there was one table I loved to sit at as it had a gorgeous view over the countryside. But for some reason he hadn't booked that table. When we arrived and I saw it was free, I asked if we could move. He refused, insisting the table he had chosen had a better view. I didn't push the matter, sensing there was something on his mind. He seemed quite edgy and when we sat down, he continually tapped his foot. And when we ordered our drinks, he insisted he was just having water, which was highly unusual.

I was about to tentatively question his choice, when he said there was something he needed to ask me. Before I could even respond, he got up out of his chair and knelt on the floor – on one knee. In his hand was a small box, holding the amethyst ring I had tried on nine months earlier.

'Will you marry me?'

The restaurant burst into applause, customers smiling and clapping, dozens of eyes looking straight at me, excitedly waiting for my response. It was the last thing I had expected, or particularly wanted, but blown away in the moment, I smiled and said, yes, despite something telling me this was exactly the opposite to what I should have been saying.

He told me he had bought the ring the day after our shopping trip when we had first seen it in January. It had stayed in the jewellers until he had moved into my parents' house and then he had hidden it in a drawer, under my bed, in the room we shared. I was stunned. Despite my refusal to get engaged nine months earlier, he had ignored my response and bought the ring anyway.

That night when we got into bed, I took the ring off, genuinely frightened I would catch the delicate setting on the sheets. But as soon as he realised, he got out of bed, picked the ring up from the bedside table, and put it back on my finger.

'You're engaged to me, and this ring found us,' he said. 'You must never take it off again.'

A few days later, he paid for me to have a manicure, so my hands and nails looked nice. He insisted on coming with me and choosing the colour.

3

ALTHOUGH THE proposal had come as a shock, the four months that followed were some of the happiest of our whole relationship. There were the phone calls to family and relatives, where we stood in my parents' hallway, ringing everyone, taking it in turns to speak. Their excitement for us fuelled my own happiness. His parents weren't as thrilled as I thought they would be, in fact their response was quite cool, but I didn't let that spoil the moment.

My parents however, were very enthusiastic and wanted to get to know my future in-laws. They booked a table at the Rose and Crown, where we had got engaged.

We decided to set the date for July 25, 1998 and booked St Saviour's Church in Thurlstone, where my parents and both sisters had got married. It was also where I had been christened as a baby. When we chatted about where we would make a home together, he was keen to stay local to where I had always lived. I was more than happy, but did keep asking him if he was sure, not wanting him to regret his decision. But he said he wanted to live near the countryside and was happy if his commute to work was less than an hour. I suspected he was also keen to make a break from his family, who he claimed were quite dysfunctional.

In November 1997, a month after we had got engaged, we were out for a walk, when he pointed out a modest detached house on a small cul-de-sac in Penistone, the village next to where we were living with my parents.

'That's the one,' he said. 'Where we should live.'

That afternoon, we went back to my parents' house and talked it over, as well as looking at the numbers, to work out if we could afford it. We could easily manage the monthly mortgage payments, but the stumbling block was the deposit. I'd always been a keen saver, but he wasn't. Money seemed to burn a hole in his pocket. After the debacle with the motorbike, he had wiped out all his spare cash. I had half the amount needed for the deposit in my savings account, but when I mentioned he needed to save more money, he got frustrated. The atmosphere changed and the excitement vanished. As we talked to my parents, he tapped his foot incessantly and when he realised things weren't going exactly how he wanted them to, he slammed his hands down hard on the table. Then, angry, he jumped up, knocking his chair over.

That night, my dad had strong words with him, and the following day at work, I received a huge bouquet of flowers – his signature apology. An expensive one at that. There wasn't a card and there wasn't any sign of a written or verbal apology. My work colleagues assumed he was making another grand, romantic, gesture and I was too embarrassed to correct them.

In the end we used the money my parents were giving us towards the wedding for the deposit. It wasn't how I would have wanted to progress, but I didn't want it to overtake the plans for the wedding either. So, like any excited bride-to-be I put all my efforts into our big day, planning everything from the flowers to the seating plans, and what food we would serve the guests. As our wedding inched ever closer, everything felt harmonious for a while, but that's not to say tensions didn't occasionally rise. Both sets of parents wanted to be actively involved and had set roles, but my mum often felt my future mother-in-law overstepped the mark. My mum was looking after the seating arrangements, but my mother-in-law wanted to be involved, despite having different jobs to do. When Mum would politely try and push back, my future husband would get angry and accuse my mum of being a bully. Naturally, my dad would get cross, and there were a couple of incidents when he warned my future husband about his aggressive tone.

A month before we were due to walk down the aisle, things began to get tetchy again. Money was tight and to top it off, the bank was taking an initial double mortgage payment. This coincided with him wanting an all-singing and dancing stag party in Dublin. We couldn't afford it, but he kept going on about it. I refused to just concede and eventually he reluctantly backed down, opting for something local. But two weeks before the wedding one of his mates suggested a joint stag do. I'd gently aired my thoughts, explaining there was no need for a second party, but I could tell he wanted to go. Unbeknown to me, on the day of the stag do, while I was at work, he had rung my parents and told them he was going. An almighty row broke out. Both my parents and fiancé had said the other wouldn't be welcome in each other's homes after the wedding. By the time I got home, my parents were furious. They were also devastated and told me they couldn't tolerate his behaviour and the way he spoke to them. I was torn between my fiancé and my parents, who had only ever shown me love and support.

'I think you should call off the wedding and sell the house,' Mum said.

Claire Throssell

I was crushed. This was supposed to be one of the happiest times of my life, but instead I felt like I was standing on the precipice of a disaster. By the time I went to bed, I was distraught and exhausted. My head was spinning, I couldn't think straight. My mind was a myriad of conflicting emotions and when my eyes finally closed, I still had no idea whether to marry the man I thought I loved or to listen to my parents who had only ever wanted the best for me.

In the middle of the night, my mum gently woke me. I assumed she had struggled to sleep too. We weren't a family who liked confrontation. But instead, she explained my future mother-in-law was on the phone. This was before the days of mobile phones so, half asleep, I went downstairs to where the house phone lived in the hallway and picked up the receiver. In the background I could hear my fiancé sobbing uncontrollably. He was calling my name and saying he was sorry, repeatedly. When he finally came on the line, he explained his best man, and his best man's dad had pinned him down and shaved off all his hair. A fight had broken out as he tried to stop them and he had been punched in the face. I couldn't believe what I was hearing. My mum and dad were already at their wits' end with him, and now he was begging for me to go and get him. By this point, both my parents were standing in the hallway, looking at me, as they overheard every word that had been said. My head was telling me to hang up the phone, but my heart was saying he was in pain and he needed me.

'I'll come,' I whispered into the phone. *How could I not?* As I clenched my eyes shut, I prayed I was making the right decision. My dad looked at me and his eyes were full of sadness, but instead of getting angry or upset, he said I wasn't driving the 25-mile journey to Leeds alone.

'I'll come with you,' he said, quietly but firmly, despite the fact he had to be up again at six o'clock in the morning. He hugged me tightly then went upstairs and got dressed. When we arrived at my future husband's family home, I insisted Dad went home, knowing I would end up spending the night in Leeds.

'I love you,' I said, before I got out of the car.

Dad nodded and smiled, without a hint of judgment. I felt an overwhelming sense of guilt, knowing how much it had taken for my dad to do this for me.

I knocked on the door and his mother answered. She and her husband had persuaded their son to go to the police, even though it was his best man and his dad who were responsible. Not only that, his best man was training to be a police officer. I suspected from how worn out his mum looked this wasn't the first time she'd had to deal with her son's drunken antics. Then, as we waited for him to get back from the station, his mum also told me she too had been on the receiving end of her son's temper in the past, explaining he had once held her by the throat and pinned her to the wall. She had forgiven him because he had been distraught afterwards. If only, at that moment, I had seen his behaviour followed a well-worn path and was unlikely to change. I will never forgive myself for not walking away then. Hindsight can be as cruel as it is insightful.

He was signed off work sick for two weeks due to his head and facial injuries and we came back to Thurstone to collect his belongings from my family home. My parents had made it clear he was no longer welcome there and I couldn't blame them. So, that's how we moved into our new house. Hardly the romantic and happy occasion I'd envisaged. It all felt like a bad dream. I was supposed to be getting married two weeks later, but I felt as though my life had been turned on its axis. I didn't know what to do for the best.

My wedding dress, and those of the bridesmaids, which had been made by my mum's best friend, were ironed and hanging on a rail, specially made by my dad, in my old bedroom. The men's suits were ready to be collected, as was the cake. Table plans had been meticulously created, checked and double-checked.

It should have been one of the most exciting times, filled with happiness, but instead we no longer had a best man, my parents were distraught, divisions had been created, and I had no idea what to do.

My parents were still talking to me, their loyalty and love held no bounds, but they had nothing left to say to the man who they had welcomed into their home only months earlier. They had gently told me they didn't want to come to the wedding, or even for it to go ahead. I was utterly heartbroken.

In a complete daze of confusion, I dragged myself through the next day, just praying a miracle would happen, and everything would get resolved. I went to work and left him in our new home, nursing his wounds. But that night, when I got home from work, his family were all in my new kitchen, organising my cupboards. Even that task, as mundane as it is, had been taken from me. I felt like a stranger in my home. The following night followed a similar pattern. This time when I got in, after a long day, his family were rearranging my living room, under my fiancé's instructions. I hadn't even been consulted.

'It would have been nice to have been asked what I thought,' I said.

His foot started tapping and I instantly regretted saying anything.

'You are so ungrateful,' he stormed. 'You should be thanking me for doing this when I'm injured. I'm saving you work and now you are causing my head to hurt.'

I knew there was no point in arguing. I was tired and just wanted everything to settle down. Then I questioned whether I was really being ungrateful, and guilt coursed through me. Ten days before the wedding, he called me at work.

'Is everything okay?' I asked. 'I'm really busy.'

'Guess who I'm sat next to right now?'

I knew there was no point trying to push the point that I would get into trouble for taking a personal call, as it would put him in a bad mood, and I would bear the brunt of it later.

Hoping to get the conversation over and done with, I said: 'Your mum.'

'No. Try again.'

Of course it was 'try again'.

'If it's not your mum or sister, then I have no idea who it is,' I replied.

'It's your Mum. I rang her this morning and paid for a taxi to bring her to the house. I didn't drive because of my head injury. I've also left your dad a message asking him to drive over after work. What do you think to that?'

What did I think? I really wasn't sure. On the one hand I was pleased that my mum and dad were being shown the respect they deserved, but the other part of me was still furious that he had treated them so badly in the first place. I was also wondering how on earth he had persuaded my mum to go to the house, but deep down I knew she would have only done it for me.

Dumbfounded, I didn't know what to say. I certainly wasn't

going to thank him for putting my family through days of upset or praise him for now being kind to my mum. But I knew I had to say something and it would have to be something he wanted to hear. In the end I went for middle ground.

'Oh, that's a surprise,' I finally said, through gritted teeth. 'I'm glad you and Mum have put your differences to one side and are talking again. Just Dad to make amends with now.'

'Yes, I'll talk to him when he gets here. Your mum is going to meet him at the gate first. Oh, and don't worry about coming home and cooking tea. Your mum is going to do it as I'm feeling dizzy again, because of my head injury.'

I put the phone down feeling utterly flummoxed. I was astounded by his audacity, as well as being worried about my dad, who had no idea what had happened. I wasn't sure if he would be as forgiving as Mum, either. I drove home from work that night, not knowing what I would be walking into, but to my surprise I was greeted with a bear hug from my dad and a smile from my mum. As we all sat down for dinner, my heart leapt. The wedding, as I'd envisaged it, was back on. I hoped this was a turning point and life would calm down. We had a house which I felt sure would become a home. I think I knew, by then, he wasn't my soulmate, but I was too old to believe in fairy tales and had made the decision to get married. The future was set.

The night before our big day, I went back to stay at my parents' house. The following morning, July 25, 1998, I woke up to clear blue skies and the sun was shining. It was the only Saturday that month it hadn't rained. A good omen. As my parents woke up and my sisters arrived, the house filled with an infectious excitement. I was getting married! My eldest sister, Christine, a hairdresser, set my hair, as well as that of all five bridesmaids, who had silk flowers and ribbons weaved into their plaits. They all looked absolutely beautiful. As they had their photographs taken by the vintage cream Model-T Ford car we had hired, I got dressed into my white satin gown. The dress was long sleeved with pearls sewn into the bodice, and I had agreed to a long train, as my soon-to-be husband had asked for one. At the time I'd simply thought it was romantic that he had thought about how I would look on our special day. Only time would tell me a different story. After everyone had left for church, and there was only Dad and I remaining, the house was suddenly quiet and calm. Dad poured me a brandy.

'You look beautiful,' Dad said, his eyes glistening.

'Thank you,' I whispered.

'It's still not too late to change your mind,' he said. 'You can always come back home.'

I didn't say anything, but a pang of sadness coursed through me, that my dad's heart wasn't full of happiness on the morning of his daughter's wedding. I also felt ashamed that I had put my dad through so much, but more than anything, I wished I was as brave as him. Although I knew my dad would support me if I called the wedding off, I believed in my heart of hearts the moment had passed. I just kept thinking 'it is too late'. We had bought a house, I was in my dress and there was a church full of people waiting for me. I didn't trust myself to speak. Dad must have read my mind. Without saying another word, he came over to me and wrapped me into a tight hug, and as I fell into his strong, protective, arms I felt safe.

'All I have ever wanted is for you to be happy,' he whispered, before releasing me from his embrace and pouring us both another brandy. After we drained our glasses, Dad took my arm.

'Time to go,' he smiled, as he led me out of the house.

A few minutes later we had arrived and were getting out of the car. As we stepped onto the church path, the Millhouse Green Male Voice Choir, which my dad was a member of, burst into song. The lyrics of *Love Changes Everything*, filled the air and my heart filled with joy. My dad had been a founder member of the choir and most of the members had known me since I was a baby. I turned to my dad and gripped his hand a little tighter. His bottom lip trembled, and tears rolled down his cheeks.

Somehow, despite how emotional we both felt, we managed to walk into church. My dad had arranged the choir without telling a single guest, apart from myself, so as I walked down the aisle, the congregation were surprised by the gesture, which brought them to their tears as the beautiful harmonies and heartfelt lyrics filled the church.

As I looked at my future husband, his face erupted into a huge smile, an indication, I assumed, of how happy he was. In that moment, all my worries faded away, and I felt like the happiest woman alive.

4

THE DESIRE to be loved and to feel happy shouldn't be anything to worry about, but I know I'm not alone in saying it can also lead you down a dangerous road. The first few years of our marriage were okay. When I say okay, I mean they weren't horrendous.

After the wedding, my new husband suggested we should have joint bank accounts.

'It will be easier to pay the bills,' he insisted.

I naively believed he was being thoughtful. Again, hindsight is a wonderful thing.

Initially there wasn't much money left at the end of each month to play with and the wedding and deposit had wiped out all our savings. We couldn't afford a fancy honeymoon so my parents agreed we could borrow their caravan to go to Cornwall.

But when we arrived, he decided he wanted to buy a £400 stunt kite. I was baffled. He knew how tight money was and in the whole time we had been a couple, I had never so much as heard him mention a kite, let alone fly one.

'That's half of what I earn in a month,' I said, flabbergasted.

But my protests fell on deaf ears. He refused to stop going on about it and despite my concerns about how skint we were, he went and bought it. I was furious that he could be so selfish. That night at dinner I barely spoke to him as every mouthful of food stuck in my throat and a knot formed in my stomach.

For the next year, I saved as much as I could, determined that we could eventually enjoy the fancy honeymoon we'd never had. I suggested a holiday to the Dominican Republic, but he scowled at the thought.

'I was hoping we would have a baby,' he said, matter-of-factly.

It's not that I didn't want to become a mum, I really did but I had just started a new job at Mamas and Papas and just wanted to have one luxurious holiday before we began a family. For the first time, I dug my heels in and reluctantly he eventually agreed and we booked the holiday for July 2000.

But in March 2000, I developed a serious kidney infection, something I had struggled with since being a teenager. I was completely wiped out and was in so much pain I could barely get up off the couch. I assumed he might take care of me, but how wrong I was. He was more disgruntled that I couldn't take care of him. A feeling of disappointment enveloped me. I was deeply hurt that the man I had married and vowed to spend the rest of my life with didn't once lift a finger to help me, let alone keep on top of the household chores.

As always, my dad was worried. On his day off, he came around to the house to check on me. He found me fast asleep on the couch and a huge pile of dirty dishes in the sink as well as scattered across the worktops. As I slept, he started cleaning up, then waited for his son-in-law to get home from work.

'You need to pull your socks up,' my dad reproached, appalled by how little he had done to help me. 'A real man looks after their wife when they are poorly.'

I suppose I shouldn't have been surprised that my dad's words were ignored.

'Make sure you tidy the house in case your dad comes round,' my husband said a couple of days later as he got ready to leave for work.

Then, almost as an afterthought added: 'Keep taking the antibiotics. You will be fine.'

But I wasn't fine. An hour later, I collapsed in excruciating pain on the landing between our bedroom and the bathroom. Somehow, I managed to crawl downstairs and ring my dad. Luckily, he was at home and came straight round. He took one look at me and called for an ambulance. I was hospitalised for five days.

My dad was furious that my husband hadn't thought to stay with me when I was so ill or even had the foresight to ask my parents to come and look after me. But I knew the real reason – he hadn't lifted a finger around the house in all the time I'd been ill and didn't want my parents to see how unsupportive he had been. My parents rang him to explain I was in hospital. That night, he arrived at the hospital, raging.

'Is this your way of getting attention?' he ranted, not seeing my dad, who was sitting in a chair in the corner of the room.

'Where are the doctors? I want to find out what's really wrong here.'

I was too weak to even think about arguing, but my dad was livid. Instantly he was on his feet.

'Don't you dare speak to my daughter in that way ever again,' he warned. I had never seen my dad lose his temper but the fury in his voice was palpable. 'You and me are going outside of this room right now,' he stated firmly.

When they returned there was no more talk of speaking to doctors, but nor was there an apology. Instead, another bouquet of flowers arrived the next day, which did little to dampen my sadness. When I was discharged, it was my dad who picked me up from hospital and stayed with me until my husband came home from work.

But again, I tried to put it behind me. I was married now and really wanted our relationship to work. Spring turned into summer and the holiday to the Dominican Republic turned out to be idyllic. I got to dive to the bottom of the ocean and it gave me an overwhelming sense of being at peace with myself that left tears rolling down my cheeks. During the holiday, we didn't have a single cross word, and I felt the happiest I had in a long time. When we got home, my husband suggested one more big holiday, on the condition we try for a baby afterwards. But his tone wasn't one of love, more of an order.

'I'm not prepared to be blackmailed into having a baby,' I rebuffed. What I didn't say was I was beginning to have reservations about starting a family when I knew how volatile he could be. In September, I ended up taking a position at head office at the same company as my husband, which meant we were working and living together. Christmas of 2000 passed, surrounded by friends and family, but on New Year's Eve, the atmosphere changed. I had booked a restaurant to bring in the New Year with my family, but suddenly it wasn't to his liking. My husband made out that he would only eat the food I cooked for him and was still getting used to more elaborate meals.

'You know I don't eat many foods and I'm still only trying the food you cook for yourself off your plate, so it's your fault not mine that I don't like restaurant food,' he moaned, sounding like a petulant toddler.

The words hung in the air as I tried to fathom how a grown man could come out with such utter nonsense. Not prepared to just bow down to his childlike protests, I calmly explained he had known for months where we were going and had eaten in the restaurant before without any complaints.

'You'll cancel it right now because I'm not going,' he snapped, his mood instantly changing.

'Don't go then,' I retorted, furious. 'We'll go without you.'

Within seconds he had run downstairs. I heard him lock the front door, and just as quickly he was back in our bedroom, wildly dangling both sets of keys in front of my face.

'You are not going anywhere,' he shouted, his cheeks reddening. 'Understood?'

It was a statement, not a question. Not prepared to put up with his outlandish behaviour, I pushed past him, went into the spare room and found my suitcase. I quickly started pulling my trousers and blouses out of the wardrobe and haphazardly threw them into the case. But as I picked out my clothes, my husband raised his hand and rained down a hard blow to my arm with his clenched fist. Once, twice, a third time. This was the first time he had ever assaulted me.

'Stop it, you b*****d,' I yelled.

'Well, stop being a mad bitch then,' he retaliated.

Ignoring his rebuke, I picked up the suitcase and ran downstairs. I reached for the home phone and dialled 999.

'Police please,' I panted.

As quickly as his temper erupted, it dissipated.

'What the hell are you doing?' he asked, worry etched across his face. 'I was only joking.'

Moving to the front door, he added: 'Look I'm unlocking the door now. Just put the phone down.'

'Please,' he pleaded.

I looked at my arm. The red blotchiness from the impact was already turning purple. To this day, I don't know why, but I put the receiver down.

'I'm going to go and get ready,' I said quietly, as I took my keys off him. 'You can do what you like.'

In the bedroom, my heart racing with adrenaline, I changed into a red velvet halterneck top. My arm, which was now swollen and throbbing, wasn't a dissimilar colour.

'Cover up,' he insisted, when he saw what I was wearing.

I refused. I still had some spirit in me.

'If it makes you feel uncomfortable seeing my arm, that's your problem, not mine,' I retorted.

'If you hadn't booked that restaurant, none of this would have happened.'

There it was again – absolving himself of any blame and pushing it all on me.

Despite his despicable actions, he insisted on coming to the restaurant. When my dad saw my arm, his face turned red, and my husband's turned white. I went and spoke to my mum but could see my dad speaking to him. Their body language told me all I needed to know. My husband didn't say another word for the rest of the night and we didn't wish each other a Happy New Year.

As the clock struck midnight, I knew things would never be the same between us again.

5

ANOTHER SPRING came round and we started talking about making some renovations to the house. The downstairs living space was quite small, but I knew the building work wouldn't be cheap.

'I'll do the labouring,' he insisted, still trying to make up for his past despicable actions.

We had booked a holiday to Venezuela and the nearby Isla de Margarita and a couple of days before we were due to go, I announced I was going shopping to buy some new clothes.

'I'll come,' he insisted.

I didn't have the strength to argue, but knew how the day would turn out. Everything I bought was only paid for when he had approved it. I didn't object, determined to avoid a confrontation so close to our trip. But when we got home, my parents were waiting for us.

'We've got bad news,' my mum said.

'What is it?' I asked.

She gently explained that my husband's nana had died. Understandably, he was very upset. I did my best to comfort him and when he suggested we cancel the holiday, I didn't object. I wanted to support him.

A week after the funeral, I realised my period was late. Unsure how I was feeling, I did a home pregnancy test and was stunned when the two lines turned blue. I had come off the pill as it was impacting my periods, but we had always been careful, apart from one night.

'Hit the bullseye in one attempt,' he boasted, smugly, as we looked at the white plastic stick.

It was the last thing I wanted to hear. There was no emotion or words about how wonderful it would be to have a family together and I berated myself for being so stupid. It's not that I didn't want to become a mum or have a baby of my own to love and cherish, I just wasn't convinced my husband was the person I wanted to have a family with. We went to see my parents, but instead of oozing happiness, I burst into tears as I broke the news.

My dad wrapped me in his arms. 'It's going to be all right,' he whispered.

'What's the matter with you,' my husband snarled, as it dawned on him my tears were not ones of joy.

My dad squeezed me a little tighter. 'It's a lot to take in,' he said, trying to soothe me.

My mind was a flurry of conflicting emotions, but my gut instinct told me this wasn't a good marriage to bring a baby into. In a daze we told my sisters and nieces. They were ecstatic and I tried to feed off their delight, but a niggling feeling gnawed away at me.

I didn't tell my colleagues and I told myself I was waiting for the three–month scan, just to be sure everything was okay. In the end, though, that decision was taken away from me when he walked into work wearing a T–shirt with 'I'm going to be a dad' emblazoned across his chest. I resigned myself to the fact I just needed to make the best of things. I was quite traditional and wanted our baby to be brought up in a home with a mum and dad, just like how I'd been brought up. I suppose I also hoped that having a baby would change my husband and bring out a kinder and more considerate side.

Then one morning in November, I was at home when the phone rang. It was my dad.

'I've bought cream buns for later when I see you,' he said.

'Lovely,' I grinned. 'What are you up to today?'

'I'm off to do my computer course.'

I smiled. He was 65 and still learning new skills.

'Love you Dad,' I said before we finished the call.

But at two o'clock, I was standing at the sink washing dishes, when I saw my husband walking down the garden path towards the house. He should have been at work and instinctively I knew it was bad news.

'What's happened?' I asked as soon he walked through the door. 'Why are you home?'

'I need you to sit down and stay calm otherwise we might need to call a doctor,' he stated.

'Stop being dramatic and tell me what's happened,' I said impatiently.

'Claire, your dad's died.'

I couldn't make sense of what he was saying. I thought it was a horrible joke, but as the words sunk in, and I saw how serious he looked, I started to shake. I'd only spoken to my dad five hours earlier.

'How?' I muttered, barely able to think. I could still hear my dad's voice from this morning, promising to bring cream buns this evening.

'We don't know yet. Your brother-in-law just told me that he had died.'

I swallowed hard, but there was a lump in my throat, which refused to move.

'Do you need a doctor?' he asked.

'Will he bring my dad back?'

'No.'

'Then I don't need a doctor.'

The phone rang, making us both jump.

It was my sister, Carolyn, or Caz as she was known. She was checking I'd heard the news.

'We're going to Mum and Dad's now, if you want to come over?'

A few minutes later, we pulled up on my mum and dad's drive. I saw Dad's car. I instinctively thought, *He must be home.* But the thought vanished as quickly as it arrived; the cruel reality consumed me. In the hallway both my sisters were waiting for me. Their arms extended, we came together as one, our heads resting on each other. The next few days passed in a complete blur. It's hard to explain the pain of losing a parent, apart from feeling utterly lost in life, like a safety barrier had been swept away.

A postmortem revealed Dad had died from a heart attack. A few days later I had my five-month scan. I wanted to be excited, but the tears that flowed down my cheeks as I watched my baby's shape appear on the screen, were out of sadness not joy. My dad would have made the perfect grandad.

'You're having a boy,' the sonographer explained.

Only then did I manage the smallest of smiles, because I knew my son would be named Jack, after the grandad he would never meet. But over the following months, I struggled to come to terms with Dad's loss. We had always been so close, and I felt like a part of my heart had been ripped apart. Days at a time would

For My Boys

pass, and I couldn't tell you what I had done. I was living on auto-pilot.

In February 2002, I turned 30. A celebratory meal was organised, but as I walked into the bar at Cubley Hall, I had to steel myself. The last time I had been in the pub was for my dad's wake.

Then when I was six months pregnant, a female member of staff made an official complaint of sexual harassment against my husband.

'She's lying,' he claimed, when he told me about the accusation.

'I only ever speak to her when she is outside the warehouse having a smoke. And there are always other people about.'

I eyed him suspiciously. I knew how much my husband loved the sound of his own voice and could be over familiar and had no filter.

'I had to stand close to hear her because of my poor hearing,' he said, rationalising his own actions.

I felt torn. I wanted to speak to the woman and ask her what had happened, but an official investigation was launched so no conversations were permitted. It was a month before the verdict came. It was concluded my husband had not committed gross misconduct, but was advised not to approach the woman again. Less than two months later, he left the company, claiming his colleagues hadn't been supportive, but my gut instinct was they had seen right through him.

At eight months pregnant, I was diagnosed with a condition called cholestasis, which affects the liver, and can be particularly dangerous in pregnancy. I was rushed into hospital and induced. On March 31, 2002, at 4.30am, my beautiful boy, Jack Graham Sykes, was born.

Claire Throssell

As soon as the midwife placed Jack in my arms, it was love at first sight. As I took in every detail of his perfect little face and every one of his tiny features, I couldn't believe how much love was in my heart. I didn't realise I could love someone so much. It was all-consuming, and the happiest I had ever felt. I couldn't imagine ever feeling more protective towards another human being and I cherished those early days, just gazing at my son, in between feeding and nursing him to sleep. It was the most magical feeling.

I had to stay in hospital for six days while I recovered, and doctors kept an eye on my liver. During that time, my husband hardly visited and when he did, he didn't stay for long, opting to delay his paternity leave until I got home. It meant he wasn't there to change a nappy, to help with Jack's first bath or help to wind our son after a feed. So, it was the midwives who brought me cups of tea while I was feeding or helped me soothe my baby. One midwife told me: 'All a baby needs is to be close to their mother's and father's hearts and hear them beating just for them.'

Those words never left me, and now haunt me.

It was in those first few days that, although I was overcome with love, another onslaught of emotions coursed through me. The grief I was feeling after losing my dad hit me like an avalanche as I realised he wouldn't be there to hold his grandson or watch him grow. And I felt unbelievably sad that Jack would miss out on all the love my dad would have offered.

On the day Jack and I were due to come home, our boiler broke down. My mum suggested we go and stay there, but my husband refused, nor would he call a plumber. Instead, he and his dad spent all day repairing the boiler, so it was 8pm by the time he came to collect me. And to top it off, he arrived with clothes and underwear that didn't fit, so I ended up having to leave the hospital in my nightdress. I had stitches and collapsed veins in my arms due to the amount of blood nurses had taken to check my liver. Exhausted, and still in pain, I burst into tears, to the complete bewilderment of my husband.

He did have two weeks off, though, and was keen to show Jack off like a prize. When visitors came to the house, he would hold Jack in his arms and announce: 'Look what I made. Look at how clever I am.'

'He's not a toy,' I quietly admonished, horrified by his behaviour, but too exhausted and weak to cause a scene. It's a shame he didn't give our son the same attention when he cried or needed a nappy change. Instead, he was all too quick to hand our baby back. During that fortnight, it was his sister's 30th birthday and a family meal had been planned at their parents' house in Leeds. I was still very sore and weak but told myself it would be nice for family who hadn't met Jack to see him for the first time. What I didn't realise was taking a newborn baby out isn't as easy as you imagine. Jack woke up halfway through dinner and needed feeding. Afterwards he wouldn't settle and cried when anyone tried to hold him. Not sure what else to do, I took Jack upstairs, hoping he would fall back to sleep if he was away from all the noise. Not once did my husband come upstairs to check if we were okay, let alone bring me a drink or the dinner that I had completely missed. I think I knew that my idea of teamwork was very different to his. On the way home, he explained how much fun he'd had playing cards with his family, telling jokes and having a laugh.

'They missed not being able to talk to you,' he said.

'I was only upstairs,' I said, desperately trying to bite my tongue. 'They could have come to see me.'

That night set the tone of how little my husband was willing to be a hands-on parent. I learnt quickly; I was going to be navigating the baby years by myself. Nobody gives you an instruction manual of how to cope with those early days. Nor do they tell you in the first few weeks it feels like you are winning in life if you manage to dress you and your baby, and get out of the house, by 10am. Or that if you eat garlic and onions, while breastfeeding, your baby will be up most of the night screaming with agonising tummy cramps – and that you might have to cope with that alone, while your husband sleeps on, oblivious. But somehow Jack and I got through those first few months, and no matter how hard it was at the time, I knew I'd been given the greatest privilege in life when I became a mum.

As I became more confident in my own skills as a parent, I suggested to my husband that maybe I could use the family car, instead of him taking it to work where he was employed as a carpet estimator. Also, it meant if I wanted to go anywhere of an evening I had to empty the car of heavy carpet samples.

When Jack was six months old, I had to take Mum to view care homes for my gran. Every night, my husband would let me empty the car of all the cumbersome samples, never lifting a finger to help me.

'This is becoming a real pain,' I said. 'You need to get a work van.'

As usual he imploded. Picking up the remote control, he launched it at my head. I ducked and it hit the newly plastered wall.

Furious, I picked up Jack.

'I'm going to collect Mum,' I said. 'And that wall is now your problem.'

For My Boys

I didn't tell my mum how difficult things were at home. It hadn't even been a year since Dad had died and now she was trying to find a care home for her mum. My conscience wouldn't allow me to give her anything else to worry about. A few days later I was told a works van had been ordered, but in the meantime, he had been given a black sports car to use.

'So, you can go and swap the hundreds of samples out of your precious car into the one I have to use,' came the order.

I should have refused, but I didn't have the energy. I was just relieved to have my car back.

Jack's christening was planned for a couple of weeks later, but a few days before, my husband had given me a lift in the interim sports car. As I got out, I tripped over the seatbelt, fell onto the pavement and ended up with a broken kneecap. I hadn't imagined being in a plaster cast for Jack's christening, let alone while trying to look after a baby, but thankfully I could still walk, and the day was as beautiful as I'd hoped. We had booked the reception for the same country pub where we'd held Dad's wake and been for my 30th birthday celebration. I managed to carry Jack to the field where my dad's ashes had been interred and with my son in my arms whispered how much we loved and missed him.

That Christmas, we spent the day itself as just the three of us, but as New Year's Eve approached, the atmosphere changed again. I didn't want to go out. Jack was only nine months old, and I knew I would miss my dad. In the past we had spent so many years bringing in the new year together. I suppose I knew my husband wouldn't understand, but I wasn't prepared for the onslaught of insults he hurled at me as December 31 rolled into January 1.

'You don't dress sexy anymore,' he sniped after a few drinks.

I didn't respond, desperate to avoid a row, but I was also hurt by his lack of compassion and empathy. I'd had a baby, my body had been left battered and bruised, stretched and stitched beyond all recognition. On top of that, I was the one who was always up in the night, surviving on a few hours' sleep at a time. Then, to put another nail in my self-esteem, my unbelievably insensitive husband added: 'If you put any more weight on, don't expect me to be interested in you.'

And of course, he then turned the conversation around to make it all about him.

'Now that you have got Jack, you have got what you wanted, and you aren't interested in me.'

I didn't even know where to start with that conversation, and there was no point trying after he'd drunk himself into such a state. But his words still cut deep. Over the following year, I lost five stone. Then, as my return date to go back to work edged closer, his usual comments of: 'I've been working all day. Someone has to keep the money coming in', gradually stopped. The irony was I had been on full pay during my maternity leave, but as I prepared to go back to work, the rhetoric changed.

'I don't want you to go back,' he whined. 'And not to Carpet World.'

I resented his words. He'd left the company under a dark cloud, but that wasn't my storm. I had always loved my job.

Then, suddenly, after him trying to say he had been the one keeping our family together financially, he changed tactics.

'Take your time going back to work,' he insisted. 'And why don't you look more locally for a job. Something that would suit us as a family.'

The statements pierced me. There had never been an 'us' when he was trying to dig the knife in about him being the only one working. Then it was only 'me' and 'I'. But he wore me down with his continual nagging, coupled with how guilty he made me feel about the fact I would be working an hour away from home, and I wouldn't be there for Jack. And that was the straw that broke the camel's back in the end. I handed in my notice, but even that wasn't enough for my husband. When my leaving card, full of lovely, heartfelt messages and gifts arrived from my colleagues, he sulked. He hadn't received a single thing when he'd left.

When Jack was 18 months old, I applied for a job at Voluntary Action Barnsley, less than ten miles away from where we lived. My mum had agreed to look after Jack. She adored her grandson, but I also knew it would help fill the huge void left in her heart and life, since Dad had died. On the day of the interview, Mum and Jack came with me in the car and when I went into the building, they stayed outside on the grass. I could hear Jack screaming, but had to just pretend he wasn't my child, as I was being interviewed (Sorry Jack!). I was delighted when I was offered the job and I can safely say my years working for the organisation and with so many amazing people, were the best of my professional life. It felt like a turning point. I had lost weight, loved being a mum and adored my job. But as had become the pattern, when things were going well for me, my husband began to sulk, like a spoilt toddler, who was having a temper tantrum because he wasn't the centre of attention. By then we had mobile phones, and the number of calls I received from my husband every day increased with each week that passed.

'When will you be home? Who have you been talking to?' The questions were always on the same theme.

Claire Throssell

When digital banking began to become the norm, he switched our accounts to online, but somehow always forgot the pin codes and passwords for me to have access. I was just left with my debit card.

At the same time, he started saying he wanted another baby, which I was slightly taken aback by after how much he'd griped about my attention being focussed on Jack, and not him. I had always envisaged having at least two children. I was the youngest of three and loved having my sisters, but I was worried about what my husband's intentions really were and our marriage wasn't the loving partnership I had hoped for. *Did he just want me at home? Another way of being in control of me?* I was also scared of developing cholestasis again. He would always come back at me with the sentiment that it would be nice for Jack to have a brother or sister, which I struggled to fight against.

In the end the decision was taken out of my hands. During one night of love-making, I am convinced he was deliberately careless. I must have been worried, as I rang the GP surgery the next day, and spoke to a nurse. She tried to reassure me saying at the stage I was in my cycle I was in the 'safe window'. She did ask if I would like the morning after pill, but it felt wrong, so I declined the offer. Five weeks later I found out I was pregnant and when I showed my husband the result, the response was a resounding: 'Yes. Get in!'

As the news sank in, despite worrying about the state of my marriage, I was delighted, knowing how much love and joy a baby brings. Although I knew in my heart of hearts that my husband wouldn't change his ways, I couldn't help but hope that maybe that now he had also got his wish to have a second baby, that he would go a little easier on me. How foolish I was.

When I was eight weeks pregnant, we were doing some renovation work in the bathroom. I was passing him a hammer, when I stood on some unsupported, exposed plasterboard and fell through the ceiling. I managed to grab one of the beams, but then my hand slipped, and I plummeted downwards, landing on the kitchen floor in a heap. Shaken, my first thoughts were for my unborn baby, but instead of showing any form of concern, my husband's first thoughts were about how the fall would affect him.

'You're an idiot,' he yelled. 'This will hold all the work up now.'

Thankfully our baby hadn't been harmed and I'd escaped with just cuts and bruises. But after the insurance company came out and surveyed the damage, they discovered the wrong asbestos had been used in the cavities and needed to be removed. This was obviously my fault, and yet more insults were hurled at me. But as well as being attacked with words, this time a kitchen chair was hurled at me.

Jack, who was at my side, put his tiny little hand in mine.

'Oh dear, Mummy. Never mind,' he said, full of love and affection. 'I still love you.'

These were the exact same words I used, when Jack had done something naughty. I prayed the only learnt behaviour Jack would replicate was from me, not his father, who after hearing his son's response, turned round and walked out the door.

While the bathroom renovations were finished, Jack and I spent a lot of time at Mum's house, where a voice was never raised and furniture never thrown. It became a place of sanctuary. Thankfully, the first pregnancy scan showed our second baby was growing nicely, unaffected by my fall through the ceiling. The next scan revealed we were having another precious little boy. I was told I would have to be monitored closely to keep an eye on my liver. Fortunately, I didn't get poorly and on January 9, 2005, I went into labour.

This time there were no medical emergencies. I didn't need any pain relief. It was all very serene. My husband opted to stay at the foot of the bed, as opposed to holding my hand. It was a midwife who wiped my forehead with a cool flannel and dabbed my lips with water, all the time softly speaking reassuring words of comfort. Then, without any trauma, our second little boy entered the world. As the midwife placed him in my arms, once again the love I felt for this tiny little thing consumed me.

'You're a bloody hero,' my husband announced, tears falling down his cheeks.

But when I looked up at him, I felt nothing. Instead, I held my son a little closer, amazed I had so much love to give to a second child. I think it was then that I realised a mother's heart is as vast and deep as the ocean. Part of me was entwined in both of my sons forever. The umbilical cord may have been cut, but the bond was unbreakable. We named our son Paul David Sykes, and like his big brother he was perfect in every way.

While I had a bath, my husband held Paul for the first time and when I got back to my bed, a huge bouquet of four dozen roses, sprayed blue, had been delivered. He took a photo of the flowers, as opposed to of Paul, and sent a text to his family and friends, announcing the news.

Although the delivery had passed without any problems, doctors decided I should stay in hospital overnight, just to keep an eye on my liver. My mum brought Jack, who was nearly three, to the hospital to meet his baby brother for the first time. I was sitting on the bed when they arrived, and just like he always had, Jack came and snuggled in next to me. I carefully placed Paul in Jack's lap and as I gazed down at them both, I felt so lucky to have two beautiful boys. My life felt complete.

The following day, I was discharged. This time I had packed my own and Paul's clothes to go home in and Jack was with us, dressed in a little shirt. As we walked down the corridors, full of smiles, we must have looked like the perfect family, but it's true what they say – appearances can be deceiving.

6

AFTER PAUL was born, I told my husband in no uncertain terms we were not travelling back and forth to Leeds visiting family. I was very happy for relatives and friends to come to us, but I had learnt by experience that I just needed to be at home and adjust to having a new baby to care for. I also was adamant that Jack needed time to get used to having a baby brother and the new family dynamics. I'd worried Jack might resent his brother demanding my attention, but like me he quickly adjusted. He would sit next to me while I fed Paul and would laugh when his brother burped afterwards and talk to him gently when Paul cried. Jack was the perfect big brother in every way. He was caring, kind and instantly protective.

He was such a warm-hearted little boy but it made things difficult when he started nursery just after turning three. When I dropped him off, he would sob and cling to me and we would both end up in tears. I found it so hard as the nursery staff would coax him away from me, his little body quivering. In the end my husband offered to take him. Interestingly, Jack didn't cry once as his dad said goodbye.

I planned for Paul's christening, hoping this time, things would all go smoothly. Apart from wrangling both boys into their outfits, after Paul was sick and Jack decided he didn't like his clothes, we finally got in the car to drive to St Saviour's Church in Thurlstone.

It was a lovely family service and all the children sat around the font. Jack wanted me near him, and I was more than happy to sit on the floor with him. My husband had been holding Paul, but within minutes a flash of white indicated my youngest son was furiously crawling towards me. That moment set the tone for their short lives; they always wanted to be near me.

That September, when Paul was eight months old, my husband was going away on a trip with the choir he attended. Mum and I used the opportunity to take the boys to Lytham St Annes, near Blackpool, for a few days. We loved being on the coast, the walks along the pier, and playing on the beach. We would fly kites, let the boys play, have picnics on the sand and paddle in the sea. It was idyllic and every year we made more and more memories. I'll never forget Jack's astonished little face the first time we took him to the circus, or his look of awe as he saw the trams, let alone how much he waved and grinned when we took him on a horse and carriage ride. Those trips away were always full of joy and as the years passed, associated with love and laughter; a place to be happy and a place to feel safe.

Paul's first Christmas was also the first year Jack understood the magic that came with Father Christmas. It was just enchanting. It was also the year Paul's passion for running emerged. He learnt to run before he could walk. We'd bought him a little toy vacuum cleaner and he spent the whole day running up and down the lounge, his tiny hand clamped around his new toy. I embraced every single moment, knowing how short those special years are.

A couple of weeks later, we celebrated Paul's first birthday in a flurry of cakes, candles and more toys. I couldn't believe how quickly the past year had gone. I'd thrown myself into being the best mum I possibly could be and my two boys had filled my life with love and happiness.

Unfortunately, my dedication to our boys wasn't replicated in my husband. His attention was always somewhere else. When Jack was three, his dad had taken him to a haberdashery store to buy a patio cleaner. Instead of giving his attention to his curious toddler, who saw the shop as an Aladdin's cave of curiosities to explore, my husband stood and talked to the female shop assistant. In doing so, he failed to keep an eye on our eldest son, and didn't spot the fact the shop owner's dog wasn't on a lead. Nor was he close enough to intervene when the dog clamped his jaw around our little boy's arm, or able to help when Jack, terrified and screaming, tried to pull his arm away as the dog tightened his grip.

The first I knew was when I got a phone call at work from my husband telling me I needed to come home straight away. He told me a watered-down version of what had happened to our precious little boy. That night as I held our son, who had puncture wounds up his arms, in my lap to ease him to sleep, there was a knock at the door. It was the police. The dog owner had called them. It was then I heard what had really happened, as opposed to what my husband had told me. I was shaking with rage, as I thought about how terrified Jack must have been and that it could have all been prevented if my husband was only doing what should have come naturally to him – looking after our son. It took every ounce of my self-control not to scream and shout. It was only the fact Jack was sleeping on my knee that stopped me.

It was decided that although the dog had bitten Jack, and therefore the offence came under the Dangerous Dogs Act, our son was not being properly supervised, so the owner was only given

For My Boys

a warning. I know accidents happen and it only takes a second for a child to get into danger, but my husband had lied to me and showed little remorse. It took days for me to even look at him, let alone speak to him.

Eventually things did go back to a kind of normal for us, but other parts of family life had started to become strained and, while my love for the two youngest members of my family grew with each day, my husband's relationship with his own parents was deteriorating. The previous year, they had celebrated their Golden Wedding anniversary. They had decided young children couldn't come to the celebration, so Jack and Paul were the only members of the family who weren't there. It was upsetting but I didn't kick up a fuss – I didn't need to; my husband was angry enough for the four of us. Then just after Easter, the year Paul had turned one, my husband came home from work in a vile mood. No hellos for me or the boys. Instead, he immediately began ranting.

'I was going to call in to see my parents today, but they were out,' he stormed.

'Where were they? Were they doing something?' I asked innocently.

But my comment, which was intended to diffuse the situation, inexplicably fuelled his bad mood. Throwing his briefcase on the floor, my husband dropped onto the couch, firmly crossed his arms across his chest, and began tapping his foot – a sure sign, he was incandescent with rage.

'My mum told me it was none of my business and wouldn't tell me,' he finally responded.

'Oh,' I said, not sure what else to say. His mum regularly called me for a chat.

'Well, that's the last time I'll show any interest in their lives. They're clearly not interested in mine,' he scowled.

I noted he'd said 'mine' not 'ours', making the situation solely about him, but I knew better than to say a word. I just hoped with time the situation would resolve itself.

But that summer his Grandad, his father's dad, who had been frail for years, passed away. I'd always remembered my husband saying he needed to stay in touch with Grandad 'to stay in his will'. So, I was shocked when he initially stated he wouldn't be travelling to Inverness for the funeral. Despite the bad feeling with his parents, my father-in-law went out of his way to persuade my husband to travel to the final farewell. When he finally agreed, nothing was actually said, but it was clear the boys and I wouldn't be going. I was secretly pleased. It would be hours and hours in the car, which would be hard for the boys, and I really didn't want to be in the middle of a war with my husband and his parents.

Afterwards, he received a formal letter stating he had been included in his grandfather's will. I overheard phone calls between my husband and his dad, who said he'd had to work hard to keep him in the will and hoped the money would be used wisely.

'I'll be giving it to charity,' he sniped.

I knew he was lying -- my husband would never give money away. And I was right, it was used to landscape the front and back garden, and to have a dining room table and chairs, none of which my in-laws ever saw as my husband's relationship with them disintegrated.

That September, his parents went away for their wedding anniversary. While they were on holiday, my husband came home from work one day, his face like thunder. I couldn't face a row so I ushered the boys into the car and drove to my mum's house. After an hour, my phone bleeped. It was a text message.

'*Get home now.* Don't you dare take my boys away from me.'

Terrified of making the situation worse, I did as he ordered. My heart was racing as I nervously walked through the front door.

'Don't you ever take Jack and Paul away from me again,' he yelled, his face flushed with anger.

Then, he told me that before he'd come home that evening, he had used his key to let himself into his parents' house. He'd gone into his dad's office, unlocked the filing cabinet, and found his grandad's will.

'My sister is getting double what I am,' he stormed.

'And my mum is getting even more than that.'

I didn't say a word, appalled by his actions.

'Nothing to say?' my husband jeered.

Still, I remained silent, knowing no matter what I said would only make matters worse.

'Well, I have,' he stormed.

With that he picked up the phone and rang his parents' landline. When the answer machine clicked in, he began ranting down the line.

'This is the last time you will ever hear from your son again. Goodbye.'

Then he hung up.

'Still got nothing to say?' he urged.

'Actually, I have,' I said desperately trying to keep my tone calm and neutral. 'Only thieves go into people's houses without them knowing. What you've done is wrong. It was your grandad's decisions, not theirs. Also, they won't understand the context of the message because you haven't told them you have just broken into their home and read the will.'

As soon as the last words passed my lips, a pen was launched at me, only missing by a centimetre or so. Despite his temper causing me to flinch, I stood my ground.

'You have violated their privacy, and you have violated their trust. Also, they might think you have harmed yourself and you mustn't let them think that, especially when they have just returned from their holiday.'

My husband just glared me.

'I haven't broken in. I had a key,' he retaliated. 'From now on, they are dead to me. I want nothing more to do with them.'

His parents never saw Jack and Paul again. They did try ringing, but my husband refused to answer the phone and forbade me to speak to them. I did receive a letter from my husband's parents, saying how much they were missing him, but when I showed it to my husband, he just screwed it up and threw it in the bin. He made it very clear I was not to get involved.

The same month, Jack started the primary school which adjoined the nursery he had attended and grown to love. But the night before Jack was due to start school, he woke up in the early hours, calling for me.

'I'm frightened,' he whispered, as I sat on his bed, gently stroking his hand.

'Everything will be okay,' I promised, doing my best to reassure Jack. Whenever he was nervous, I always sang *Somewhere Over The Rainbow* to him to calm his nerves, so that's what I did, until he fell back to sleep.

The next morning, I dressed Jack in his little school uniform, which I had laid out on the bed the night before, but when I tried to take the obligatory first day photo, he refused to smile. I didn't want to make the morning any harder for Jack, so I let it go, and did my best to gee him up for school, but as we arrived at his classrooms, his little face crumpled. Bursting into tears, Jack clung to my legs.

'This is your fault,' my unsympathetic husband admonished, in front of all the other parents. 'You shouldn't have come.'

My heart sank. Of course, I was going to bring our son to school on one of the biggest milestones of his life, but instead of supporting me, Jack's dad opted to publicly criticise me. I blinked back the tears and reassured my scared little boy he would have the best day, as the teacher coaxed him into school. I'll never forget the fear on his worried little face as I waved goodbye.

That night, I started a routine that would last their entire lives. After their baths and they had cleaned their teeth, I helped the boys into their pyjamas and the three of us snuggled up in my bed and I read them a story. I wanted them to feel secure in the knowledge that no matter how hard their day had been, they could fall asleep feeling safe and loved. Now, all these years on, as I write these words, I have to pause. Closing my eyes to recall those precious moments, I can still smell the scent of their shampoo as they rested their heads on my shoulders.

While the routine helped, it still took Jack a while to settle in school. He was such a homely boy and would rather have been with me. He saved his biggest smiles for when I picked him up at 3.15pm. Paul, on the other hand, was coming on leaps and bounds. With a big brother to emulate, he did everything quicker than Jack had. He ran before he could walk, climbed before he could scramble, and was brimming with confidence. In soft play centres, he would dash up to the top of the climbing frames without looking back, once losing his trousers halfway up, but didn't even pause. His ability to learn amazed me, and while I was helping Jack with his homework, Paul would sit on my knee at the kitchen table, quietly absorbing it all. Desperate to be just like his big brother, he copied everything Jack did, and as a result knew his two and five times table before he started nursery.

As a mum, I learnt very quickly that in many ways children are like computers, in the sense you only get out of them what you put in, and you have to give before you receive. A child's trust must be earnt along with respect. Throughout Jack and Paul's early years, at the time they were most receptive, there was very little input or involvement from their dad, unless it was to show them off like performing puppets.

And yet again, his ambivalent attitude caused one of our sons to get hurt. This time it was Paul who fell victim to his dad's negligence. He had taken Paul to some friends and one of them had placed a scalding hot black coffee on the top of a CD rack to cool. My husband had left our 18-month-old son to play in the room by himself while he was busy talking in another room. Paul, the eternal climber, had pulled himself up onto the CD rack, causing the mug to topple. Luckily it had missed his beautiful little face, but the red-hot liquid had splattered down his arm. Once again, I came home from work, to one of our children hurt and upset.

Horrified, by how neglectful my husband had been, I no longer trusted him with our two, lovely, boys and I went back and forth arguing with myself about leaving him. He definitely wasn't the man I'd hoped he would be and I was annoyed at myself for falling for his charms, for not seeing how controlling and manipulative he was. But I also knew, hindsight was an amazing thing. Humiliated, isolated and scared with no self-esteem, I couldn't just leave. There seemed to be barriers that I couldn't overcome and I didn't know how I would cope if I tried to walk away from our marriage – it felt like such a mountain to climb.

Financially, my husband controlled our bank accounts. We had a joint account, but he monitored every penny I spent, and since the boys had come along, I earned much less. I had no idea how I would save enough cash to just leave, and I certainly wouldn't be able to manage the mortgage on my salary. I would have to move in with my mum, and I knew my husband wouldn't just let us go, in fact I had no doubt in my mind he would make my life a living hell. My husband definitely had the power, physically and financially, and I felt trapped.

So, I did what so many other victims of what I now know was coercive control do. I stayed and hoped things would get better. I focussed on being the best mum I could and showering the boys with all the love and support they needed. Their dad's blase attitude to parenthood meant it was me they called out to in the night, if they woke up feeling unwell or had a bad dream. It was never their dad's side of the bed they appeared at, asking for a cuddle. I didn't mind at all and I cherished every moment with my sons, knowing they wouldn't be children forever. Being a parent is a gift and one I treasured with all my heart. So, when it was my arms they ran towards, whether they were happy or sad, angry or laughing, hurt or proud, I was always there.

Throughout his life my dad had often said: 'It's the hand that rocks the cradle that rules the world. It's a big responsibility but also the biggest joy and greatest honour to raise children.' Never a truer word said.

But that didn't mean I was ready to bring more children into this situation and so when Paul was two, and my husband asked if we should try for another baby I responded with a firm 'No'.

For weeks he pestered me, but my mind was made up. I loved Jack and Paul with all my heart, and I felt complete. Besides which, I was virtually raising them alone. My husband had never done any of the hard work, let alone looked after them in a way that instilled any confidence in his abilities as a father. Changing a nappy, washing clothes, or clearing up toys was not in his thought process. I could just about juggle and didn't want that perfect little bubble with my boys to burst. So, when I announced I was going to see the GP about a sterilisation, my husband was horrified. But I needed to take control of my life and my body, knowing there was every chance his slack idea of contraception would result in me falling pregnant.

In the end, things flipped on their head; call it karma or some form of divine retribution for my increasingly controlling husband insisting on coming to the doctors with me. When I explained to the GP that I would like a sterilisation, reassuring him my life was complete with two children and I didn't want to risk any more complications with my liver, he nodded acceptingly. Then the doctor turned to my husband.

'Why are you putting your wife through a major operation when it's quicker and easier for you to have a vasectomy?'

'She doesn't want to have any more children,' he coldly sniped in response.

'Well since you are married, do you see yourself having children with anyone else in the future?'

'No!' came his retort.

'Then why the reluctance to have a vasectomy, which is a very simple procedure?'

My husband had never appreciated being confronted or questioned.

Staring at the doctor, he said: 'Well you have it done first and I'll go to whoever you go to.'

I suspect he thought the doctor would then back down, but maybe my GP had dealt with characters like my husband in the past, or maybe he sensed things weren't great in my marriage.

'I had the procedure at the medical centre in Lundwood, so I can make you an appointment there as soon as possible,' he responded, very calmly.

A date was arranged, and my worries were placated. I could have hugged the doctor.

But as one problem was solved, another was waiting in the wings. Cutting his ties with family seemed to accelerate how poorly my husband treated me and our boys. He never spoke to his mother again, and I'm not sure what reaction he was expecting from me, but I couldn't support his behaviour. And with each week and month that passed, he became more emotionally needy and when he didn't get what he wanted, it was me that suffered.

7

IN THE years after Paul was born, I started suffering with severe stomach cramps, and I was eventually diagnosed with endometriosis. For a long time, sex had been very painful and always resulted in me bleeding. Not that this ever seemed to concern my husband – as long as he got his fix, that's all that mattered.

When Jack was five and Paul was three, he was going away on his annual choir trip, this time on a boat. I had an exploratory colposcopy procedure booked for the following week, but the night before my husband was going away, he hinted he was in the mood for sex. He could never go more than two days without wanting intercourse and I knew if I said no, he would make my life a misery, insult me, be bad-tempered and make it clear I was failing as a wife. In his eyes, being married meant sex was freely available whenever he wanted it, with no consideration to how I felt. But that night, I really couldn't face it and, in one of the very few times I dared to refuse his animalistic urges, I said no. I knew, from years of experience, how much having sex would physically hurt and I wouldn't be able to sleep afterwards. As predicted, the punishment came quickly. Glaring at me, my husband couldn't resist insulting me for daring to refuse his sexual needs.

'Thanks for not giving me my leaving present,' he barked sarcastically.

When I didn't retaliate, he stuck the boot in a bit further.

'You're as attractive as a limp lettuce anyway,' he snarled, before stomping downstairs, like a petulant toddler. When he finally came to bed much later, he slept as close to the edge as possible.

The next morning he made a big show of hugging the boys. Holding Paul in his arms, he said: 'I'm going to miss you baby boy. Are you going to miss me?'

'No,' Paul replied, without an ounce of malice.

Needless to say, the goodbyes my husband and I exchanged were cool and distant. But, that evening, I had just got home after picking the boys up from school and nursery when my mobile rang. It was him.

'I've forgotten my choir uniform,' he said. 'You will need to bring it to the boat.'

The boat was 60 miles away in Hull.

'The boys can wave me off on my big boat.'

As usual, there was no consideration of how late I would get back, or the fact the boys would be exhausted. And I knew if I refused, there would be hell to pay. So, I piled Jack and Paul into the car, and collected mum, as I knew there was a chance the boys would have to stay in the car while I went through the terminus security. When we arrived at Hull, I took the uniform to the ferry security. I was told by the guard, my husband had decided not to come and collect it personally, despite the 120-mile round trip I had felt obliged to do. When I got back in the car, I could see my husband on the deck waving frantically. I asked the boys if they would like to get out and wave at daddy. They both refused.

'Are we going to McDonald's now?' Jack asked, desperate for the quick and easy dinner I'd promised, after being forced to abandon their normal teatime routine.

Maybe I should have insisted they got out of the car to keep their dad happy – that way I would have spared Jack the later barrage of contempt when he was accused of loving McDonald's more than his father. But how could I have predicted those words?

And soon it was my turn to face his ire again. On the day of my colposcopy, the atmosphere between myself and my husband was still frosty, to say the least. I'd told him I was going to the hospital alone, but again my wishes didn't count for anything and he got in the car. I suspected he didn't believe there was anything wrong with me and hated the fact he might not be in control. It didn't even occur to him that I might not want him there while I went through an incredibly invasive and personal procedure, where all sense of dignity had to be abandoned.

Apart from one female nurse, everyone else in the room were men. They were all clustered around the screen watching as a cotton bud gently touched my cervix, which split open and started to bleed. I later discovered all my defective cells had reacted to the solution they had used to examine me. The room fell silent. Even my husband was lost for words. I was told I would need gynaecology surgery within days. In a state of shock, from the brutally undignified procedure and the news, I quietly got dressed, thanked the medical staff, and left.

I couldn't find it in me to speak to my husband for days. He'd gone off to Hull after hurling a barrage of insults at me, been mean to our eldest son on his return, and then attended a deeply invasive appointment against my wishes. Of course, a huge bouquet of flowers arrived, and my meals were cooked, but as always, none of it came with an apology, and what was left of my fragile self-esteem shattered.

For My Boys

I knew my husband wouldn't be able to find the courage to say sorry. Narcissists never can. This was anybody's fault but his, but I didn't even have the strength to fight. Alongside endometriosis, I was diagnosed with pelvic inflammatory diseases and precancerous cells had been found on my cervix. I was told sex wasn't advisable and I knew my husband would be furious because the one word he refused to accept or obey, was 'no'. He would hate the fact that he could no longer call me a liar when I said I didn't want to have sex because it was too painful. His spiteful accusations that I was 'frigid' and 'cold' could no longer be used as a justification on his part.

Gaslighting wasn't a term that was used 20 years ago, but my husband was the master of it. After being vile to me, he would brush off his insults by saying, 'I didn't mean it' or 'You just took it the wrong way, like you always do'. This was still my fault, as it was me with the 'problem'.

So, rather than trying to comfort me, my husband quite brazenly, without a single care, told me: 'You will have to think of different ways to be able to keep the desire alive'. This wasn't a suggestion, but an order. Oral sex was demanded at least once a week and I felt violated. In a healthy relationship, based on love and respect, you would turn to your partner, but he had left me utterly broken.

I had to undergo a laparoscopy, so surgeons could take a closer look at my ovaries. It was discovered the lining of my womb had come away and completely covered my left ovary. My right ovary and bowel were also partially covered. It all had to be lasered away, which then revealed a lump on my left ovary, which was removed at the same time, taking away half the ovary, too. It was no surprise I had been in so much pain.

The surgeon was stunned I'd managed to fall pregnant at all and once again, I felt so blessed to have my wonderful boys.

In between treatments, we took the boys to London for the first time. Everyone we met, from the doorman at the Savoy to the police officer outside Downing Street, commented on the boys' huge, happy smiles and their gorgeous blue eyes. When we went into Harrods, a member of staff saw me staring in admiration at the Grand Piano. 'Have a go,' they encouraged.

I had always been a keen pianist, but still felt very self-conscious as I sat down on the stool, with Jack and Paul by my side. Then as soon as my fingers touched the keys, everyone and everything melted into the background, as I had the privilege of playing this magnificent instrument. I enjoyed every second and when I finished, a group of people were applauding. I looked round to see what was happening.

'Mummy, they are clapping us,' Jack whispered.

I was stunned when I realised customers had stopped shopping and gathered around the piano to hear me play. Jack and Paul were equally as shocked, as they sat perfectly still, either side of me.

That late September summer evening, we walked through Green Park, collecting pinecones, sticks and conkers – I drew the line at worms and snails, despite my sons' protests. As ever Paul was racing down the pavements, birds taking flight as he speedily approached. On the bus on the way back to the hotel, Jack asked me if I would massage his feet.

'They are pssting, Mummy,' he said, using his own unique word for 'aching'.

Instantly, Paul tried to copy the word, but of course it all came out the wrong way.

'Piss. Piss, Piss,' he repeated, his voice increasing by a couple of decibels each time he repeated the word. The bus erupted into laughter, as my youngest and unintentionally funny son gave end of the day commuters a reason to smile.

After we returned home, my treatment continued. For six months I needed steroid injections, given alternatively into each of my ovaries. I was prescribed medication to stop the heavy blood loss I had suffered with for years, but a second laparoscopy revealed new blood had attached to my scar tissue – a hangover from my previous operation. I started gaining weight, which my husband was all too happy to point out.

'All that money I have spent on clothes, and now they don't fit,' he scowled.

And whenever I put on something that was slightly more loose-fitting, he would look at me in disgust.

'That's not a dress, it's a tent,' he said, coldly. 'Look at yourself in the mirror. You need to think more carefully about the food shopping and stop eating treats from your mother. You are two fat cows together.'

The insults were cutting and relentless in equal measure.

But while the words left my self-esteem even more battered, my thoughts were consumed with my health problems. Unsure the treatment was working, as I was still in a lot of pain, I paid for a private appointment to secure a second opinion. I told my husband I wanted to go to the appointment alone, but of course I was ignored. I knew there was no point in arguing, it would make no difference, and I didn't have the energy to cope with the argument that would follow. The doctor agreed the treatment wasn't working and suggested I change hospitals urgently. He also explained it would be virtually impossible for me to lose weight while I was having steroid injections and all I could do was maintain a healthy, balanced, diet. He pointed out I had two young children so it was no surprise, on top of the treatment, I was so tired. The doctor also reiterated that it was close to miraculous that I had coped for so long without much stronger pain relief drugs and hadn't spent weeks on end in bed. But, throughout the appointment my husband continually interrupted the doctor, until the specialist put his pen down.

'This is your wife's consultation not yours,' he said firmly.

I just put my head down, not daring to vocalise the fact I had been criticised for months about my weight and not wanting to have sex. I knew I would pay for the fact my husband had been chastised and as soon as we left the surgery, the accusations started.

'You enjoyed that didn't you?'

'What?' I asked, exhausted by his self-centred proclamations.

'The doctor taking me down and making me look bad.'

I didn't retaliate, knowing if I did, I would pay the price – the best option was to stay silent. Once again, I retreated into myself, but I had underestimated his rage and a split second later, I heard his foot connect with my shin and a sharp pain soared through me. The pain was so severe, my leg gave way, but as I tumbled, my arm caught on a metal bar that surrounded one of the industrial size council bins. I looked down and there was a huge gash on my arm, which was already bleeding. I tried to stand up, but my leg was paralysed. A few people had seen me tumble and started to come over.

Humiliated, I allowed my husband to help me up, not wanting anyone to realise he was the one responsible. I went back into the

GP surgery and a nurse cleaned up the cut before telling me I should get checked out at A&E, in case my arm needed stitches. I didn't go to hospital, but I didn't get back in my own car either. My husband drove off in our car so I rang a taxi and went to my mum's house, where she was looking after the boys. I told her everything and she was understandably furious. Mum's gut instinct about my husband had been right all along. I told Jack and Paul we were having a surprise sleepover at Nannan's house, which they were delighted about and happily went along with. I turned my phone off and we all snuggled up on the sofa. For a few precious hours, life felt peaceful and tranquil, but it didn't escape me that Jack, Paul, and myself now all had scars on our arms caused by the man that was supposed to love and protect us. They were the only visible scars he left. The rest are too deep to see.

The next morning, I dropped the boys off at school, deliberately waiting until I knew my house would be empty before going home. When I turned my phone on, I had 30 missed calls from my husband. I wasn't surprised, he could never leave me alone, even when he was the one who had caused the problem. Within minutes, the house phone rang. I knew who it would be, and I knew the calls wouldn't stop until I answered, so when I picked up the receiver, I didn't even say hello.

'I've rung the landline because you're not answering your mobile,' my husband announced, matter-of-factly.

Mustering up all my courage, I vocalised what I'd been thinking about all night, when sleep had evaded me.

'That's because I have nothing left to say, except that the marriage is over. I can't and won't take any more.'

And then before he had a chance to respond, I put the phone

down. Half an hour later, he arrived at home holding his signature apology bouquet of flowers. I couldn't even bear to look at him.

'I'll change,' he promised tearfully. 'I'll do anything you want. I can't live without you.'

I didn't know what to think. He might have needed me, but could he love me if he could cause me so much pain? His pleading went on, the tears carried on falling and his promises were repeated and repeated, over and over again. Worn down, I finally said: 'If you go on an anger management course, I'll stay. If you don't, we will go.' He booked an appointment at Mind, but I will always regret not taking my boys and leaving that day.

My leg and arm didn't heal, so I booked an appointment with the GP.

'How did you get these injuries?' she asked kindly.

I looked down. I had always been a terrible liar and knew I couldn't look her in the eye.

'I fell down the stairs,' I muttered, hating myself.

The doctor didn't argue with me but gently explained I should have had my arm stitched at the time. My leg was badly bruised, but thankfully nothing had been broken.

'If you can grin and bear it over the next couple of weeks, they should both heal,' the doctor explained.

'Everything but my marriage,' I silently thought. I knew that was now broken beyond repair.

8

I BROUGHT my children into the world and taught them the same morals and values. They were showered with the same amount of love, yet Jack and Paul's personalities were so different. Jack was quiet, diffident, and a deep thinker. He only spoke if he had something to say, while Paul was energetic, cheeky and unintentionally loud.

But they did have things in common too. Neither of them wanted to be taken to school by their dad, preferring the hugs and kisses I bestowed upon them before they got into line. So, we got into a routine and it was one I kept until it was cruelly taken from me. As the three of us walked to school, I would tell them 'I love you'. Their reply always came in unison; 'To infinity and beyond', they happily chirped back, coining a phrase taken from *Toy Story*, one of our favourite movies. I loved those moments. And at the other end of the day, I would be waiting in the playground for my precious boys, as Paul belted towards me and dived into my arms and Jack's face lit up when he spotted me.

When I was poorly, they would worry, so when I explained I needed a hysterectomy, following a laparoscopy during the Easter holidays, Jack in particular got upset. He'd had his grommets – tiny tubes put into the eardrum to help restore normal hearing – inserted when he was six. He had been allowed to look around the operating theatre ahead of the surgery to try and put his mind at ease, but unfortunately it had had the opposite effect.

'Are you going to die, Mummy?' he cried.

'No, of course I'm not,' I reassured him.

But as I recalled my surgeon's words, about the cancerous cells and the fact I would need a full hysterectomy, I swallowed back my own fears.

'This way you'll be around to watch your sons grow up,' he had said.

As I held Jack in my arms, tears pooling in his eyes, I felt like my heart was being ripped into 100 pieces. Over the next few weeks, I hugged my eldest son tightly and held his hand as I sang him to sleep night after night. The evening before my operation I let him sleep in our bed, despite the disapproving objections from my husband.

Jack turned out to be far more supportive than his father. He rang me on my mobile as I was on the way to hospital, and then when I was waiting to go down for theatre, while my husband hot-footed it out of the hospital as soon as I had arrived on the ward. The boys had also chosen me some comfy, fluffy pyjamas for my stay. Unsurprisingly, it wasn't my husband, who was by my bedside when I woke up from the surgery. Instead, it was my eldest sister, Christine, but in a way, I was relieved, knowing they were there out of love, and not because they had to be.

I was allowed to go home after three days on the condition that I had at least two hours' bed rest every afternoon. I was signed off work for eight weeks but, of course, my husband still expected the house to be immaculate and he didn't lift a finger to help. I ended up cleaning up with blood oozing out of me.

The boys were absolute angels though, tidying up after

themselves and even doing little household chores, making their beds and clearing their plates after mealtimes. Friends helped with school pick-ups and drop-offs, offering to have the boys for playdates and tea. They were like a parade of umbrellas, keeping me dry throughout the storm – a storm that within a few years would leave me shrouded in fear and darkness.

As I recovered, I put any reserves of energy I had into my boys. Jack was struggling to engage at school, he liked having something physical to do with his hands, but really didn't enjoy writing. Jack felt all the information was in his mind and he didn't see the point in writing it down. I lost count of the hours I spent with him at the kitchen table trying to gently encourage him to write, and then many more, sitting alone, thinking of ways to try and help my son. Of course, my husband didn't give it a second thought. Then, when Jack moved into Year 3, something magical happened. I picked him up from school and he came dashing across the playground.

'Mum. Mum. Guess what?'

'What sunshine?'

'A mister came into class today and played a trumpet. I really want to play one, but you have to fill a form in. Can I play it, Mum?'

'Of course,' I smiled.

You could have knocked me down with a feather. Jack never talked about school. It was like he locked it away in his mind come 3.15pm every day, yet here he was full of enthusiasm for something he had enjoyed.

That day transformed Jack's life. Through music and playing the trumpet he learnt it was okay to make mistakes and as the months passed, Jack started putting his hand up in class and contributed more in his lessons. It was as if music had unlocked an element of his mind that had been shut away. At home, that trumpet barely left his side, he practiced for hours on end. The sounds turned to notes and the notes became the most beautiful mix of musical pieces. More than once, I saw people stop and listen on the street, as Jack's music emanated through the windows.

He was asked to join not one, but two bands, and I became a 'taxi mum' – not that I would have had it any other way. I had always loved music and to see Jack follow in my footsteps made my heart implode with happiness. Jack had found his own little community, who supported and believed in him. He felt valued and as though he belonged, surrounded by like-minded people, who became a second family. He also had some talented male role models to look up to, who encouraged Jack to be the best musician he could be. As he started playing concerts, it wasn't just me, as his mum, who would be moved to tears by his recitals; I would turn round and see people he'd never even met dabbing their eyes.

Of course, my husband liked to show Jack off, now he was becoming recognised for his talent. At concerts he would march into the hall ahead of me, holding up Jack's uniform and trumpet as if they were trophies, but it was me who took our son to every rehearsal and listened to him practice for hours on end when his father was 'too busy'.

Paul was the opposite of his big brother, in so many ways. At school, he absorbed information like a sponge but also raced around everywhere at breakneck speed, a bundle of energy and emotion, sometimes to his own detriment. When he wanted something, he would just go for it, at full pelt, which could occasionally lead to him and Jack getting into the odd sibling fight. Paul would go for Jack, arms and legs flaying in every direction, but Jack was taller and calmer, so inevitably won the battle.

On the sports field, Paul was like a whippet. By the time he was in Year 2 he was faster than the children a year older than him in school races. When I asked Paul if he wanted to join an athletics club he simply pointed to the school track and said: 'That's where I want to be'. I found a club about 40 minutes away at the Dorothy Hyman Sports Centre, on the other side of Barnsley. The first night I took him, Paul ran over to the track, knelt down and touched it.

'Thank you,' he smiled, looking up at me.

Paul was never happier than when his trainers were on, the track under his feet, the wind in his face and the finishing line in sight. He became a sprinter and loved the 80 and 150 metres, especially the latter, as it included a bend. Whenever he ran, he lit up from the inside out. Initially, he trained twice a week, but quickly increased to three nights a week and I'll never forget watching him race around the track. One evening just before Bonfire Night, a firework exploded into the sky behind him. His whole face was a mirrored explosion of colour and that image is forever imprinted on my mind. Paul was at his calmest and serene after he had been training.

'It's the closest feeling to flying,' Paul told me.

He took the principles he learnt from running into every element of his life. He treated every challenge like a finishing line; to conquer and cross. He just wanted to be the best he could be and always looked ahead, not sideways, never backwards, but always towards the winning line. Paul had heart, determination and the will to succeed.

9

IT TOOK months for me to recover from my hysterectomy, but as I gradually got better after the surgery, my personal life was plummeting in the opposite direction. You can never actually pinpoint exactly when abuse starts – it's like a tap that at first has a steady drip but then the tap turns on. Not only turns on, but turns to full blast and before you know it you are battling against a torrent and drowning with no way to escape the tidal wave. It affects every part of your life.

To the outside world, it looked like I had a perfect life; a husband, two amazing children, a lovely home and a job that I loved. But it was all an illusion; the reality carefully hidden away, invisible to everyone except my mum and close colleagues, and the boys, who had grown up watching the cracks in our marriage get wider and wider.

Jack and Paul would see the difference in how their friends' parents treated one another, compared to how their dad spoke to me. They began asking questions when they realised other dads didn't scream at their mums, nor did they throw things at their wives or push them about or call them terrible names.

My husband had also started getting increasingly annoyed if Paul didn't eat every single morsel on his plate. When our son moved vegetables around with his fork, he would shout at him, then he started deliberately putting more and more peas on his plate. Paul was forced to eat each and every one until he felt physically sick. Jack would then get upset, seeing his brother suffering, and would consequently be called a 'cry baby' by his father.

This wasn't the only way my husband made our sons' lives a misery. If their bedrooms weren't immaculate, he would grab their toys and dump them on the patio. If they were a bit silly at the dinner table, he would make them eat their meal sitting on the floor.

'Why does Daddy shout as much?' Jack asked.

'And why does he throw things?' Paul followed.

My heart sank. I knew the answers. My husband liked to be in control and he made our lives hell, because he could. He humiliated, scorned, and belittled me, because he could. There was no one to challenge him, except my mum, but I didn't tell her everything, desperate to protect her and knowing how worried she would be. I had no real friends of my own and if I did meet up with the other mums from school or work colleagues, my husband would turn up unannounced. And if he didn't arrive, he would interrogate me for hours afterwards. Worn down and exhausted, unable to cope with the relentless questioning, I simply stopped going out.

You don't notice the little signs to begin with, the sporadic comments or the odd bit of criticism. It's only after you have become so deeply rooted into a relationship, and so worn down, that you suddenly become aware your self-confidence has been crumpled into dust around your feet. Not only that, but your abuser's actions have become the norm, embedded into every part of daily life.

In the house, I did all the cleaning, washing and ironing, but even that was scrutinised. My husband insisted his socks had to be put away in colour order. Even today, I get anxious if I even see anyone wearing odd socks. There had to be a perfect crease down the arms of his shirt sleeves and work trousers, and his underwear had to be organised in his drawers in colours and brands. He would lose his temper if different items of his food were touching on the plate, and then the insults would come thick and fast.

'You're fat,' was one of his favourite lines of attack.

At first, it would bring tears to my eyes, let alone ebb away at my already diminished self-worth. But if by some miracle I didn't crumble and therefore create the reaction my husband was hoping for, he would start on the boys.

'Jack is too fat. Paul is too thin.'

Those words cut me like a knife. I couldn't understand how any parent could be so horrible about their own children. I tried to make sure every other element of their lives was full of joy and four nights a week, I would take Jack to band practice or Paul training, but even then, there was no respite. My husband would ring me every ten to 15 minutes, demanding to know exactly what the boys and I were doing.

'I'm stood at the side of the running track,' I would reply, honestly.

On other nights, my response would be: 'I'm reading a Beast Quest book with Paul while Jack is at band practice.'

He would call me the minute I finished work to ask where I was.

'Walking to my car,' I replied, exhausted.

I would receive on average 40 calls and text messages a day, demanding to know exactly what I was doing, who I had spoken to, when I would be home. Stalked and harassed by my own husband. My mobile phone felt like a way to keep me under lock and key, it was another stick to beat me with, another way of controlling me. My home, which should have been a safe haven, a sanctuary your heart leads you back to, was actually a place of oppression and fear.

I stopped singing, unless it was for the boys. I stopped playing my flute and my husband sold my childhood piano, claiming we needed the space, something I could never forgive him for. He seemed to get so much pleasure from ripping away all the things I loved. I stopped offering my opinion on anything, knowing he would just berate me if he didn't agree. I even stopped buying clothes, after I had treated myself to a beautiful dress for my niece's wedding. My husband didn't like that it wasn't skintight and drove me back to Meadowhall, where I'd bought it, to exchange it for a smaller size. I hated how it clung to me and vowed to never allow my husband to make me feel so cheap again.

Every Christmas, he bought me a nail salon kit. On the surface it sounds like a lovely gift, but he would insist on painting my nails and then wherever we went, my husband would force me to show them off.

'Do you like them?' he would ask smugly. 'I designed and painted them.' Piece by piece, my identity was being taken away.

After my hysterectomy, I struggled to lose weight and even though I was already at rock bottom, my husband couldn't resist sticking the boot in a bit further. 'You're so ugly,' he repeated, day after day. He didn't care that our sons could hear him, or that they got upset at seeing their dad hurl such nasty insults at their mum.

Another favourite was labelling me a 'green eyed monster',

not due to the fact I got remotely jealous of anything he did, but because he wanted to depict me as something alien. My eyes would slightly change colour with my mood, which the boys loved, claiming I was a secret member of The Fantastic Four, but now instead of it being a thing to smile about, it was being used to further diminish me.

Once your self-respect and self-esteem cracks and crumbles, it feels impossible, while you are with the person who destroyed it, to rebuild it. On a daily basis I was told I was ugly, to be quiet, and that I was no longer sexually attractive. My husband took great joy in comparing me to a 'limp lettuce' or a plank of wood, but once he got into bed, he wouldn't leave me alone, insisting we had sex. But it wasn't making love, a special and intimate moment shared between couples who adored and respected one another, it was humiliating and degrading. My husband, after he had been sexually satisfied, would take great pleasure in urinating on me. The first time it happened, I was stunned and completely humiliated. I couldn't actually understand what he had done at first. I could just feel this warm liquid on me. It was only when the smell of urine hit me, that I realised the vile act he had committed. In shock, and disgust, I jumped out of bed and ran into the shower and scrubbed myself. He reduced me to nothing. I don't think I will ever be able to put into words how hard it became to not completely loathe myself.

The next morning, my husband just got up as normal, as if nothing had happened. I was too numb to confront him - he had reduced me to nothing more than an object that he could abuse in the most degrading of manners. I guess, by then, I was also too weary to fight back.

But it wasn't the last time. I never knew when it would happen, because I couldn't ever predict which version of my husband would be getting into bed with me. At least once a fortnight, he repeated his disgusting act. Afterwards, feeling utterly humiliated, I would stand in the shower at two and three o'clock in the morning, scrubbing myself, until my skin was red raw, because I felt so dirty. The irony was he always demanded expensive bedding, but then would destroy it with his unimaginable act.

My only salvation was being a mum. I would get up the following morning, paint a smile on my face to wake up Jack and Paul, take them to school, then go to work. I may have looked calm and together on the outside but underneath, I was falling apart. I became a master at internalising everything. I refused to engage with my husband, as he rained one derogatory remark on me after another. I don't know if it was strength of character or just the opposite and I had no strength left, but either way I somehow managed to lock my mind and soul away. I stopped looking in the mirror, as I no longer recognised the person I had become. I still can't look at my reflection, as I can't bear to see the damage that man has done to me.

After every verbal or physical attack, the boys would snuggle up to me, hold my hand tightly and tell me how much they loved me. I hated the fact they witnessed how cruel their father was and prayed they wouldn't end up replicating his behaviour, thinking it was normal. Thankfully, they seemed to instinctively realise their father wasn't a role model to aspire to and in spite of the unkindness and cruelty their dad displayed every single day, they refused to mirror his actions and found joy and happiness in their lives with me. They were still both succeeding at school and their teachers constantly told me they were well behaved, polite and caring.

But that's not to say they were immune to their dad's volatile actions. In 2011, when Jack was nine, we were on a caravan holiday in Norfolk. As we sat down to eat dinner, my husband suggested we go to watch the circus. The boys quietly, but politely, said they didn't want to. They associated it with our trips to Lytham St Annes, and said they only wanted to see the circus in the Big Top at Blackpool. I steeled myself, knowing this would infuriate their dad as he hated how close the boys were to me. Possibly out of nerves, Jack started fiddling with his fork at the table, further irritating his father, who went to knock Jack's hand but missed and knocked his large glass of red wine everywhere. Instinctively, Jack, Paul and I froze, knowing how quickly their dad could explode. And then, in a split second, everything happened at once. My husband went to get a cloth, but as he did, he flicked Jack around the head and hit him so hard his grommet became dislodged. Paul hadn't done a thing, but he could see what was coming and as his dad raised his hand to him, Paul ducked, causing my husband's hand to crash to the table. By this point I was on my feet and standing between my precious sons and my bullyboy husband. He tried to push past me, but I refused to budge.

'If you lay another finger on Jack or Paul,' I said, holding up my mobile phone, 'I am calling the police.'

He stormed out of the caravan, grabbing the car keys as he left, to ensure I couldn't go anywhere. The anger management course he had completed years earlier had done nothing to dilute his temper and with each month that passed, he exerted more and more control over us all. We were scared to say the wrong thing or look in the wrong direction and could never relax. We were constantly on our guard.

Jack, Paul, and I cherished the weekends or holidays when we could spend time with Mum. Only then could we really be ourselves, laugh, have fun and chat without repercussions. Mum would pay for everything, and I would pay her back in cash, so there was no paper trail for my husband to examine and question. He was never interested in how we had spent our time together, so we never told him, keeping those special moments to ourselves. I would store them up in a jar in my mind and get them out every time I needed something to help me smile. It's a coping mechanism I use to this day.

On the occasions, my husband did know we were meeting Mum, the tension at home beforehand was palpable so, to try and dilute any potential explosions I would make sure the house was spotless, as his go-to attack was 'Yes, you go out for the day, even though the house is a mess'. But even that didn't make any difference. He would start hiding my car keys and handbag to make it harder for me to go out until just getting out the door was a monumental task that would leave my heart racing and me physically shaking.

In 2012, Paul had been nominated to watch the Paralympics, and I was allowed to go with him. We were both so excited, but I knew Jack was anxious. He didn't like me not being there when he woke up of a morning.

'Will you leave a note under my pillow?' he asked.

'Of course,' I smiled, wrapping him in my arms. 'And I'll be back before you know it.'

I felt so torn. The trip was such a big treat, but I hated seeing

Jack worried. It made me so sad, that he dreaded a day with his dad, as opposed to being excited that they would have some quality time together. As I wrote Jack a little message, knowing it would be the first thing he reached for when he woke up, my husband sneered as he looked over my shoulder.

'You're turning him into a mummy's boy!' Something he took great pleasure in chiding our son with too. 'I never write notes for him.'

'And therein lies the problem,' I thought, but didn't dare vocalise my thoughts.

Then, in his paradoxical manner, my husband insisted on getting up at 3am to make the sandwiches we were taking, even dipping strawberries in chocolate for me. I wasn't deceived by what could appear to be a loving gesture though; it was just another way of him taking control.

Paul and I had a wonderful day. I was so touched his friends had nominated him to go, which was topped off when one of the Olympic volunteers gave Paul one of his commemorative pin badges because he was 'the nicest, and most polite child he had spoken to throughout the Olympics'. Those words have always stayed with me. Despite their father's aggressive and nasty behaviour, my children didn't replicate him, which they would have been forgiven for. Instead, they remained true to themselves, weathering the storm and torrential abuse.

When the coach was late back that night, the shower of text messages started.

'Where are you?'

'Jack needs you.'

'He won't go to bed until he sees you.'

For My Boys

My husband knew how guilty I felt about being away and this was his way of making sure the end of the day was ruined. When I arrived home at 1am, nearly 24 hours after I had set off, holding a sound asleep Paul in my arms, I nipped upstairs to check on Jack. He opened his heavy eyes. 'Mum,' he whispered, a smile appearing. He had fought sleep until I got back, never able to settle unless my mum or I were in the house.

My husband's aggression wasn't limited to just me and the boys; he had a knack of annoying most people. Within a few years of moving into our house, he had managed to alienate everyone on our street and was constantly falling out with our next door neighbours. They were lovely people, but my husband had gone out of his way to find fault with them. In 2013, he received a police caution for assault after attacking the neighbour in a row over his dog. I was mortified but my husband's awful actions only served as a catalyst to further alienate me, Jack and Paul too. Although we got on with everyone and the boys had lots of friends on the street, I didn't want them to come to the house in case my husband was rude or aggressive.

My husband's techniques to control me impacted every element of my life. He hated me going on work socials and would either sulk or make life difficult. In December 2013, I was supposed to go on my work Christmas do, which consisted of a meal and going to a few pubs.

'Get a taxi home after the meal,' my husband ordered, insistent I didn't stay out a minute longer. There was obviously no encouragement for me to have a good time; just a barking instruction, a hidden warning for me not to push my luck. He wasn't even prepared to finish work early to help with the boys so a friend agreed to pick Paul up from school, while Jack, who was at senior school, was old enough to walk home on his own.

It would have been nice to go out for a few drinks with colleagues after the meal, but I knew if I dared, it would cause an almighty row, so I did as my husband instructed and got in a cab as soon as we left the restaurant. That morning, I'd checked my purse to ensure I had enough cash, but when I came to pay, it was empty. I couldn't prove it, but I was sure my husband must have taken it out without me realising.

The start of 2014 began badly. My husband had insisted on taking the boys to an indoor dry ski slope after booking a family skiing holiday in Austria during February half term. I hated the cold and the snow. I'd suffered a head injury a few years earlier and was advised not to ski or ice skate. The trip also meant we couldn't afford a summer holiday. Not that it bothered my husband; my feelings were irrelevant.

So, on New Year's Day, while the boys were at the ski slope, I sat at the kitchen table studying. I knew my husband would never change and had decided to try and find a way out of the marriage. I didn't earn enough to support the boys by myself, so had embarked upon training courses at work to try and enhance my job prospects.

A week later, tensions were still running high. Paul's birthday and our traditional trip to the pantomime, which my mum and her friend had started 20 years earlier, had come round. But a few days before, my husband said he wanted to redecorate our bedroom. I wasn't keen, desperate to save as much money as possible. I was done with making plans in a house that was full of abuse, let alone in our bedroom where my husband had destroyed all my dignity. I didn't know how and when I could escape, but I couldn't carry on.

For My Boys

I was exhausted, sad and scarred, but fundamentally I knew I had to get my boys away. They deserved a better life. And so did I, but I was frightened. Any confidence had long been knocked out of me.

I refused to engage with his plans and didn't look at the brochures he'd ordered, full of expensive bedroom furniture. As usual my husband retaliated in the only way he knew how. He started tapping his foot, then picked up a chair and launched it across the kitchen at me. This time I wasn't quick enough to avoid the assault and the chair bounced off my arm and legs, leaving me battered and bruised. When I went to see my GP, I lied and said I'd slipped.

My husband slept on the settee for two nights following the attack, assuming removing his physical presence from our bed would be another punishment, but it was a relief. It was two whole nights free of dread and free of humiliation. Of course, the usual bouquet of flowers was delivered; only this time I didn't ring and thank him. I was adamant I wasn't going to thank him for hurting me anymore. I had realised, out of confusion and fear, for years I had enabled my husband's behaviour, by gratefully thanking him for the flowers. It's easy to call a florist and have a bouquet delivered; it's a lot harder to look at yourself and acknowledge your flaws, then change them or apologise for your evil actions.

At the end of January 2014, we were at home one afternoon, when yet again, my husband started telling me how fat I was.

'Get on the scales,' he ordered. He had become a master of humiliation.

'My mum's not fat,' Paul, who had overheard the conversation, said. 'She's beautiful.'

My husband turned to face our youngest son.

'Your mum is fat,' he reinforced. 'And she is going to get ill because of it.'

Paul's beautiful, big, blue eyes filled with tears. Unable to stand the shame and hurt my husband was causing, I ran into the bathroom, sat on the toilet lid, put my hands over my face, and wept. I had never felt so broken. Then as despair was threatening to engulf me, a small pair of hands closed around one of mine and a much larger pair took my other.

'We love you, Mum,' Jack said. 'And we want you to leave Dad.'

Their words were all the encouragement I needed. That night, as I got into my bed, my husband said: 'You can sleep on the settee from now on.' It was fine by me. The next day I took the boys to stay at my mum's house and when my husband got home and realised we weren't there, he rang me.

'I'm having the boys on my next day off,' he stated.

'They don't want to see you,' I explained calmly, only reiterating what my sons had emphatically told me.

'You can't stop me,' came my husband's confident and cocky retort.

I knew he was right. He was their father and had a legal right to see his sons.

'Put Jack and Paul on the phone,' he commanded.

I turned to my son and asked them if they wanted to speak to their dad. They both shook their heads.

'Not tonight,' I said into the phone.

'You're turning the boys against me,' my husband accused.

'You have done this to yourself,' I pointed out.

The following day I took some legal advice from a solicitor, who explained it would be difficult financially and a hard road ahead.

I wasn't earning enough to support the boys or to take on the mortgage. Even though I knew he was right and had suspected that's what he would say, it still felt like a hammer blow to my heart. I would have to go back to my husband until I could find a way to be independent. The boys didn't want to go back to their dad, and neither did I, but I didn't know what else to do. And this is when I learnt for the first time how hard our society has made it for victims of abuse to escape a perpetrator. They have the power, and their victims are completely powerless.

Over the next week, I spoke to my husband. As usual he never apologised, but he promised to make some changes if we came back, assuring me he would no longer criticise Paul at the dinner table, or call Jack and myself 'fat'. I sat the boys down and explained that although their dad had behaved badly, he wouldn't do it in the future. What I didn't tell them was that in order to keep them safe, to avoid the alternative of leaving them alone with their dad, we had to go back.

So, we did and for the first few days, my husband was on his best behaviour, but it didn't last long. A few weeks later at one of my other niece's weddings, to my husband's annoyance, Paul wanted to go and talk to his friends and relatives. Out of sheer frustration, he grabbed Paul's wrist and twisted it, leaving an angry, red mark. Of course he blamed me. Apparently, it was my fault for not insisting Paul sat down at the table with us.

What I realise now, is my husband had become an expert in deflecting the blame away from himself and onto the people he abused, generally me. He denied that people found his behaviour unacceptable. He would verbally attack me, always accusing me of causing the problem. By finding a different version of events, he reversed the situation, turning the victim, me, into the offender. Exhausted and worn down, I didn't realise back then but have since learned, this is classic DARVO behaviour – deny, attack, and reverse victim and offender.

Despite all this, in February half term we went skiing. I wasn't looking forward to the trip but painted on a smile, wanting the boys to have a brilliant time. Then one morning, my husband noticed Paul had left the crusts from his toast – like loads of children, he didn't like them and at home, I always bought crustless bread as I knew he would grow out of it eventually.

'Eat them,' my husband ordered.

But Paul, who had moved away from the table, refused. I wasn't quick enough to see my husband explode. Yet again, in what felt like a second, he was on his feet, had picked Paul up by his collar, dragged him back to the table and thrown him into the chair. Jack tried to put his arm out to protect his brother, but like me, he wasn't fast enough to stop his dad – not that he should have to. I ran to my youngest son, pulled him into my arms and took him into the sitting room of our accommodation. Terrified, Jack had run to the bedroom and was hiding under the bed. Paul was so upset he was hyperventilating so I gently picked him up and carried him into the bedroom where Jack was hiding.

'He tried to strangle me,' Paul sobbed.

All I could do was hold my sons and tell them I loved them over and over again.

Six words spun around my mind, tormenting me, breaking my heart. *Could have, would have, should have.* I should never have returned, gone on the skiing trip and obeyed his selfish orders. Paul

For My Boys

refused to go near his dad for the rest of the holiday and like me, both boys were happy when we finally flew home.

Still we had no choice but to stay, I couldn't leave my boys alone with him and without money I couldn't look after them.

Soon Mother's Day approached. For the previous four years, my husband had never given the boys money or taken them shopping to choose a little gift. I didn't say a word, choosing to cherish the homemade cards the boys had made for me, but my mum was furious when she found out and afterwards ensured the boys had the opportunity to get me a little something. The presents were always lovely, but what I really looked forward to was the effort the boys went to on Mother's Day morning. Jack and Paul would always make me breakfast in bed, and I would watch with my heart in my mouth, as they proudly carried the tray into the bedroom and carefully put it on the bed. They would jump onto the bed next to me, sending everything flying, happy to be enveloped in the hugs. We would all laugh as we looked at the detritus scattered across the duvet. My husband never participated, always opting to stay downstairs. But in 2014, the month after the disastrous skiing trip, he had arranged gifts, cards and a day out to Xscape, a leisure complex at Castleford, which my mum had also been invited to.

The charm offensive didn't last long, though. A month later I was on a placement at a primary school for a qualification I was working towards. I had arranged to meet a former colleague for lunch, but the night before, my husband said he was taking the car to work, despite the fact he had a van. My friend's partner came to pick me up, but it meant I didn't get the chance to take any cash out, so I used the chip and pin facility to pay for my lunch. My husband had always monitored every penny I spent, so

Claire Throssell

I knew I was taking a risk as he had alerts on his phone whenever a transaction was made, so he instantly saw the payment go through. Despite knowing it was likely to be me, he called the bank and reported it as a fraudulent transaction. I rang the bank and confirmed the payment was legitimate, but still my husband wasn't happy. To my horror, he went to the pub where I'd had lunch and demanded to see the CCTV footage, which of course showed me eating my lunch with a female colleague. Even then he refused to back down and spent the next four days telling friends, colleagues, and my mum, I had defrauded the bank. He called me a liar and a thief to the boys and in front of my mum, repeating: 'I can't trust her with money'. All of this because I had dared to spend £13 on lunch with a friend. I knew his behaviour was inexcusable and decided to open my own bank account in secret to take my first step towards independence. But then came an incident that would change our lives forever.

10

THE WEEK before Easter, Jack had a lot of homework to be submitted before the holidays started. He had put it all in his rucksack ready to take to school.

'What are you putting in there?' my husband asked.

He had never been in the least bit interested in how Jack was performing at school, had no idea he was working at a higher level in maths and science, or had been recording his own music. Nor did he know Jack deliberately left for school early, so he didn't have to watch his little brother get interrogated by his dad for how little he ate at breakfast.

'Just my homework,' Jack replied, honestly.

This was all my husband needed to start another verbal assault.

'If you rush your homework, and it isn't of a high standard, you will go nowhere in life,' he shouted.

My heart twisted. He had no idea how hard our son worked. I wanted to scream and shout and tell my husband to just look at what a brilliant son he had, but I knew it would only make matters worse. I went upstairs to put the washing away. Jack followed me, desperate to get away from the callous diatribe he was being subjected to. I gave him a tight hug but within a minute, my husband was pounding up the stairs.

'Don't you dare walk away from me when I am talking to you,' he yelled.

At first, I thought he was talking to me, but then I realised this was aimed at our quiet, hardworking son.

'Answer me when I am speaking to you. Have you finished all your homework?' he demanded.

'I've told you already, I've done it. It's you who isn't listening,' Jack dared to reply.

Everything that came afterwards happened so quickly, but it will be forever imprinted in my memories. My husband lurched forward, his fist raised, ready to hit Jack. Instinctively, I stepped in between them, and quickly pushed Jack into his bedroom. In a bid to save my son, I bore the brunt of his dad's fury, the punch landing heavily on my arm. The heavy-handed assault was bad enough, but the force of my husband's brutality knocked me off balance, and before I could grab hold of anything, I was hurling down the stairs. Jack rushed out of his room, and ran down the stairs after me, at the same time as Paul flew out of the living room. They both reached me as I fell, crumpled in a heap. Terrified, Jack and Paul curled themselves around me, as my head spun, and my body jarred in an awkward position.

'Look what you made me do,' my husband shouted, as he looked down on the three of us, entwined together as one.

The last thread had been broken, but I knew I had to act quick.

'Run to the car,' I gasped to Paul.

'Get both sets of keys,' I instructed Jack, knowing my husband would try to lock us in the house, as he had done many times before.

Somehow, I picked my aching body up off the floor, scrambled out of the house after my frightened sons, and got in the car. Jack had already put a set of keys in the ignition. Not daring to look back, I started the engine and drove to Mum's house.

For My Boys

This time I vowed I would never go back.

Mum's house was like a second home to the boys and had been my home since I was 12. It was a safe haven to help protect against the pain life threw at us. I had been lucky enough to have parents who had always told my sisters, and I, that we could always come home whenever we needed to. Mum's mantra was: *'Whatever the weather, no matter the weather, we'll weather the weather together'*. And we certainly did.

That Easter we took the boys back to Lytham St Annes, then set about turning my old bedroom into a room they could share. I bought them new beds and identical bedding to some I'd bought them years earlier. Jack helped me erect their new beds and never once did the boys moan about sharing a room.

But as May arrived, so did trouble. My husband demanded to see the boys on his days off. Unlike, in the past, when he had begged for forgiveness after he had caused a row, this time my husband was arrogant. He truly believed that he would keep the house and have full custody of the boys, have a new girlfriend and completely eradicate me from his life. Jack and Paul were distraught when I told them I would have to let him see them. In the eyes of the law, he was their father. Six difficult weeks followed. The boys didn't like going and always ran into my arms as soon as they came back. As well as the emotional upset, the boys' PE kits wouldn't come back with them, school uniforms, shoes and musical instruments went missing. My husband was making it clear he was still in control and doing everything he could to make life difficult for us all. On one occasion, I had arranged to meet a friend for lunch. I don't know how my husband found out, but he had a spare set of keys, as we were still sharing the car, and took the car, leaving me stranded.

Jack and Paul dreaded going to stay with their dad, and their normally happy demeanour was vanishing by the day. Their little eyes were no longer sparkling, and they looked as though they had the world on their shoulders. Paul got upset that I was still wearing my engagement and wedding rings.

'Please take them off,' he begged me. 'You don't belong to him anymore.'

I knew my Paul was right, but I found it hard to detangle myself from the 18 years I had spent with his father. Separation brings with it a complex set of confusing emotions that take time to unpick.

In May, I went to see a solicitor to start custody proceedings and initiate a divorce on the grounds of unreasonable behaviour. I had to swallow my pride and apply for Universal Credit. Then I spoke to the local authority housing department, but when I explained my circumstances, I was told I had made myself and my children deliberately homeless, and that because I had a mortgage, I wasn't entitled to a council property.

Is it any surprise victims of domestic abuse stay with the perpetrators? The system makes it almost impossibly hard for survivors of abuse to rebuild their lives.

I walked out, got into my car and burst into tears. I drove to Paul's school, but when I got into the playground, my son's eyes were glistening, and I could tell he had been crying too.

'Could I have a quick word?' his teacher asked.

When my son was out of earshot, she explained Paul was upset because I was still wearing my rings, and that while he was at his dad's house, he was once again being forced to eat foods he didn't like. The teacher was kind, she knew I was suffering, but I knew I had to fight to keep my sons safe. That night, I let Paul's small hand take mine, and remove my eternity, engagement and wedding rings.

At the beginning of June, I received a call at work to say Paul had suffered an emotional breakdown at school and the safeguarding team had been informed, as they felt his father was the cause. It was a Wednesday – one of the days my husband was due to have the boys. The safeguarding team had told the headteacher not to release Paul to his father, and to contact me to collect him.

In that moment, I made the decision that my son's wishes and safety came ahead of my husband's rights. I called Jack's school, explained what had happened and that I was picking him up early. I felt sick with fear and worry, knowing my husband wouldn't just let this happen. But I also felt sick with shame for letting my sons down so badly, and sick with fear for what the future held. I picked Jack up from reception at Penistone Grammar School and explained he wouldn't be seeing his dad for a while. His face lit up.

'Paul won't have nightmares now, but don't worry Mum, I have held his hand like you do,' he said, and my heart crumbled a little bit more.

We then went to Paul's school. Jack took hold of my hand and didn't let go. We found Paul in the library, he looked so small and vulnerable and bile rose in my throat. The guilt and shame I felt for allowing my boys to be with their dad was suffocating. Both Jack and I held out our arms and Paul ran into them. We stood there, enveloping my youngest son, promising him he was going to be okay. I knew my husband would explode when he realised he wouldn't have the boys that night and I didn't want the teachers to be on the receiving end, so I rang him and told him I had already collected the boys.

'I'm stopping contact until a court hearing. Paul has made a disclosure against you,' I said, the firmness in my voice, hiding how terrified I felt.

Instantly, my husband went on the attack.

'You have turned the boys against me, but I will get them,' he roared. 'You can't stop me.'

I was starting to lose the tiny amount of confidence I had managed to muster.

'If you come here, I will call the police. Our son is at breaking point, and he should come first.'

The phone went dead. He'd hung up. An hour later his van pulled up outside Mum's house and some of my belongings were thrown onto the drive and garden. Mum's neighbours called the police. When the officers arrived, the boys told them what they had seen and how their dad had threatened me. They said they would look into it.

Later that night, my husband rang me, telling me he was going to take his own life. As much as all my feelings had vanished for this man who had caused me so much pain, I couldn't ignore what he'd said so I called the police. They went to the property, but he refused to let them in so I gave the officer the contact details of a friend who had been fairly sympathetic towards my husband in the past. Tellingly, they didn't go to see my husband, though.

Over the next week or so, the boys, myself and Mum all spoke to a social worker, who reiterated there should be no contact for the rest of June and July. Two precious months of peace where the boys could breathe easily again.

But there were dark clouds gathering. Every few days, my husband would call me, promising to destroy me, and sent vile messages to my family, saying exactly the same. I couldn't get back into the family home to retrieve any of our clothes or belongings, as he parked the car against the gate, so I couldn't get through, and left the keys locked on the inside of the front door. The police advised me to have the locks changed at Mum's house and to put a location app onto my phone, so people knew where I was at all times. I made a will and changed the joint mortgage to a joint tenancy, so if anything happened to me, my share of the house and any money would go to Jack and Paul.

As the divorce proceedings began, I was told we would have to attend mediation first. My husband insisted we went to a solicitor's office in Leeds, over 30 miles away and I reluctantly agreed, knowing this was yet another way of him trying to control me. In the end it took place in Barnsley but when I turned up, he didn't. Yet again, he was manipulating me and the process. Then he refused to sign the divorce papers, only relenting when I didn't respond to his text messages, which had now swung to him begging me for forgiveness.

Throughout all of this, I was determined to keep Jack and Paul smiling. I bought a car, and we named her Bessie. That summer we went on one day out after another; nowhere particularly special, just to parks or for walks, but we spent our time together. Those days were filled with uninterrupted happiness and love. Whether we were reading books together or laughing until our sides hurt after the boys both hurtled down a slide and landed in a puddle of muddy water, we were simply content.

Then came the family court proceedings, and once again, life came crashing down. I naïvely believed these institutions were in place to protect you and your children, but I quickly realised how wrong I was. I had applied for residency of Jack and Paul and full custody. They didn't want to be anywhere near their dad, and I really thought their wishes, feelings and voices would be heard. I had disclosed everything to my solicitor, detailing all the physical and verbal attacks against the three of us. I had also made it very clear, from the start, that I believed my husband was capable of killing Jack and Paul. I knew my husband was jealous of the close bond the three of us had.

I had watched on the news, a year earlier, how a father had driven his two beautiful children to woods, murdered them and then taken his own life. My husband had been watching the news with me. His words had chilled me to the core.

'I can understand it. Dads don't have the same rights as women do,' he'd said. 'We men will do anything to punish our exes.'

I had stepped in between my husband and our sons enough times to know what he would do to Jack and Paul. I also warned the social worker and the officer from Cafcass (Children and Family Court Advisory and Support Service) never to be alone with him. I tried to keep everyone safe, but ultimately, I failed.

Throughout the whole court process, Jack, Paul and I were invisible. Unseen, unheard and unsupported. The family court was a barbaric and humiliating place to be. Everyone is scanned for physical weapons, but perpetrators don't need them when they have their voice, mannerisms and presence.

I had to walk past my husband in the waiting area, where he was tapping his foot; the sound that had reduced me to a trembling wreck for years. During one hearing, my husband attacked me as we were going into the courtroom.

'You've turned the boys against me,' he yelled. 'You're pure evil.'

For My Boys

It's this sort of abuse that leaves you a trembling wreck. The courtroom itself wasn't a safe space either. Despite the fact my husband had a barrister to represent him, he hurled insults across the table at me. 'You're mentally unstable,' he spat. 'You defrauded the bank.' He was just four seats away from me and the verbal assaults carried on. 'You're overweight and paranoid.' He was free to say whatever he wanted. In what other court is a perpetrator of abuse allowed to carry on in such a way? His lies continued. He accused me of putting thoughts in the boys' heads, announcing I was possessive and jealous.

I remained calm, but inside I was a wreck. This man had systematically destroyed me throughout our whole relationship. He had reduced me to nothing and was still allowed to rain one insult after another at me in a courtroom. He did have to admit that he had physically hurt the boys in the past and that he had forced Paul to eat food he didn't like, as well as leaving Jack emotionally upset by insulting me in front of him. But despite all the evidence against my husband, all the testimonies of how he had hurt the three of us on several occasions, he was awarded five hours unsupervised contact a week. It did come with some clauses – no overnight stays were permitted, no mealtimes and it was agreed Jack and Paul would reside with me. A Section 7 report was ordered; to provide the court with information about Jack and Paul's welfare. The reports are supposed to include the child's wishes and feelings, as well as their physical, emotional and educational needs, along with the suitability of their home environment. The court can then use the findings and recommendations from Cafcass to make decisions about where a child should live and how much time they should spend with each parent. This is standard procedure when domestic abuse is suspected, and another hearing would take place on November 17, 2014.

I had naively believed by going to court, we would be safe, fairly represented and justice would be upheld. The reality couldn't have been further than the truth, and even more heartbreakingly, the truth was never reflected in any of the decisions made. The judge, a stranger to Jack and Paul, made a judgement on their lives, which ultimately ended them.

In August, I took the boys back to their favourite place, Lytham St Annes, for a summer holiday. They had started to regain their confidence, were feeling more at ease and their sense of humour was returning. I let them go to the shops together. They bought a fake parking ticket and secretly planted it on my car windscreen. I fell for it, hook, line and sinker and the boys howled with laughter, jubilant in the knowledge they had successfully managed to prank me. My only regret is Jack had asked if he could take his beloved trumpet so he could play it on the bandstand at St Annes, but I had been reluctant. The car was already packed to the rafters with suitcases, kites, beach toys, teddies, blankets and scooters.

'Next time,' I had promised.

If only I'd found the space.

But the break away was filled with love and laughter. We drew pictures in the sand and turned the shapes in the clouds into fantastical stories. I will never forget the look of pure delight on Paul's face as he jumped into the paddling pool fully dressed, just because he could, and there was no one to reprimand him for simply having fun. I took both the boys to the top of Blackpool Tower and captured the moment of them both letting the wind flow through their hair, without a care in the world.

For My Boys

That September, Jack and Paul returned to school happy, focussed and revived. Even though they weren't happy about having to see their dad twice a week, they were relieved they didn't have to sleep over at the house without me or their Nannan. They no longer saw our previous family home as a place of safety or love.

This became abundantly clear one morning when I noticed my favourite, expensive perfume, Allure by Chanel, was rapidly depleting. I didn't understand where it was going until I walked into my bedroom and saw Jack and Paul liberally spraying themselves with it.

'I can buy you aftershave if you want to smell good,' I said, catching them in the moment.

Their response broke my heart.

'We don't like seeing dad, but if we smell of you, we're taking a part of you with us to keep us safe ,' Jack said.

It was like a punch to the stomach. I have thought about those words over and over again. I challenge any judge not to remember my innocent sons' honest and scared sentiments when they order children to go somewhere that isn't safe. Presumption of contact was introduced into the Children Act 1989 in 2014. It is a legal principle that parents should always be given contact with their children. However, this should not be at any cost. I believe it has no place in a court of law and destroys lives, as the following month proved in the most brutal way. As a parent all you want to do is protect your children, not put them in danger, but as I was about to discover, with devastating effect the law fails to protect the innocent, including Jack, Paul and I.

11

AS SEPTEMBER turned into October, things got a lot harder. Emotionally, I was handling the separation as best as I could, with my mum's support, but financially, it was difficult, too. My husband earned far more than me, but didn't pay a penny towards necessities for the boys after we left. He would pay to take them on days out, to show what a 'fun' dad he was, but refused to buy their new school shoes or uniform.

Then, leaving me feeling like I had whiplash, I would get one answer machine message after another.

'Please come home.'

'I'm sorry.'

'I'll let you talk.'

But within minutes, another would arrive.

'You will never hear from me again.'

My emotions were a mess. I knew I could never go back, but it broke my heart to hear those messages and I felt guilty, blaming myself for tearing our family apart. In the end, I called the police and spoke to my family. They all told me not to go back or to even go to the house.

Disentangling my marriage also meant disentangling myself too, but when your self-esteem, confidence and self-worth is on the floor, it's hard to do. I was exhausted and a shadow of the woman I was before him – the woman who loved life and was always smiling. I put all my energy into fighting for Jack and Paul, in the hope they would have a better, safer, future, but my husband was putting one obstacle after another in the way.

I contacted the Child Support Agency to ask for help in terms of maintenance payments, but when they contacted him, he lied and claimed the boys and I were still living at the family home. I had to provide evidence to prove I was living at Mum's house, all of which slowed the process down, and let my husband think he was still pulling all the strings. In the first week of October, I made my sister, Carolyn, and her husband, Ted, legal guardians for Jack and Paul, if I died or was murdered.

As soon as my husband was informed of the changes to the mortgage, the relentless text messages began again, flitting from begging for forgiveness to indicating he would take his own life. I knew it was all to get my attention and as much as it was hard, I stood my ground and refused to succumb to his tactics. Of course, that only aggravated him. He started driving past Mum's house at all hours of the day and night, and began flouting the court order, dropping the boys off late or turning up early. He turned aggressive towards my solicitor and estate agent, as he realised the house would be classed as an asset and he would have to share the value of it with me. Then he tried to claim half of my car, and got angry when he realised he couldn't, as I had taken the finance out in my name alone. When that didn't work, he tried to claim he was entitled to half of my share of my mum's house. That obviously didn't work as Mum was still alive and living in the house, so there was no money or assets there to pass to me.

Desperation started to kick in and he dropped to a new low, messaging members of my family, making up lies that my brother-in-law had acted inappropriately around me. He knew my eldest sister, Christine, was battling terminal cancer, but he didn't care. Being the narcissist he was, this was all about him. I felt like I was fighting this battle from every angle and it left me utterly drained. The police had marked Mum's property as at risk, but apart from posting a leaflet through the door about domestic abuse, they couldn't offer any other support. Social Services had written to me, stating because I had been awarded residency, they no longer needed to be involved. The judge in the custody hearing had ordered a Section 7 report, to ascertain what was in the boy's best interests, yet Cafcass took weeks to make contact.

As half term and Halloween drew closer, my husband got more and more desperate. He wrote to my solicitor demanding more time with the boys to make masks, claiming he was renowned within Penistone for his face-painting skills. Thankfully, his request was refused by both my solicitor and Cafcass. The irony was, in years gone by, it was me who had bought their costumes, the masks and face paints, and on the boy's insistence, it was me who took them trick or treating, then scrubbed them clean afterwards. Their dad had always resented the fact our sons naturally gravitated towards me, frightened of his aggressive and controlling behaviour.

My husband was angry when Cafcass didn't take his side, but I knew he would be even more furious with me. Two weeks before half term our Decree Absolute arrived, officially ending our marriage. I felt like I was finally managing to take control, despite how much I hated myself for not seeing through my now ex-husband all those years earlier when he'd first love-bombed me with rose after rose.

I was on a new training course at work and the boys' teachers explained they were both feeling a lot happier and settled. Paul was running three times a week, Jack was engrossed with his music, and the bank had said I could apply for a mortgage, solely in my own name. Maybe, just maybe, we could all get through this in one piece, I told myself. I had seen a little terraced house for sale, not far from my mum's home, in Thurstone so I sat the boys down and gently asked them how they would feel if it was just the three of us living together.

'Wherever you are is home,' they both said, and my heart filled with happiness.

My mum decided we should celebrate my divorce coming through and booked a table at one of the local pubs, the Waggon and Horses. The boys loved the food there, and we knew the owner, Tony. He would listen to Jack and Paul talk about their music and running as he took our order, never once interrupting them. On that particular day, the boys had their usual access visit with their dad from 1pm to 4pm, so Mum had reserved the table for 5.30pm. As always, as I waited for my sons to come home, my stomach was in knots, hoping their visit had gone well, but no young boy coats themselves in their mum's perfume just to feel safer. At 3.30pm, I got a text from my now ex-husband.

'The boys are going to be late back tonight. Enjoying Xscape.'

I immediately sent a text back.

'No. We have a table booked at the Waggon & Horses for 5.30pm.'

The response was fast and nasty.

'Don't be a bitch.' Then in capital letters, added: 'THEY ARE HAVING FUN.'

I didn't want this to turn into an excuse for my ex to bombard me with insults. But then I got a message from Jack, from the phone I had bought him.

'We want to come home,' his message read.

By this point, they were already half an hour late.

I sent my ex another message.

'You are breaching the court order. Bring Jack and Paul home or I will have you arrested.'

I picked up my car keys, telling mum I would just go and find them, but as I was about to head out the door, another text message landed.

'On way home. As usual you have spoilt everything. At least we are divorced now. I'll throw a party and trash the house – I'll enjoy that!!'

I just took a deep breath, knowing his attacks and threats would never end. The boys arrived home at 5pm, an hour late, and as they ran into the house, they were both crying. I pulled them into my arms and dried their eyes, then I made them one of my special hot chocolates and sat on the couch in between them and let them talk. The real reason they were late home soon emerged.

He had met a new woman, a nurse with a son, four months earlier, in June, and she had arrived at Xscape late. The boys explained their dad had paid more attention to his 'old family friend' as she had been introduced, and her son. When Jack and Paul had asked if they could come home, their dad had told them: 'We'll go when I am ready'.

As the boys cuddled in next to me, I saw their dad's car pass the front of the house three times. I didn't say a word to my sons, knowing it would only upset them more. But when they took it in turns to have a shower, my phone beeped again. This time their dad's message felt sinister.

'You just can't stop lying can you. I'm watching and waiting.'

I closed the message, refusing to let him intimidate me. Instead, we decided to still go out for dinner and make the evening as enjoyable as possible, but as we pulled up at the pub, I saw my old car, which mu ex now had, parked in one of the dark corners. I didn't say anything knowing it would scare Mum and the boys. Instead, we went into the pub and ordered our meals. I spent the next couple of hours making the boys laugh, in a bid to help them forget about the afternoon they had been forced to endure.

By the time we left the boys were in a much brighter mood, but as I started to drive home, the car began veering out of control. No matter how hard I pulled on the steering wheel, I couldn't keep it straight. I pulled over, and got out of the car, to check if I had a flat, and that's when I saw it – one of my tyres had been slashed. We could have been killed. If it wasn't for the fact the boys were in the car, I would have burst into tears, but Jack sensed how worried I was.

'Put your hazard lights on and don't worry Mum,' he said calmly. 'I know how to change a tyre.' Jack, still only 12, then proceeded to get out of the car, opened the boot and pulled out the jack which he then started to use. He took the wheel off, found the spare tyre and put it on. A passer-by stopped and helped tighten the nuts and when he drove off, Jack and I shared a massive hug.

'Thank you,' I whispered into his ear, feeling incredibly proud and grateful, despite how sick I felt on the inside. I had no doubt in my mind who was responsible for slashing my tyre.

The next day I rang the pub to ask if they had any CCTV that covered the car park. They didn't. Terrified of what my husband would do next, I called the Cafcass officer and told her what had happened. She made an appointment to see Jack and Paul in school, but asked me not to talk to them about it beforehand. I understood that they didn't want me to influence them, but I knew the unannounced appointments would upset them. Against my better judgment, I did as the Cafcass officer said though, terrified that if I didn't it would be held against me in some way.

That evening, I picked the boys up as normal. Paul had been to a Halloween disco, and Jack was at band practice. Again, I spotted their father's car in the corner of the car park, and it was still there an hour later when I collected Paul. I desperately tried not to let it freak me out in front of the boys, but it made me feel sick to know he was constantly watching me.

It was Thursday before Paul had his interview with Cafcass but the representative from the service asked me to drive Jack to their office to be interviewed on Monday, October 27. I knew that was the first day of half term, and wasn't how I had envisaged Jack would spend his holidays, but knew how important it was that both my son's feelings were taken into consideration and recorded in the Section 7 order.

In the days leading up to half term, my solicitor received a message from my ex stating: 'Reach a settlement or I take action.' His words terrified me. I knew what he was capable of, and his words sent a chill through me, but I also knew I had to stay strong for Jack and Paul.

After school, on the Friday after the tyre incident, I took the boys to see the house I was thinking of buying. As soon as Jack and Paul saw the jacuzzi style bath, they were smitten.

'Can we move in now,' Paul asked.

I was delighted to see them so happy. We'd also planned to buy two kittens as soon as we moved in. I wanted to mark the new chapter in our lives and fill the house with love and laughter. That weekend, we carried on as normal. Paul and I sat together at the dining room table and got his homework out of the way, while Jack perched on the settee playing his trumpet. He was practicing a new classical piece, *Song to the Moon* from the opera *Rusalka* by Dvorak, but was struggling to understand the notes. I knew it, so sang it to Jack, hoping it would help.

Paul looked up from the table.

'Oh Mum, it's sad that only me and Jack hear you sing. You should sing to everyone, not just us.'

It was just like Paul to be so kind and his thoughtful words never failed to touch me. For the rest of the day, we watched DVDs wrapped up in the boys' snuggle blankets, did some leaf painting, and started the countdown to half term.

As I've said before, life is like a coin – there are two sides to it. There's happiness and sadness, success and failure, optimism and pessimism, joy and bitterness. But one thing that moulds and welds the two sides of the coin together is love. And it's love that gives life's coins value and worth.

On Tuesday, October 21, 2014, I got to spend some individual time with both my sons. Jack had an appointment with an ear, nose and throat specialist, so I took him out of school before lunch. At the appointment the specialist explained one grommet had been knocked out of his ear, and the other had become dislodged. We would need to keep an eye on how his hearing was affected and take him back in another six months. Afterwards, I took him out for lunch and we talked about Remembrance Sunday and Jack explained he was looking forward to playing *The Last Post* at the service at school.

'I'm looking forward to Christmas without Dad too,' he commented.

It broke my heart that their lives had been so damaged, this wasn't how I'd imagined family life would be. That night, I dropped Jack off at the community band he loved to play in, took Paul to the running track for two hours, and then we both went to pick his big brother up. When we got home it was shower time, into pyjamas, which I'd warmed on the radiator, and then into bed. I turned the light to low, and as they each climbed into bed, I sat on the chair between them and read them a chapter from *Harry Potter and the Philosopher's Stone*.

If only that night could have stood still, given me a few extra minutes, hours, or more.

12

THE FOLLOWING day I dropped the boys off at school and told them both I loved them. They each replied with their usual response; 'to infinity and beyond'. Jack had walked into school, with a final look over his shoulder to check I was still there, and of course I was. I always liked to know they had gotten into school safely. For some reason, Jack looked back twice that day. His little face, smiling back at me, is permanently etched into my memory. Paul did what he was born to do – he ran!

I went off to my training course, then to work, before coming home. Their dad had picked our sons up late that evening from Mum's house, but I had still missed them by five minutes. I always felt anxious on Wednesday and Sundays, counting down the minutes until they were home. I spotted their mobile phones on the coffee table.

'They should be with the boys,' I said to Mum. I had bought them for Jack and Paul, so they could always contact me if they needed to, especially when they were with their dad.

'I'll take them to them,' I added.

'Have your dinner first,' Mum insisted.

If only I had followed my gut instinct. I had just finished eating my dinner, when that fateful knock on the door arrived. Mum assumed it was the boys coming home early as they hadn't had a good time, but something told me she was wrong. When I opened the door, I was faced with a police officer. His car was in the road, the engine still running, the blue emergency lights flashing.

'What's he done?' I asked instinctively.

'There's been an incident at the house,' the officer, who I recognised from school runs, said. 'A fire. You need to come with me now to Sheffield Children's Hospital, where your sons have been taken. Paul is very poorly, but Jack has been able to talk.'

I couldn't fully take in what he was saying. My mind wouldn't comprehend it. The officer ushered me and mum into the car. As we sped away, I questioned why he was flying through police speed cameras. *Wouldn't he get into trouble?* It felt like the journey lasted forever, as I clung to mum's hand, praying my sons were okay.

Finally, we reached Sheffield Children's Hospital. 'Go on in,' the officer said, as he pulled in outside the entrance. Terrified, I jumped out of the car and ran through the double doors into the resuscitation unit where I saw my beautiful, but severely injured, youngest son on a bed. Medical staff surrounded him, as they desperately administered CPR. A doctor was suddenly by my side.

'Come this way,' he gently urged, ushering me into a quiet room.

'Are you Paul's mum?' he asked.

'Yes.'

He reached over and squeezed my hand.

'I'm going to take you to him now.'

I had no idea what was going on but something inside me told me it wasn't going to be good news. By the time we got to Paul's side, my heart was crying in pain. Then I saw my son's fragile body, which was virtually bouncing off the bed, with the force of the CPR.

The doctor who was working on my little boy turned to me

and repeated the question his colleague had asked a couple of minutes earlier.

'Are you Paul's mum?'

'Yes,' I nodded, my resolve crumbling.

'I'm very sorry,' he said gently. 'But we are going to let him go.'

'Go where?' I don't know if I said it or thought it, but a split second later, I realised what he meant.

'No,' I gasped. 'Please, no!' The sound coming out of my mouth was raw, guttural, unrecognisable.

Someone must have ushered me to a chair. I don't remember, but Paul was placed in my arms. I remember thinking he was naked – just like the day he was born. But back then, he was pink and healthy, this time his poor, broken body, was irreparably damaged and still. It had been my arms that had held Paul when he had entered the world, and now those very same arms were holding him as he quickly slipped away, his life over before it had barely started.

'Please don't go,' I begged, my words hardly more than a whisper, the words catching in my throat.

'I love you so much. I've always loved you and I always will love you.'

I thought my heart was literally breaking. Paul smiled one last time, then the light in his beautiful blue eyes turned grey. Their sparkle vanished. His eyes empty. My whole body reeled in a pain that consumed every fibre of my soul. It enveloped me. Smothered me. It tore my very being apart. A nurse discreetly closed his eyes, and I held my precious son in my arms, my tears falling and ever-so-subtly darkening his nearly white, blonde hair.

'Please could I have a blanket?' I asked.

Claire Throssell

Both my sons had always hated the cold, and all the heat had left Paul. I gently wrapped him up, and all I could do was hold him as the pain deep within me ripped my heart, chest and lungs apart, leaving me incapable of functioning on any level. I just wanted to stay there, holding my son tight. If I didn't let him go, then maybe none of this was real. I would wake up, realise it was all a horrible dream, and the boys would be snuggled beside me on my bed, laughing and smiling. But then I realised there were a lot of people around me, encouraging me to let Paul go. I turned away from them.

'No,' I cried internally. 'He's my son. I'm not letting you take him.'

I clung to Paul's body, bent over him, protectively. They couldn't take him from me.

'I'm sorry Ms Throssell.' The voice pierced my thoughts. 'Your son is a crime scene.'

What were they talking about?

'No!' I protested. 'He's my boy, not a crime scene.'

Two medics gently prised Paul from my arms and everything that was left inside me shattered. I couldn't process what was happening. It was all too much. Nothing felt real. Paul was taken to a side room and laid on a bed, underneath a blanket. If I didn't know the cruel truth, I would have assumed he was simply sleeping – the only sign of a problem was the smallest of grazes to his nose. Then my mum was by my side, my sisters arrived, and gradually it started to sink in. My lovely, gentle, caring boy was dead. And I knew, instinctively, his father had killed him, purely to punish me.

My brother-in-law, Ted, arrived.

'The evil bastard!' The words exploded out of him.

For My Boys

Everything was unravelling inside me. Threads were snapping one by one. I was broken beyond repair. I knew in that moment I would never, ever, heal.

A forensic examiner came in carrying a box and asked us to leave the room. I still can't remember with clarity what happened in what order, but suddenly I was officially identifying Paul's body and signing forms that proclaimed my son as dead.

'Do we need to call Social Services?' a doctor asked. It felt like he was implying I had somehow harmed my son.

My sister, Carolyn, jumped in like a lion defending a cub, and told him in no uncertain terms that there were a dozen police officers outside the door that knew different. Shamefaced, the doctor put the phone he had been holding down and explained he had been one of the team that had fought to save my son. I just nodded. I couldn't move. I could hear noise all around me. The police officer who had brought me to Paul received the news my ex-husband had just died at Barnsley Hospital. I looked at the officer, but felt nothing.

Then he took a deep breath.

'I'm sorry to ask but will you take responsibility for your ex-husband's body?'

'No,' I muttered. 'His parents are alive. They can be responsible for what they have created.'

This sounds horrible, but at that stage, my mind hadn't allowed me to think about Jack. Holding Paul as he left the world was all I'd been capable of dealing with. My middle sister, Caz, and her husband, Ted, led me to the room where Jack was being worked on. When I got into the room, Jack was wrapped in bandages with his hair sticking up.

'I'm here,' I whispered, as I stood next to him.

'I love you,' I repeated, just as I'd told Paul.

A doctor explained Jack had been sedated, to help control his pain levels, but he could still hear me. It was only later, I discovered medics had been forced to cut his chest open so he could breathe. The severe burns he suffered meant he was being pumped with plasma, draining the hospital's supply. The doctor explained they believed Jack thought he had saved his brother's life, and it would jeopardise his recovery if he knew otherwise.

'Talk about Paul as if he is still alive,' he encouraged.

I didn't know how much more I could be dealt, but there was more to come.

The doctor explained Jack was critically ill and was about to be transferred to Manchester's Paediatric Intensive Care Unit, by Embrace, a specialist ambulance service for children. Now, for the first time in my life, I had to choose between Jack and Paul. I didn't have a favourite son. I had always loved and treated them equally, but I had to decide whether to stay with Paul, so he wasn't alone, or go with Jack. As I made my decision, I felt physically sick, nausea sweeping over me, as I hoped Paul would forgive me for leaving him. As doctors worked to stabilise Jack for the journey to Manchester, I went back to Paul's bedside.

'I'm sorry,' I whispered. 'I would stay with you forever, but your brother needs me.'

I found a nurse and asked if someone could stay with Paul.

'He's only nine,' I cried.

I kissed my youngest son on the forehead and nose, then blindly walked out of the room, completely broken. It was another 90 minutes before Jack was ready to be moved. It was agreed I would travel in the ambulance with my son, a doctor, and a nurse. As we set off, I was told there were roadworks on the motorway, but the police had cleared a route for the ambulance to travel through at speed. A police car, which my mum was in, was in front. As I sat, numb, in the ambulance, I watched as the doctor and nurse worked on Jack the whole time. Time didn't seem to move or stop. I was frozen in the moment. At one point, the ambulance had to pull in so the medics could loop up more bags of blood and plasma for Jack. I had no sense of reality, all I could do was watch as the nurse lay on her back on the floor of the ambulance, as she held up the bags of lifesaving fluid. I remember thinking that apart from the Paralympics, this was the furthest Jack and Paul had ever been from one another. Like most brothers, they would fight, squabble and wind each other up, but their bond was unbreakable. They were each other's most loyal and fiercest companions.

It was 2am when we finally arrived at Manchester Royal Infirmary, where a medical team was waiting outside for us. Jack was taken straight to theatre and the next fight for survival began.

As Jack was wheeled down a corridor towards the theatre, being pushed further and further away from me, I started to scream. In my head the screams were getting louder and louder, but as I looked around no one was reacting. Nobody was even looking at me, and that's when I realised my desperate reaction was all inside me. It was as if the pain hurt too much to set free. A kind hand gently guided Mum and I to a quiet room that was usually used for medics when they are resting.

'Try and have a lay down,' the nurse said. 'We will come and get you when Jack is out of theatre.'

I looked at Mum. I knew she was suffering too, but the shock was beginning to set in, and I couldn't actually say a single word. I knew if I said anything, I would break into a thousand pieces. I had to stay perfectly still, silent, and not touch another human being, because I knew if I did all the grief and pain I was feeling would pour out of me. I could still hear the eternal screaming inside me, despite how silent it was to the rest of the world.

Someone brought in freshly made tea, but I couldn't even touch the cup, because if I touched anything I would shatter. As I lay on the bed, my whole body cried out for Paul, my beautiful little boy. I'd dropped him off at school that morning, happy and full of life. As always, I'd waved goodbye and said: 'I love you' and his usual reply came. 'To infinity and beyond' he'd grinned, before running down the path into school. It had just been a normal day, but now he was lying silent and still, and it felt like I'd lost my life too. I knew I would never be able to live again, at best I would simply exist.

A myriad of thoughts and memories were crashing through my mind. The pain of them consumed every part of me. I wanted to fall asleep and never wake up, but I knew I couldn't, Jack needed me more than ever. I must have dropped off though, because the next thing I remember was being woken up and told Jack was going back to theatre, but I could stay with him until he was taken down for the next lot of surgery. I was on my feet within a second.

When I got to the ward, I was asked to create a password that only staff, close family, and police would have. I chose the first word that came into my traumatised mind - purple, the colour that is recognised as a symbol of domestic abuse. And then I was taken into the room. I took a deep breath, but nothing could have prepared me for the sight of Jack swathed in bandages and attached to so many machines and monitors, fluids and drugs being pumped into his barely recognisable body.

No parent should ever have to see their child so utterly damaged. I had promised on the day Jack was born, I would always protect him, but as I looked at my poor boy, I felt petrified and useless in equal measure. But something inside me kicked in. I had to be strong. I had to be Jack's mum. He had to know I was there, that I was fighting for him. So, I sat down next to his bed and started talking to him. As soon as I started to speak, a monitor revealed his racing heartbeat had slowed down – Jack was responding to the sound of my voice. Not just mine; Mum's too. She was next to me, both of us willing Jack to pull through. But even as Jack's heart beat steadied, it felt like mine was smashing into pieces, at the sight of how injured my son was.

Then, suddenly, the room was full of medics. It felt suffocating. Once again, I was separated from Jack; a wall of people between us. Anaesthetists, consultants, nurses and surgeons all seemed to be talking at the same time about the best way to keep Jack alive. I stumbled into a chair and put my head in my hands, desperately trying to block out the noise and not look at the human wall that had blocked my view of Jack. They must have turned to me, because a pair of shoes came into vision. I looked up and immediately wished that they still had their backs to me. Their faces told me more than I wanted to know.

'Mrs Sykes,' someone said.

The sound of those words and being associated with my ex-husband, the monster I knew was responsible for killing my youngest son and leaving Jack fighting for his life, caused my body to convulse. I felt like I was going to be physically sick, but I knew I needed to respond; they needed to speak to me, so I simply nodded.

'Please don't call me that again,' was all I could manage.

The doctor nodded and wrote something down in his notes.

'Your son is critically ill,' he said gently. 'And I'm afraid the prognosis is uncertain. He is 56% burnt on his face, chest, arms and back. All third degree with the added complication that your son is suffering from smoke inhalation. He will be in theatre for 17 hours today.'

The words didn't feel real. How could any father inflict such brutal injuries on his own son. My poor, poor, boy. How on earth could he possibly survive? Then I was handed a form and a pen.

'I'm very sorry,' the doctor apologised. 'But I am going to have to ask you to write that surname one last time to give your consent in order for us to medically treat your son.' It was too much. All of it was too much. Hours earlier I had signed a form declaring Paul was officially dead and now Jack might die too, and I had to sign a form that inadvertently gave my permission. I took the pen, but couldn't write because my hand had started to shake uncontrollably, followed by the rest of my body. I took a deep breath, to try and bring the shaking under control, but it didn't work and the shaking increased. The doctor left the room and when he came back a couple of minutes later, he was holding tablets and water.

'These will help,' he promised.

I swallowed the pills, and the effect was almost instant.

'Keep drinking the water,' he softly encouraged. I found out later I needed to keep my body temperature stable, as Jack's room had to be kept at 39 degrees. I managed to sign the form and knowing

Jack was going back into theatre, I wanted to be near him, to kiss him, and hold him in my arms, but there wasn't a single part of my son we could kiss or touch. Mum started to get upset. Like me, she just wanted to hold Jack. A nurse gently lifted a sheet and indicated towards Jack's leg. We placed our hands on my son, and once again, began talking to him until he was taken back to theatre. As Jack was wheeled away, the all-consuming pain I had tried to keep at bay, engulfed me once again. The room was unbearably empty without Jack, and every fibre of my body ached.

Mum and I were shown to a grey and airless waiting room, with a massive clock on the wall. Just as I collapsed into an armchair, a barrage of people arrived one-by-one, to talk about what now seemed impossible – living. Two South Yorkshire Police family liaison officers came in, along with a hospital family support worker. Then more of my family arrived. A team was building around me, but all I could do was watch the clock on the wall and tell myself, as the little hand did another circle, that's another hour Jack has managed to stay alive. Another hour he's made it through. All I could do was stay in one moment at a time.

This is where my family stepped in and became the scaffolding that held me together. They surrounded me in love and support. Mum and I had climbed into the police car with the clothes we were wearing. Mum had still been in her slippers. My sisters arrived with food, toiletries and spare clothes. The hospital also did everything they could to help me. The Ronald McDonald charity had provided the hospital with rooms for relatives to stay in. As Mum and I walked inside the apartment the day after Jack was admitted, I remembered how whenever I took Jack and Paul to McDonald's, they would ask for money to pop in the donation stand, so they could watch the coins spin round and round. I had never really thought about what that money went to, but now I realised that loose change went towards rooms to help people in their darkest hours.

It meant when Jack finally came back from surgery and I had been reassured he was stable, I could have a shower and snatch a few hours sleep, cushioned from the atrocities of the rest of the world. I was back on the ward at 7.30am, only to be met by two surgeons and an anaesthetist. I was told Jack would need to go back into theatre. His injuries had been extensive, and they wanted to do more surgery to try and save his hands and fingers.

'Please, please do everything you can,' I begged. 'He's a trumpet player and it means everything to him.'

Tears flowed down my cheeks at the thought of what it would do to Jack if he couldn't play his beloved trumpet.

'We will do our best,' one of the surgeons said, as he glanced at his colleague.

When Jack was taken back down to theatre, I went back to the all-too-familiar grey room and watched the hands on the clock slowly turn. But the bad news kept coming. A different doctor came into the room, along with the police officer who had been assigned to my family, and the barrage of questions began.

'Can I ask you to describe the ladder that goes into the attic for me?' the officer asked.

'Why?' I was confused. I didn't understand the relevance.

'Your son has a deep laceration to his left buttock.'

I closed my eyes and swallowed.

'It's a metal loft ladder and where it extends it has sharp bits.'

I had asked my ex-husband to buy a new one, several times, as at different points all four of us had been caught on it and ended up with cuts and scratches.

'Thank you,' the doctor said, and left the room.

I looked at the officer, my eyes searching for an explanation.

'I'm sorry, Claire,' he started. 'But from initial investigations Jack and Paul were in the attic when your ex-husband deliberately set your property alight. He used an accelerant, and although investigators and forensics are still compiling evidence, we believe fires were started in more than one place, using some of your clothes and possessions.

I listened in horror as the officer explained firefighters had located my ex-husband at the far end of the attic, but Jack and Paul hadn't been with him. Police believe when the fire had taken hold my sons had tried to escape from the loft through the hatch, but Paul had collapsed. Jack had tried to help his little brother and pull him through the attic opening. From the evidence gathered, it was thought Jack had fallen through the hatch, onto the landing, and caught his body on the ladder as he fell, hence the deep cut to his bottom. When the firefighters got to Jack, he was in a bad way but managed to say: 'My dad did this and he did it on purpose.'

It felt like a hammer blow to the chest. I was so proud of the young man I was raising, but those feelings were drowned out in the guilt I felt for not being there for Jack and Paul when they needed me the most. The pain that overwhelmed me was like nothing I had ever felt before, as I thought of how terrified my beautiful boys must have been when they realised what their evil father had done.

In a state of shock, I kept looking at the clock on the wall, the hour hand fast becoming a talisman connected to Jack's life.

The clock slowly ticked into the afternoon. Work colleagues, who over the years had become friends, arrived at the hospital; news quickly spread about what had happened. They held my hands as we cried together.

Just when I thought I couldn't cope with anything else, a third hammer blow was forced on me. The police officer, who we had come to know as DC Dave, explained the media had heard about the fire and reports were being published. Jack and Paul were going to be on the national news.

'Would you like to provide a photo of your sons?' the officer asked.

My mind was a complex mess of emotions. Everyone would know what Jack and Paul's father had done to them. I couldn't think straight, barely able to comprehend my youngest son was dead and my eldest was fighting for his life. The officer was still talking.

'It's probably better that you don't use any special photos of the boys as it might ruin the memories of when they were taken.'

The hurt hit me all over again, knowing I could never again make any more special memories with Paul. My abusive ex-husband had delivered the cruellest blow. I would never be able to take a photo of my kind-hearted youngest son again. The life he should have lived had been stolen from him. My chest felt like it was in a vice that was squeezing all the air out of me. Once again, I couldn't breathe. Doctors were called, tablets were administered, and everything went numb.

Unlike the previous time, Jack wasn't stable when he came back from theatre. I have never prayed so hard for anything, as I willed my son to hang on. I couldn't let him leave this world. I just couldn't. My sister had brought some David Walliams books to the hospital – he was Jack's favourite author. So, in the still of the night, with only the background noise of monitors and life-saving machines, I tried to give my son some normality in the scary world we had been plunged into. I sat as close as I could to Jack, and started reading, just like I had every single day since he was six months old.

Jack's heartbeat steadied, once again, as he heard my voice, which brought me a little bit of comfort. But it was short-lived. At 1am, nurses told me to try and get some sleep. Reluctantly, I agreed to go back to the apartment, but two hours later, I was woken up. Something was wrong and Jack started overheating.

'Jack might not survive the night,' a nurse told me gently.

My heart raced, as she explained consultants were on their way back to the hospital. I couldn't be with Jack, as they worked on him, so all I could do was sit with Mum and wait. It was 5am before I was told Jack was now connected to a dialysis machine, but he was stable. The machine was taking blood out of Jack's body, cooling it, and then putting it back in. My brave, brave, son was holding his own, and he made it through another night. By 9am Mum and I were back by his bedside. We were both trying so hard to keep it together, but emotionally and physically we were broken. We weren't alone; our whole family was struggling to cope. My middle sister, Carolyn, and her husband, Ted, travelled to Manchester every day. Even my eldest sister, Christine, who was battling cancer, came to be near us.

By then it was Friday and no surgeries were planned for the weekend and those two days were the strongest Jack had been since he had been admitted to hospital. My nieces and I covered my eldest son's room with photos of him and his brother. The nurses found me a radio, so I could play Classic FM, the boys' favourite channel. Ever since being tiny, it had helped lull them to sleep after I had read their bedtime stories.

Of a night when everyone else went home, Mum and I took it in turns to read David Walliams' *Awful Auntie* to Jack. I'm not sure my sister had really seen the title of the book when she had bought it for him, but it had always made him belly laugh. What I would have done to hear that infectious laugh in those desperate hours. But despite how hard those long days were, reading to Jack felt like a little bit of normality amongst the pain. I felt close to him and wondered if it made Jack feel better knowing I was there reading his favourite book, but it was bittersweet, knowing he couldn't respond.

13

THEN CAME Monday, October 27, the day my life ended, and my existence began.

That morning, Mum insisted I had something to eat in the apartment before we went back to the ward, knowing I'd barely touched a morsel of food since arriving in Manchester. I knew she was right, but I was desperate to get to Jack. By the time we arrived, the medical staff seemed tense. Jack needed another huge operation. Extra blood and platelets had been ordered, which had to be infused into my son before surgery, but it hadn't arrived, delayed after the weekend.

To everyone who gives blood and the men who give platelets, thank you. Know that your generosity and time saves lives and gives others a chance of survival when the odds are stacked against them. I am eternally grateful to every single person who helped try to save my son's life. There are not enough words in the world to express my gratitude.

Before he was taken down to theatre, I told Jack repeatedly how much I loved him. Medical staff explained it would be 8pm before he would be back, so I went back to the grey room and, yet again, watched the clock. Family arrived and after a few hours insisted I went back to the Ronald McDonald room with them, and away from the big clock on the wall, to get some rest. I reluctantly agreed, but only after the medical team assured me they had both the apartment and my mobile phone number.

As the afternoon wore on, I looked at what information the police had revealed to the media. All the world knew at this point was that there had been a fire and that Paul had died and Jack was fighting for his life in hospital. I felt angry and frustrated. I wanted people to know the truth, not some sanitised version. One of my nieces, Chloe, suggested I start a Facebook page to keep people informed on Jack's condition. My sister, Caz, had read an article in the *Sheffield Star* titled, Pray For Jack, and there my Facebook page under the same name was born.

I typed my thoughts and prayers onto my phone. I explained I wasn't allowed to say much but explained Jack was undergoing an 18-hour operation. I asked people to keep Jack and Paul in their hearts, minds and prayers. I hoped people would now understand the gravity of the situation. I was stunned when it accumulated over 100,000 views. In many ways asking people to pray for my son was the easiest of my writing tasks that day. My next job involved a pen and paper, as I started making notes on what I wanted for Paul's final farewell. I knew my son had been moved to the Medico-Legal Centre in Sheffield, where the coroner was based. It felt so cold, and I was desperate to see Paul. I hated the idea of him being alone in a mortuary. Every time I thought of him there, another part of me crumbled.

A few days earlier my sister and brother-in-law had taken the clothes I had requested to the staff at the centre. I'd asked for Paul to be dressed in his running skins and top, with his Heelys on his feet. Paul had only had them a month and was still getting used to having wheels attached to his feet, but he loved them. Before that, the one and only time he had been roller skating was at a friend's birthday party and he had set off like a rocket, just like he did when he was running. Only this time Paul couldn't turn and had catapulted into the wall. I smiled at the memory, and knew his nickname of 'Danger Mouse' was perfectly apt.

'I can take you to see Paul whenever you want,' my brother-in-law, Ted, offered.

Once again, I was torn in two. How on earth could I choose between either of my sons.

'I can stay here with Mum and be with Jack,' my sister, Caz, reassured me.

I was just coming round to the idea, when I noticed a missed call on my mobile. I had accidentally let the battery drain, and it had only just charged back up. It was the number for the ward. I frantically rang the number back, but as I waited for someone to pick up, I went icy cold. I just knew something was wrong. The nurse who answered said she couldn't tell me anything about Jack's condition, but he still wasn't out of theatre. My sister and her family had been getting ready to go home for the night, but something about the look on my face must have prompted them to stay. They insisted on walking back to the ward with me, past Jack's empty bed, to the grey room. A sense of fear had crept over us all. I stared at the clock. 8pm came and went. Jack wasn't back on the ward, but a nurse explained he was out of theatre.

9pm. The clock was becoming a harbinger of doom. At 10pm a ward sister burst into the room. Without a word, she grabbed my hand, and we ran. I think I already knew deep down what was happening, but my heart and mind were screaming 'No!' When we got to Jack's room, it was like history repeating itself. Doctors, nurses and anaesthetists were performing CPR, but only this time it was on my oldest son. I tried to be strong. I willed myself to be brave. 'I love you, Jack,' I shouted, hoping to give him my strength. I resolutely refused to give up hope. I couldn't give up. I couldn't.

But then the surgeon cut off Jack's bandages, and I saw Jack's chest and torso for the first time. That's when my heart and soul cracked open. When I saw how badly injured my son was, I knew I couldn't beg him to fight any longer. His poor body had literally been ripped apart. The longer the CPR continued, I knew the less of my son I would ever get back. After 20 minutes, I couldn't watch anymore and left the room. At 45 minutes, I forced myself to go back in. An exhausted doctor looked at me. He was drenched in sweat, shaken and visibly upset.

'I'm sorry,' he said.

He didn't have to instruct the other medical staff to stop. I think they must have been waiting for me, and just parted so I could get to my son. My whole body was consumed in pain. Somehow, I walked to Jack and climbed onto the bed next to him. I took my lovely boy in my arms and held him tightly, just like I had with his younger brother five days earlier.

'I love you to infinity and beyond,' I whispered, repeating the phrase the three of us had told one another for years.

The medical staff discreetly stepped out, leaving me to envelop my son and hold onto our final moments together. The room was silent except for the single flat monotone of the machine, confirming the life of my gentle boy, who had the heart and courage of a lion, had been stolen away from him. But even worse, this wasn't some tragic accident. Both Jack and Paul had been murdered at the hands of their father; a man consumed by anger and hatred. Anger and hatred towards me, and he had committed the final act of cruelty, by taking away the two people I loved most in the world.

As I lay on Jack's bed, his body still warm in my arms, guilt overtook me. Jack and Paul were dead because of me. This was the punishment my ex-husband saw as fitting after I had dared to leave him and take our sons with me in the hope they could finally live a life where they didn't have to walk on eggshells or be abused on a twisted whim. They were just young boys, at the start of their lives, but had been robbed of a future. In those horrible and dark minutes, I accepted my guilt, suffocated by the thought I had failed to fulfil the one responsibility I had as a mum; to protect my boys. The thoughts tortured me, and I no longer wanted to live, but something told me I had to carry on, so I made one final promise. I quietly whispered into Jack's ear, I would do everything I could to prevent any more children dying, at the hands of a parent. Then I silently vowed to myself that no other mum or dad, not one, should ever have to hold their child in their arms as they die, knowing it's at the hands of the other parent.

14

I WAS vaguely aware of people filling the room, though I barely recognised their movements. I was, however, acutely aware of the awful, deafening silence when all the machines and monitors were switched off, and a simultaneous pain raging through my chest, like a gale force wind. I couldn't let my son go and I curled my body closer to Jack's, tightly encircling him in my arms. I couldn't let him go. I needed him. I had to keep him close, because I knew as soon as I let Jack go, my life as I knew it was finally over. I would have to face a new, unbearable, reality. 'DC Dave' arrived. His eyes were red, betraying an upset he was trying to hide, but somehow, he took charge. Kindly and compassionately, he gently prised me off Jack, allowing the medical staff to do what they needed to. No longer physically connected to my son, I found I couldn't hear. Instead, a roaring sound filled my ears and my vision blurred as my eyes flooded with tears. Then everything went black.

When I came round I was on the floor, attached to an ECG monitor, which was taking readings of my heart. It was erratic, not that it could measure how severely broken and cracked I really was. When the doctors were finally happy to let me stand up, DC Dave quietly asked me if I felt strong enough to formally identify Jack's body. I nodded and he held my hand as I did what he asked and signed the form to officially end my son's life. He helped me hold the pen with my free hand and once I'd signed the document no parent should ever have to write their signature on, he quickly took the piece of paper out of sight. It was a small act of kindness that meant so much. As he guided me out of the room, I noticed a uniformed police officer by the door, just like there had been when Paul slipped away. Now both my children were crime scenes.

'I promise I will look after him,' DC Dave said. 'And bring him home.' I found out later, he worked a 36-hour shift to keep that promise.

We retreated back to the grey room, but I couldn't bear to look at the clock. The clock that had given me hope, that had signalled my son had survived another second, minute, hour. It was heartbreaking to know that time was now passing, without Jack and Paul in it. I was given a sedative to help me sleep, and shouldered by family, I made the journey one last time from the hospital to the Ronald McDonald apartment. Before the tablet took effect, my mind raced with cruel reminders of what should have been. It had felt like the longest day ever, yet it was still Monday, October 27; the first day of the half-term holidays. The boys should have been relaxing, enjoying a sleep-in, and looking forward to Halloween. Jack should have also had his appointment with Cafcass – his chance to explain how scared he was of his dad, how he dreaded going for the unsupervised visits. Instead, I'd held him in my arms, as he'd taken his final breath.

I was angry. Social Services had been told how dangerous my ex was, but they hadn't done enough to protect my sons. Cafcass had never heard Jack's voice, his fears, wishes and feelings. Their involvement had come too late. Far too little had been done to save the lives of Jack and Paul. A judge had wrongly presumed five hours unsupervised contact would be better than none, despite knowing their father was a perpetrator of domestic abuse, and that it wasn't just me who had been physically and emotionally attacked. Now my sons were silent forever, their voices unheard, because the rights of an abusive parent had been put before the rights and fears of two innocent children.

I curled under the bedclothes, waiting for the sedative to kick in. Finally, a peaceful oblivion embraced me. Until I woke up the next morning with an overwhelming and crushing sense of disappointment when I realised I was alive. I tightened myself into a ball, like a wounded animal, and decided not to move; to remain cocooned in my shell of sheets and blankets, protected from the harsh reality of my new existence. Mum got up and made us both a cup of tea. I curled up even further. The family co-ordinator arrived and I pulled the bedding over my head, so only my eyes and nose were visible. I could hear Mum getting upset, but I was frozen. All I could hear was incessant screaming inside my own head, which drowned out everything else. Carolyn and Ted arrived and began packing up our clothes and belongings. I didn't move a muscle. Ted came and sat next to me on the bed. He had loved his nephews deeply, and had looked forward to watching Paul race and Jack play his trumpet as they grew older. I knew he would have done everything he could to help Jack rehabilitate.

'It's time for me to take you home,' he openly wept.

Maybe it was hearing those words. Maybe it was the compassion in which they were said. Or maybe I just knew I couldn't stay crumpled in a hospital apartment forever, but I nodded. I knew it was time to leave. Christine, and my nieces, were all waiting at Mum's house. As we were getting ready to leave, my mobile phone rang, it was Lyndsey, one of my nieces.

'Auntie Claire, there's reporters and photographers at the bottom of the road, near Nannan's house,' she said. 'What do you want us to do?'

My response was instant.

'Go and tell them Jack has died. They will probably leave.'

It was raining when we set off from Manchester. None of us spoke. I was drowsy; the sedative I had been given still hadn't worn off. When we arrived in Thurlstone, we saw the first TV van. Photographers took pictures of our car as we drove past. As we approached the bottom of mum's road, Ted virtually had to stop the car, as camera flashes filled the windows. I hadn't been outside the confines of a hospital for six days and it all felt so overwhelming, but I still had another mountain to climb. Somehow, I had to walk into Mum's house, knowing Jack and Paul weren't there, and would never be again.

I was blinded by flashlights and the roaring in my ears began again. Ted managed to get past the huddle of reporters and photographers and pulled onto the drive. I got out of the car. Shaking and emotional, I put one foot in front of the other and got over the doorstep into what had become a haven. I was home, but as the enormity of it hit me, I fell to the floor.

The day after we got home from Manchester, a journalist knocked on the door. I've since discovered the press call this type of practice a 'death knock'. Jack had died less than 48-hours earlier and I was still heavily sedated. Mum told the journalist to leave, but in my desperate and confused state, I insisted on talking to her. I wanted the world to know what my ex-husband had done, and how much I loved my boys. I don't really remember much about the interview, apart from the look of concern on my mum's face, as I spoke to the reporter. She felt it was too soon. It probably was, but I didn't want anyone to think what had happened to Jack and Paul was an accident.

That first week after Jack lost his battle for survival was a haze of indescribable pain. Both my sons were dead and there was no purpose to my life anymore. I just wanted to die, so I could be with my boys. I didn't want to open my eyes, because every time I did, the crushing reality of what had happened came flooding back. As a mum, the whole point of my life had been to look after Jack and Paul, to cherish our special moments together and watch them grow, but that had been robbed from me in the most vindictive of ways.

Every morning my mum dragged me out of bed. It was her way of keeping me alive. At the time I hated her for it, but I know she was only doing what I would have done for Jack and Paul. Even after Mum got me out of bed, I would just curl up on the couch, unable to move. I wrapped myself in Jack and Paul's cuddle blankets. The blankets that had once been a symbol of happy times; the three of us snuggled up watching movies and drinking hot chocolate, or on early mornings before school, when they were still half asleep. Game nights, pick-me-ups, heart-to-hearts, laughter and moments of hope, but now, I clung onto those blankets, because they smelt of my precious boys. And there was another reason I hid under those blankets too. I couldn't see the world anymore, and if the world couldn't see me, it couldn't hurt me more and I could go back to somewhere only the boys and I knew and loved.

Few people were brave enough to try and join me under those blankets, in my defence against the world. The first was Father

David, from my local church, and second, a lovely lady called Lisa, from Victim Support, but even they couldn't break through to me in those early days. Those blankets were my barrier against the rest of the world. GPs came and gave me tablets to numb the pain, but they also kept my heart beating; something I resented and knew no matter how hard they tried, the doctors would never be able to fix how utterly broken it was. They told mum to hide all tablets, knives and keys. I looked at the people who were trying to keep me alive and silently screamed.

The fact Jack and Paul were still in a mortuary in Sheffield added to my agony, another form of torture. We had never spent more than three nights apart, and I needed them close to me. Peter, from the local funeral parlour, came to see me. There were so many forms to sign. He knelt next to me, and kindly showed me where to sign, not once but twice. One signature for each son. The hardest part was I had to sign to give Peter permission to collect my sons' ashes in the future. I hadn't even brought Jack and Paul home, but I was already consigning them to dust. My hand began to shake, but Peter caught it in his and held it tightly. I genuinely didn't think I could take anymore. It was over a week before Jack and Paul were brought back to Penistone and placed in the care of the funeral parlour.

In rare moments of lucidity, it became incredibly important to me that I thanked everyone who had tried to save my boys; the fire crews, the paramedics, the emergency transportation teams. I don't know how, but I wrote thank you card after thank you card.

Father David and Peter explained how the close-knit community we lived in were grieving too, shocked that two innocent boys could be so cruelly murdered by their own father. Two-minute silences were held at sports and music events, and tributes, in the form of flowers and cards, were left at both of the boys' schools, as well as outside what had once been our family home.

It was the lead-up to Halloween and Bonfire Night. Peter explained there was talk of the community bonfire, a huge annual tradition, being cancelled. Apparently, it didn't feel right. I understood but Jack and Paul had always loved Bonfire Night. I clicked onto the Pray for Jack page on Facebook and asked people not to cancel events. The community had been dealt a huge enough shock and I wanted children to have normality, just like my own sons would have, if things had been different. Every year I had bought costumes for the boys to wear to go trick or treating and pumpkins for them to carve. So, I asked everyone locally to do the same, and enjoy the special time with the children, making memories.

'Think of Jack and Paul,' I wrote, devastated I would never get the chance to watch their faces light up, ever again, as the night sky changed colours. I could never have imagined the ripple effect my post would have on the small town my boys had lived in for their short lives. Over the next few days, hundreds of people carved pumpkins for Jack and Paul and posted their pictures on Facebook. It was a moment of light amongst the shadows, a bright reflection of love and remembrance. Every shop and farm sold out of pumpkins, to the extent people were decorating turnips and peppers. Parades were held and runners at the Dorothy Hyman sports centre, where Paul had trained, ran around the track holding their carved pumpkins. A community was united against the darkness, illuminating the love people had for my two boys, whose smiles made the sun look dull and the stars ordinary.

For My Boys

St John's Church in Penistone opened its doors every day for people to go and light candles, say a prayer, or just have a moment of reflection. Throughout those early days, Father David was a constant presence and offered continual support. He walked with me through the darkest of times, a keeper of my unbearable thoughts and feelings, braving my pain that held no bounds. When Jack and Paul were brought back to Penistone, it was Father David who blessed them both, just as he had when he'd christened them years earlier.

Not only was I grieving for my sons, but I was also trying to hold together the fragments of my life as I faced the full extent of what their father had done. Double murder, arson and I would later discover financial abuse, but he wasn't the one serving a life sentence – I was. Every time the police family liaison officers visited, their unfaltering kindness was tempered by another hammer blow to the heart. On their first visit to the house, I popped my head over my sons' blankets and asked if they could arrange for me to have a lock of hair from each of my boys. There was an uncomfortable silence as both of them avoided looking at me. My stomach lurched. More bad news was coming. DC Dave came and sat next to me.

'We can do that with Paul,' he started. 'But in one of Jack's operations, they had to shave off his hair.'

I tried to swallow back my anguish, but I suspect I did a pretty bad job of hiding how distraught I was. All I could think about was Jack's thick, fluffy hair with the bits that stuck up. The memories were visceral. I could smell his hair, the scent of his shampoo, and could still feel the weight of his head as he rested it on my shoulder as I read stories to him each night. I was quickly learning that pain can hurt beyond tears or words.

'Can you use forensics to take his footprint, please?' I asked.

Claire Throssell

I took DC Dave's nod as a yes.

I had already decided what I wanted the boys to be dressed in for their final farewell. Jack should be in his band uniform, with his favourite white shirt, which he always said was softer than his school shirts. When I told my sister, Carolyn, about Jack's hair, she went out and bought a purple beanie to match the piping on his band uniform. The gesture was so thoughtful, but it was bittersweet. Jack hated wearing hats, arguing his hair, his beautiful hair, kept his head warm. We'd gone to a ceilidh once, when everyone had to wear hats, but by the end of the night Jack's had mysteriously disappeared.

My sisters and nieces had also bought two cat teddies to be with Jack and Paul in their resting place. Again, my heart ached. I had promised the boys when we moved into our new house together, they could both have a kitten. Jack wanted an orange tabby and Paul a silver one. Paul had even researched where we could get one and announced we would take the cat everywhere on a lead, including training. Paul had decided his cat would, rather appropriately, be called 'Flash' and be the fastest cat in the whole world. Except it never happened.

Guilt gushed through me, yet again, as I recalled how I had told the boys we had to wait until we moved into our new home before we bought them. They pleaded and protested, claiming 'it's not fair'. To my shame, I'd replied 'life's not fair'. Why hadn't I just agreed? Did it really matter? I had reasoned that the kittens would be young and moving from Mum's house to our new home would be too much, but to this day that decision still haunts me. I would do anything to go back in time and buy the kittens, just to see the look of joy on Jack and Paul's faces.

DC Dave did come back, as his previous nod indicated he would. In his usual caring manner, he sat down next to me, holding two small boxes in his arms. I saw Jack's name was on one and Paul's on the other as DC Dave placed them in front of me.

'Open them,' he gently coaxed.

I'd had so much bad news; I was frightened that whatever was inside them would only cause me more pain and heartache.

'It's okay,' DC Dave encouraged, sensing my trepidation.

I picked up the first one. Inside was another beautifully decorated box. I carefully lifted the lid, and inside was a plaster cast of Paul's foot, a glass angel, a candle, a balloon and forget-me-not seeds, alongside a personal message from a charity called *4Louis*. I was touched beyond belief at the kind and thoughtful mementos of my precious son. When I opened the second box, with Jack's name on it, the gifts were replicated, only the glass angel was holding a trumpet, pressed to its lips.

I placed a plaster cast foot in each hand and closed my eyes. As I ran my fingers down the feet, it felt like one last precious gift from Jack and Paul. I will always be grateful to the police for contacting the charity, who work relentlessly to provide families with treasured and personalised gifts. The work *4Louis* does for bereaved families is amazing. The founders, father and daughter, Bob and Kirsty, are very special people and set up the charity after losing their own grandson, and son, Louis. I had the privilege of meeting them both several years later, and couldn't thank them enough for the work they do to bring a little bit of joy to people whose lives have been ripped apart, in the darkest of times.

That visit from DC Dave was special in so many ways, but as I had started to expect, it also came with yet another 'hammer blow', as I now referred to the relentless difficult news I had to cope with. No-one had yet formally identified my ex's body. 'I think I know the answer to this, but I have to ask you,' DC Dave began. 'Will you identify him?'

'No!' I was resolute in my answer.

He also explained at some point the police would need a statement from me about what happened on the day of the fire. It was the last thing I wanted to do but agreed on the condition I did it alone. My family had suffered enough.

I did the interview two weeks later. I don't know how, but I recounted all the post separation abuse my ex-husband had hurled at me, after I left. Then explained on the morning of October 22, I had dropped the boys off at school and told them both I loved them. They each replied with their usual response; 'to infinity and beyond'. I clenched my eyes shut as I explained they were the last words we ever said to each other.

After I finished retelling the awful events of that day, I was dealt yet another hammer blow.

15

THE OFFICERS explained that throughout that Wednesday, my ex-husband had continually sent texts to Jack and Paul, telling them he'd bought them new trains for their trainset and they were waiting for them in the boarded-out attic.

'They just need two drivers,' his messages read.

He had also put a bowl of sweets in the loft and when the boys had got up there, their dad had acted fast to carry out his sadistic and evil plan. He'd already parked his van away from the house, to make it look like no one was home. Then, once the boys were in the house, he'd barricaded the patio doors leading into the back garden with a bike chain, placed a mattress in the doorway between the kitchen and the lounge, and wedged a chair against the door between the kitchen and the hallway. He had piled my belongings on our old marital bed and put another mattress at the top of the stairs. He had used five full canisters of petrol to set the house on fire. He'd then locked the front door and pocketed the key before creating a spark which would turn the house into a blazing inferno. There was no way for Jack and Paul to escape.

The officers explained when the firefighters managed to get into the house, Jack was on the landing. Despite his extensive injuries he told the firefighters: 'My dad did this and he did it on purpose.' Paul was still in the attic, with his one arm dangling down through the hatch.

Claire Throssell

I am haunted to this day about how terrified my sons must have been. My mind still fills with harrowing images of Jack and Paul desperately trying to escape that leave me crumpled on the floor.

When the firefighters arrived, they began tackling the blaze externally until a neighbour's CCTV showed my ex-husband, along with Jack and Paul, entering the house. Those brave firefighters risked their own lives to try and rescue my two precious sons, and it was only when they went inside that the distinct and overwhelming smell of petrol hit them. An investigation revealed 14 fires had been started around the house. Jack had been right when he'd told firefighters: 'My dad did this and he did it on purpose'.

How on earth could any parent do this? His hatred of me must have been all-consuming to carry out such a despicable act of revenge. The screaming inside me was getting louder and louder, but I had to control it as the police still hadn't finished talking to me – there were still more hammer blows to come. The police couldn't find any evidence the house was insured. My ex-husband, who looked after all the insurance, hadn't renewed it when the policy had expired in June.

When police discovered my ex-husband's work van, they found copies of suicide notes, alongside a letter to the bank, informing them I was now responsible for the £50,000 mortgage, because he would be dead. There was still more. Over the last six months, he had built up £15,000 worth of debt on credit cards.

The police also explained that at 6.30pm he murdered our sons, he had sent text messages to several people stating, 'I'm now at peace'. For reasons I'll either never understand or know, not one person responded. Maybe they didn't know he was with Jack and Paul, or maybe they just didn't think. I found it hard to comprehend. The overpowering thought that they didn't care enough for my two innocent sons was overwhelming. Unable to hold it together anymore, I ran to the toilet and vomited. I have no recollection of being guided back to the police car or the journey home. I was a broken shell.

A few days later, on the Friday before Remembrance Sunday, I was invited to Penistone Grammar School, where Jack had been a pupil. The school has its own Cenotaph for ex-pupils whose lives have been lost in war and Jack had been given the honour of playing *The Last Post* the year before and had been asked to perform the tribute again this year. As I stood at the memorial, the memories of the previous year came flooding back, how my heart had filled with pride. There was a tree next to the Cenotaph and around it a white ribbon had been tied. Nestled below the branches was a photo of Jack, his smile beaming towards me. *The Last Post* was played by a Reverend from Barnsley. As the poignant notes filled the air, I closed my eyes and allowed the memory of Jack's music and the Reverend's to blend as one. Marquees had been erected to protect us from the rain, but it felt like I was in tune with Mother Nature, both of us crying together.

The school had provided a wreath of white flowers for me to place on the Cenotaph. The purity of it was perfect and as I laid them down, I kissed my fingers and then touched the photo of Jack's beautiful face. It takes courage to fight on a battlefield, but I knew it took as much strength for Jack to go to his brother, when they were thrown into darkness, engulfed in thick smoke, and took his hand in a bid to lead Paul to safety. Over the years they had fought, argued and wound each other up, but when it counted Jack was always there when his little brother needed him the most.

Claire Throssell

By then the boys were in Dyson's funeral parlour in Penistone. I was advised not to see Paul, which was hard, but I knew there must have been a very good reason why they didn't want me to. I was allowed to see Jack and I was desperate to see him one last time, to hold him in my arms without all the tubes, wires, lines and bandages. But still I had to steel myself, not sure how I would react. When I arrived at the funeral home, my lovely boy was lying on a table, bathed in purple light. He was impeccably dressed in his band uniform, ready to go to his last concert. Although his face had been badly injured, to me Jack was still my beautiful, brave, boy. I put my arms around him, pressed my cheek to his, consigning those moments together to memory. I knew it was time to say goodbye, that this would be the final time I held my eldest son, but the pain of leaving Jack was indescribable. Unable to tear myself away, and blinded by tears, it was Peter from Dyson's who gently took hold of my hand and led me away. I gave him my favourite perfume, the one the boys had secretly used, and asked him to spray Jack and Paul with the scent. In the same way, it had always brought my sons comfort when they were scared and upset, it now helped me knowing a part of me would be with them, to infinity and beyond, on their final journey.

The day before their final farewell, I went back to the funeral home. After my previous visit, I'd asked for the boys' coffins to be sealed. When I walked into the room, they were resting on trestle tables, sleeping side by side. The room smelt faintly of my perfume which brought me comfort, and this time I didn't have to choose which son to go to as there was room for me to stand in between them. Bowing my head, I placed my hands on the simple white wood, and, along with the tears, I let the memories of the precious years we had shared together flow through me. In truth, I was desperately trying to reconnect with my children, who I had carried inside me, given life to and nurtured, but the cruel reality was I now felt horribly disconnected as a mum. In the space of three weeks, I had gone from doing everything for the boys to nothing.

I looked at the plaques and realised they were just engraved with their first names. No surnames had been used. As parents we never own our children, they are always only ever on loan to us, and in that time, it's up to us to love and care for them, show them the difference between right and wrong, and to use the time we have together wisely.

My ex-husband's name certainly had no right to be on their final places of rest, but I also knew the precious times I'd shared with Jack and Paul, wouldn't die with them. They would continue to shine bright in my heart and memories. Nothing and no one could take them away from me, but I also didn't want to leave them. The physical foundations of my life were crumbling away. I would have stayed with Jack and Paul forever, but at the right time, a familiar and gentle hand rested on my shoulder.

'They are Peter Pans forever,' Peter whispered.

The thought of them never aging, never being scared or hurt again, was bittersweet. I allowed Peter to lead me out of the room, took a deep breath, and tried not to think about what the next day would bring.

The night before the boy's final journey I didn't sleep a wink, tortured by the thought I would never see my sons ever again, hear their infectious laughter, or hold them in my arms. In the end, I climbed out of bed, went downstairs and wrapped myself in their snuggle blankets. I sat with my back against the radiator on the floor, shaking at the prospect of the day ahead. I wished with all my heart it was still yesterday, because the boys would still be physically here. After today there would be nothing. I would be nothing, and I wished that I couldn't feel anything either. Grief suffocated me, but I had to face the day ahead.

I knew the town had come together to help prepare for the service. The local cinema had loaned their PA system to St John's Church, so it could be heard by people who were outside. My employers had kindly produced an order of service, adorned with beautiful photos of the boys. Children at the primary school Paul had been at had recorded *I Will Pray For You* to be played during the service, and the senior school were holding their own ceremony at the same time for their students. I was so grateful for the care and thought that everyone had put in, but as I sat on the floor, my back to the radiator, I just wanted to die and to be with my boys. Without them, my life was non-existent. I didn't have a future.

When it got to 9am and it became apparent I wasn't going to conveniently die, I knew I had to find the strength to stand up, to get dressed and face another torturous day. I had asked everyone who was attending the final farewell to dress in colours. Jack and Paul were just children, I didn't need people to wear black to show their respects. I wanted them to celebrate my sons' lives with the brightness they had lived by.

I wore a green dress and a flowing bright red cardigan I had bought to wear for my niece's wedding, which felt perfect. The only shoes I had were black, so I borrowed a pair from my eldest sister, Christine. I stuffed the back of them with newspaper, as they were too big, and I couldn't afford or face going to choose a new pair. I'd spent every spare penny I had on legal fees, trying to keep

Jack and Paul safe. The irony. My sense of failure covered every part of me.

The day itself felt like an out-of-body experience – it was as though I was looking down on it from a faraway place. It was probably my mind's way of trying to pretend it wasn't happening to me. By 10am my family had gathered around me. I remember looking at both of my sisters' husbands, who were wearing identical pink shirts, and thinking how funny Paul would have found that. But for Ted and Tony, it was their way of showing solidarity and strength. They were my protectors, a reminder I wouldn't be walking alone.

Then the cars pulled up. Jack and Paul had come home for the final time. As we stood on the driveway, Ted took hold of my hand. I glanced at the garden and spotted foam Nerf gun bullets still stuck in some of Mum's plants after the boy's latest battle; now they would never play again. Their laughter resigned to a memory in the breeze.

The police held the traffic back on the short journey to the church, ensuring the cortege stayed together. Officers wearing white gloves lined the streets and saluted as our cars went past. But it wasn't just police officers. As I stared out of the window, I realised the pavements were full of people, all bowing their heads, paying their heartfelt respects to my lovely boys. Shops and businesses had also closed and when we came to a stop outside the church, nearby workmen stopped what they were doing, removed their hard hats and placed them over their hearts. Penistone had fallen silent.

Then as I looked at the huge, stone, church, I saw people had formed a circle, three deep, and everyone was connected by hands, elbows and arms. A circle of love, to give my lovely boys the protection and care they deserved, as they softly slept. I can't express how moved and touched I was, that so many people created such a beautiful gesture of love for Jack and Paul. The circle was only broken to allow the boys to be carried into church and then was immediately closed again. Friends and strangers alike had wrapped the boys in their arms. The community had come together to help me shoulder the burden of pain which engulfed me.

As I followed Jack and Paul into church, and over the rainbow, my brothers-in-law were either side of me. My legs gave way and they physically lifted me up. I held their hands tightly, determined not to let my sons down. Not today.

The boys' headteachers both gave beautiful speeches; Jack's music teachers performed a special arrangement of *What A Wonderful World*. I remembered how my eldest son had once played a solo of the same piece and knew he would have felt honoured his teachers did that for him.

I don't know how I survived the service. Maybe it was the circle of love, maybe it was the fact I had to do it for my sons, or maybe it was a mixture of both of those things and knowing I had no choice. But then came the hardest part. I didn't have the strength to face the crematorium. I had chosen the songs to be played; *Shine* by Take That and *Roar* by Katy Perry, which Paul always insisted on listening to before he went onto the running track to compete in a race. He would sing it to me too, understanding the meaning of the lyrics. It's still the ringtone of my mobile phone, and I hear his voice every time it plays.

So, as I stood outside the church, I said my final goodbyes to my two perfect, sweet, boys, kissing my hands and placing them, for the last time, on the white wood of their resting places. My brothers-in-law formed a shield with their bodies, to keep me hidden from the watching world, as my heart ripped out of my chest. Then Jack and Paul slowly moved away from me and they were gone.

16

THE NEXT few weeks passed in a blur, as I tried to come to terms with the fact that Jack and Paul had really gone. The inquest date was still to be set and I was dreading it – no parent ever wants to hear how their children died in forensic detail.

In the meantime, I had Christmas to contend with. I used to be one of those annoying parents who had everything bought by October, then a month later I would spend the day at Mum's house, wrapping everything up and hiding the gifts in cupboards. On Christmas Eve, I would wait for the boys to be fast asleep, then nip to Mum's house to get the presents so they could all be ready and waiting for Jack and Paul around the tree on Christmas morning. For me, the magic was everything, and what made the day so special.

But a month after the boys were murdered, their presents lay unwrapped in one of Mum's cupboards – a cruel reminder that there would be no excited guesses of what might have arrived under the Christmas tree. Never again would I be able to watch as Jack carefully removed the wrapping paper to see what surprises lay in wait or laugh as Paul ripped off the gift wrap at a rate of knots. Instead, I knew Christmas morning would deliver a deafening and heartbreaking silence.

I had given all Jack's sheet music to the music service for other children to play and enjoy, but I had kept the piece he was practicing, *Song To The Moon*, just before he was killed. It was such a beautiful melody. I was thinking about this as I looked at all the gifts in Mum's cupboard and it hit me what I needed to do. I wanted to make other children smile, like Jack did with his music, so I contacted Bluebell Wood Children's Hospice, in Sheffield, and arranged to take all the boys' presents and donate them.

It was a decision that would eventually help save my life. When I arrived, one of the women who worked there showed me around. It was humbling to see the amazing things that the staff did to support such desperately ill children, and the things those children and young adults achieved with such life-limiting illnesses. As I talked to the member of staff, she explained they offered counselling and asked if I would be interested. I agreed instantly and my counselling, with Angie Beasley, began in January 2015.

In the meantime, the fire investigation was concluded but the police hadn't finished their work and the house was still a crime scene. With each day something new would hit me, but there was kindness too. The house fire had destroyed virtually everything, including all the boys' school photos. The company who takes them, Tempest, heard about what had happened to my sons and sent me a selection of their latest photos, including lots of keyrings with Jack and Paul's pictures in, which I gave to family members. I sent one of the medium-sized photos of Jack and Paul to my ex-husband's parents and wrote them a letter. They hadn't seen their grandchildren for years, so I explained to them what the boys had been like and all about Paul's passion for running and Jack's love of music. DC Dave promised to deliver them, but I explained I didn't want them to reply. It would be too painful.

On Christmas Eve, DC Dave came to see me and explained the

inquest was due to be opened in January and then asked about the possibility of my ex having a will because nothing had been found. I hadn't and it meant I even ended up being charged for the funeral costs from the estate of a man who murdered his children.

But more hurt and pain was still to come. On one of DC Dave's visits, just before Christmas, he explained he needed to show me the photos of the remains of my house. He didn't want to do it, as much as I didn't want to see them, but he explained they could be shown at the inquests and he didn't want that to be the first time I saw them. As I looked at the charred remains of what should have been a happy family home, knowing my sons had been trapped in there, it felt like more than I could physically take. I could almost feel how scared they must have been. The police had already explained how my ex-husband had blocked all the doors to prevent my sons escaping and making it harder for the rescue services to enter. The images revealed how all my belongings had been piled on top of our marital bed and set alight, the mattress in Jack's room had been set on fire, and my ex-husband had used towels and bedding to intensify the flames in Paul's room. Photos revealed the green petrol canisters and the 14 different sites where the fires were started. But the one image that has never left me, and still haunts my dreams to this day, was of Paul's glasses on the floor, in the wake of all the devastation.

I didn't think my heart could take any more. Christmas Day passed in a blur. I spent it with Caz, Ted and Mum, but it felt horrifically empty. Without Jack and Paul, life was very bleak and the day was like a dark insight to what the future would look like.

On Boxing Day, I attempted to take my own life. I couldn't see the point of being alive anymore. All the light had gone out of my life, leaving it in darkness. I just wanted to be with my beautiful boys. I tried to cut my own wrists, but Mum found me in the kitchen bleeding and quickly wrapped a towel around my wrist. Thankfully, the following month, the counselling, which would go on to save my life, began.

Despite how dark life felt, I somehow managed to make my way into January. I was told all three inquests for Jack, Paul and my ex-husband had been opened but adjourned until February. But with bad news came a little bit of light, as the credit card companies, which my ex-husband had built up £15,000 worth of debt with, had agreed to write off the money owed, due to the fact we were divorced.

A will still hadn't been found, which meant Jack, as his eldest son was his next of kin. But after Jack died, I was his next of kin, so I legally inherited the uninsured ruins of our home. I didn't know where to start. I couldn't afford to pay for the repairs.

I had to handle one punch to the stomach after another, but the one thing I couldn't reason with was that I hadn't been there to protect my sons. It shouldn't have been Jack trying to save Paul. I should have been the one taking care of both of my sons. Not only that, but my boys had also died because of me. My ex-husband had killed them to hurt me – it was his final act of revenge. Their lives had been sacrificed to punish me for daring to leave the abuse I had endured for years. My ex-husband was blinded and consumed with anger, jealousy and hate towards me. Even though he had found a new partner within two months of me leaving, he had been hell-bent on destroying me and very nearly did.

Claire Throssell

Existing felt very lonely without my boys. I spent day after day, followed by night after night, wondering what sort of men my brave, courageous sons would have become. I was consumed with guilt that their lives had been taken away, and I was still alive. There were so many milestones to endure. On January 9, 2015, Paul should have celebrated his 10th birthday. The silence of the day felt unbearable. He should have been revelling in the fact he had now reached double figures. Instead, with my family, I released blue balloons – his favourite colour.

By the time I met my appointed counsellor, Angie Beasley, who had been arranged by Bluebell Wood, for the first time, my existence couldn't have gotten any darker or more overwhelming. As I talked, despite how painful it was, I felt like my feelings, emotions and thoughts were being validated for the first time. Counselling isn't easy, it's painful and for it to work, it requires brutal honesty, trust in your counsellor and commitment to work through the tangle of emotions, trauma and the huge mass of feelings that come with missing your child and the yearning for what can never be.

The counselling sessions helped me cope with the continual tsunami of bad news that came one wave after another. When you hit rock bottom, there's only one way you can go, and that's up. Week after week, Angie picked up the pieces of my broken self. There was no magic cure and I was in a very dark place, but instead of being on the floor, I had a chair. And that chair made it a little bit easier to get back up. Angela didn't try and glue me back together, instead she showed me ways to build around the gaps that had been created, to live with the torn edges of my existence and constantly reminded me of the light within me. She taught me there was still a beacon of hope and a tiny flicker of illumination that glimmered, no matter how faintly, in the darkness, that shone through the cracks and the tears, the scars and the pain. The pieces might no longer be intact but somehow, with determination, they could hold together. It wasn't a quick or easy process. I saw Angie for five years and she became an anchor in the sea of raw grief I was drowning in, as well as a safe space to throw the anger and despair away.

It was still very tough in the beginning, though. I did, however, try and find comfort in every way I could. I had been told you could use loved ones' ashes in the ink for a tattoo. I know it's not to everyone's taste, but the idea of being able to have my children with me permanently gave me strength. The only problem was making the ashes fine enough to mix with the ink. My mum was given the job. It's strange where you find light and humour. We both laughed that Jack and Paul would be furious with her for giving them a banging headache, as she pounded their ashes with a rolling pin.

The task done, I booked my appointment with the tattoo artist who carefully penned the words 'Jack and Paul love you to infinity and back' on my chest, in memory of the phrase the three of us had shared. When I traced the letters with my fingers, I could feel the boys' ashes and knew they would be next to my heart forever. On my arm, I had the Hawaiian word 'Ohana', which means family. Famously followed by, 'No one gets left behind or forgotten' in *Lilo and Stitch*. My mum at the grand age of 74 had the same word tattooed onto her arm, just without the ashes.

I also had some of the boys' ashes turned into a ring – that way I would have something tangible I could touch. Again, I know it's not to everyone's taste but for me being able to take my children with me, have a part of them close, helped me to carry on living. I only had to touch the glass on the third finger of my left hand to know my boys were with me – Peter Pans forever. Without my tattoos and ring, I don't think I could have withstood the pain of having the boys interred.

On the day we interred Jack and Paul's remaining ashes, I was barely hanging on. I knew I couldn't take the rest of the boys' ashes home – they would be a constant reminder of what had happened to them. I'd had Jack and Paul's ashes carefully and lovingly mixed together and then I had them interred with my late dad. I had wondered if the boys would be cross with me; like most brothers they had their arguments and fall outs, but despite their differences they were never far apart from one another, and I couldn't bear for them to be alone now. I took some comfort in the fact they were together, but on stormy nights or when the wind is howling and the rain is pouring, I've had to stop myself going to their resting place and digging them up to take them home, knowing how much they hated the cold and dark.

My birthday came round in February and I sobbed into my sister's arms, guilty that I had lived to see another year, but my sons hadn't. You feel terrible as a parent, when you have to leave your children to go to work, but the guilt a parent feels for outliving their children penetrates every fibre of your soul.

That same month, my niece, Elizabeth and her fiancé, Tom, got married. It broke my heart to see Jack and Paul's suits hanging unused in the wardrobe. After Jack had died, staff at Penistone Grammar School, where he had been a pupil, had paid for white wristbands for students and our family to wear. At the wedding our wrists were all adorned with one, and Elizabeth had one sewn into her dress. It was her very special and thoughtful way of including the boys.

On the day of the wedding, I found myself instinctively putting my hands out for Jack and Paul to hold and looking around every room I entered to check where they were. It was a habit I was finding heartbreakingly hard to break. The rituals of a mum die hard. The cruelty of my hands remaining empty was indescribable, as was not seeing their smiling faces. It was like a slam to the chest when my brain caught up that I would never see their faces or hold their little hands again.

In the lead up to the inquests into my sons' deaths, I had to meet up with the investigating officer, Detective Inspector Stuart Hall. Caz came with me, insisting I shouldn't go alone. Thank goodness she did, as I was dealt yet another hammer blow. DI Hall explained that my ex-husband had a meeting with the Cafcass officer on October 20, two days before the fire. She tried to terminate the meeting early, but my ex-husband had barricaded her in the office, by blocking the doorway, and refused to let her leave. In previous meetings with her, I had warned the officer never to be alone with my ex-husband as he wasn't safe to be around whenever he was challenged or angry.

Not only had my warnings gone unheeded and disregarded, I felt sick to the core that despite seeing how dangerous my ex-husband was, she did not put anything in place to stop the access visit with my sons two days later. Instead, she informed senior members at Cafcass that she wanted senior colleagues present in future interviews with their dad. It was too little too late. In my eyes, I had tried to protect the Cafcass officer, but they had utterly failed my sons. Half an hour after her meeting with my ex ended, he was filmed on CCTV buying five cans of petrol.

As I was still taking in what DI Hall had told me, he asked if I would like to read the letters my ex had sent to me and my mum on the day of the fire. They had been intercepted by family and handed in to the police. My sister was shaking her head at DI Hall, but I said yes. No matter how hard, I needed to know everything, even though as I saw the letters, and recognised his handwriting, I felt sick. Each letter started in the same way. *I'm sorry it had to end this way, but they are in my arms now. Forever away from your evil eyes.* I handed the letter back to DI Hall, wordlessly. For all the vengeful, hateful and derogatory words that had been hurled at me repeatedly for over a decade, it would appear my ex-husband had finally run out of them when he took the decision to end his and our sons' lives.

'I want you to know,' DI Hall said. 'Jack's last words have been taken by the police as his dying testimony.'

The kind detective promised to make sure they were recorded and used when he was called to the witness stand during the inquest. I was so grateful. Jack's voice would be heard.

In the week leading up to the three inquests, which would all be heard one after the other, in March 2015, I was full of angst. I barely slept a wink and struggled to eat a thing. The thought of hearing about how Jack and Paul had died in minute detail was horrifying, but as a mum, I had to be there to represent my sons. It didn't help that the inquests were being held in the same building where Jack and Paul's postmortems were carried out. Just hearing those words made me want to cry.

The police had prepared me for what I might see and hear at the inquests, but I don't think you can ever be ready to hear, in detail, about how your children had been murdered. Caz came with me and we were shown the seats reserved for the family, and where the press would be seated. I'd expected the media to be there and I understood it was their job to report on what was said at the inquest, what I didn't envisage was coming face-to-face with my ex-husband's parents. I was just grateful my vicar and a police officer were sitting between us.

My ex-husband's inquest was heard first. I have no idea how his parents must have felt when they heard their son described as an abuser, bully, and arsonist. You could have heard a pin drop as the truth of my ex-husband's cruelty was read out. In that moment, I hoped that all the friends and family that had come to represent him, now understood what a monster he really was. The coroner recorded a verdict of death by suicide in relation to my ex. I would have liked 'murderer' stamped across his death certificate, but unfortunately the law doesn't allow for that.

Hearing the details of his death was hard, but much worse was still to come, as I had to listen to how my sons died. But I was a lioness there to protect my cubs. Thankfully, my ex-husband's parents were no longer sitting near me and as the inquest started, Caz leaned into me.

'Imagine Jack and Paul are sat on the bench swinging their legs,' she whispered.

It helped me block out the room and focus on what the coroner was saying but hearing the details of Jack and Paul's deaths being read out was to feel something beyond the normal realms of pain. As a parent, it shatters something inside you knowing your children's broken bodies have been examined piece by piece. In turn, it tears you apart piece by piece. Knowing my boys hadn't been physically tortured in the attic was little consolation, but I still worried what their dad had said to them. Did he tell them they were going to die? Did he taunt them? Did he blame me?

When DI Hall took to the stand, he kept his promise, and read out Jack's last words, ensuring they were recorded on the court files. Social Services and Cafcass both had legal representatives present, the latter arriving late; a total disregard for how difficult this day was for me and my family. When the Cafcass officer, took to the stand, I felt my whole body shake. She hadn't even brought her notes with her, and ended up using DI Hall's. Unaware of the protocol, I stood up and asked her why she had made the decisions she did. I didn't realise you couldn't just interrupt proceedings. DC Dave, the liaison officer, gently encouraged me to sit back down.

I sat through all the awful details of how the fires had started, how my sons had fought for life, how they didn't stand a chance. Because my ex-husband had never stood trial, the coroner couldn't label him a murderer, which felt like an injustice, but I understood. Instead, the coroner ruled Jack and Paul had been unlawfully killed, then looked at me, and reiterated none of this was my fault.

But as I left the court, I was still riddled with guilt that I could have done something more to protect my boys. I was a mum – it was my only job. Then I had to face the press, who had just heard all the horrific details of how Jack and Paul had died. The police had prepared a statement to be read out on the family's behalf, but as I looked at the waiting reporters, I knew it was time for my voice to be heard. I let the police read out their piece, but I knew a prepared statement couldn't possibly convey my feelings; the things I felt deep in my heart. And there was something else too; I wasn't prepared to be silenced for a minute longer.

For My Boys

I took a deep breath and started answering their questions, one after the other. *How was I feeling? How had I coped? How would I remember Jack and Paul?*

Then came one question that struck deep.

'What's your response to the coroner absolving you from any part in your son's murders?'

It was then I knew what I had to do.

'My sons' names are Jack and Paul.' Their names had to be known. I would not allow my precious sons just to be another two anonymous victims of a Serious Case Review. Then I added: 'The coroner was very kind with his verdict and subsequent ruling. However, I let them go on that contact visit. I wasn't there when they needed me the most. Therefore, the blame lies with me.' As I said the words, I touched the tattoo on my chest; the one that would permanently connect me to Jack and Paul.

The journalists' gasps were audible, their shocked and sympathetic shakes of their heads visible, but they didn't carry the guilt that I bore every day. Knowing my strength was about to succumb to tears, I politely thanked them and walked away, my vision blurred. The inquests had filled in gaps, the truth had been heard, but there was no closure. There never could be. My life sentence had begun.

17

A COUPLE of weeks after the inquests should have been Jack's 13th birthday, the day he would have become a teenager. When your babies are born, everyone tells you to savour every moment, that time goes too fast, but you never envisage your children won't be there. It's the wrong order of things. Instead of rejoicing in my eldest son reaching such a monumental milestone, I stood and wept at his and Paul's grave. This time we released red balloons — Jack's favourite colour.

By April I was facing up to the ruins of my life, as well as the physical ruins of my house, something else I couldn't fix. But then Father David suggested setting up a fund to help rebuild my home. A journalist, Michelle Rawlins, who I had been working with came up with a name — Care for Claire, and an appeal was sent out to the media, local businesses and trades people to see if anyone could help with skills or materials. A press conference was set up at St John's Church. I was terrified at the thought of TV cameras, and told Michelle I didn't think I could do it. She gently squeezed my hand.

'You will be fine,' Michelle promised. 'You are in safe hands and we are all behind you.'

It was hearing the words 'we are all behind you' that made the difference. For 16 years, I had battled alone.

I was humbled by the results of the media appeal, so many

people got in touch, all wanting to help. The worry and complexities around the house, which I had assumed were mine to carry alone, were lifted by the whole of Yorkshire, who heard about my plight and offered to support me. Once again, the circle of love that got me through the boys' final journey, stepped in. Hundreds of people came forward to help or donated materials to renovate the house, something I will be forever grateful for. It allowed me to kneel, and eventually stand, against the rubble of what had once been my life. Their humanity and compassion restored my faith in human nature and reminded me to never allow the hope inside me to fade. There is one person I must mention specifically and that is Ged Brearley Jnr, who took on the role of project manager. Despite having a newborn baby and commitments of his own, he managed to organise everyone and somehow coordinate rebuilding the burnt-out shell of my home.

There were so many who offered a hand to help me heal, to help me stand again, including the Sunday Times bestselling author, Milly Johnson, who wrote an e-book, The Barn on Half Moon Hill, and donated the proceeds to the Care for Claire campaign. I don't think I can ever say thank you enough times to show how much that meant to me.

In the months that followed a wealth of labourers, trades people and volunteers set to work on renovating the house, most of them giving up their time to do it on a voluntary basis. Once again, I was overwhelmed with gratitude to everyone who had come together to help me.

In June 2015, one meeting after another was scheduled. I was invited to talk to the chief executive of Manchester Royal

Infirmary regarding Jack's treatment, as well as being asked to attend an interview in relation to the Serious Case Review with Cafcass, and an appointment had been made with HSBC. I was still deep in grief, and it all felt too much. I wanted to pull a blanket over my head and ignore everything. I was so angry at my ex-husband too. It felt as though he was leaving me to pick up the devastating pieces of what he had left behind, taunting me from beyond the grave. The lyrics of an ABBA song, 'The Winner Takes It All', seemed to play repeatedly in my head, competing with my endless, silent screams. I felt like the loser who had to fall, and shouldn't complain.

But I did have to complain because so many people had let my sons down. My ex had tried to destroy me and had succeeded in taking everything that mattered away from me, but the one thing he couldn't snatch was my love and determination to build a lasting legacy for Jack and Paul. I had promised them, as they died in my arms, I would fight to make sure they were never forgotten, and it was that vow which got me through the battles ahead.

My first meeting was with the hospital and I was told there was going to be an external investigation into Jack's treatment, carried out by staff from a Birmingham hospital, who also have a specialist burns unit. The news came as a shock as I hadn't even realised Jack's care was under scrutiny. Out of all the organisations involved in Jack's life, I had really believed Manchester Royal Infirmary was the one who hadn't let me down, and more importantly hadn't failed my son. This was definitely one of those hammer blows I hadn't seen coming.

At the meeting I was handed a brown envelope. Why is bad news always delivered in brown envelopes? This one contained the painful details of Jack's final hours and as I held the vessel of what I knew was going to be more bad news, I started to shake. I dropped it onto the table, almost repelling the information. Maybe it was my defence mechanisms, my body's way of protecting me, but I needed a few minutes to steel myself.

Once I'd gathered myself, I opened the envelope and read the details. It revealed on the day of Jack's final surgery, he had not been in a stable condition, but the decision had still been made to take him to theatre. He was removed from the machine that was cooling his blood because the theatre couldn't accommodate it. From that point on, he began to struggle. Sepsis seeped in, his organs began to fail, and because of his severe burns, potassium built up in his beleaguered body, and his heart stopped. By the time medics reconnected Jack to the cooling machine, it was too late. CPR on his burnt, damaged, chest was all they could do.

I put the papers back in the envelope and looked across the table at the CEO of the hospital, who was also a surgeon. He'd asked me a question, but in a state of confusion and shock, I hadn't heard it.

'Could you say that again?' I asked, utterly bewildered by what I'd just read.

'Do you understand everything you have just read?' he asked.

I nodded, too numb to speak. He explained he would meet with me again once the external investigation had taken place and a report had been completed.

Would that be in a brown envelope too? It took all my strength not to utter those words. Instead, I stood up, proffered a strong handshake, and left.

Next came my interview for the Serious Case Review, which had been set up at the Victim Support office in Barnsley. This was the meeting I had been dreading. I knew it had to happen but my anger, fury and despair at the system which had deemed my sons should see their dad, had ultimately killed them. As soon as I was guided into the room by Lisa, my victim support officer, my chest began to pound, and I felt like my airways were closing, preventing me from breathing. Looking back, I realise I was having a panic attack, but I was determined this meeting went ahead. This was where my fight for Jack and Paul had to begin.

I was introduced to a man called Peter Ward, who would conduct the interview. I could tell he was nervous, but I was too het up to make him feel at ease. Instead, I explained in great detail the abuse I'd suffered, before and after I left my ex-husband, and the barbaric and humiliating experience of the family court that ultimately led to his opportunity to play out his unspeakable revenge in a last act of evil vengeance.

I'd been forced to learn fast and knew that unlike when a crime is committed and the onus is on the police to prove exactly that, when it comes to domestic abuse and child abuse, despite this being the police's responsibility, it all too frequently falls to the victims, adults and children, to prove their case, even with how exhausted, broken, scared and traumatised they are.

After I'd said my initial piece, a break was called, and I went outside so I could try and breathe more easily. My blouse was sticking to my back, and I felt shaky – my body was in fight or flight mode.

I went into the toilets and splashed my face with water, pulled my shoulders back and returned to the room. But the break did little to alleviate the tension, which once again peaked when I explained very clearly I'd received no support from the police during the abuse, separation and post separation abuse. I also stated that although Social Services had interviewed my sons, they hadn't, in my opinion, done enough to help them.

And then I spoke about Cafcass. This was my opportunity to explain what had happened. Determined not to let my sons down, I made myself cold, calm and measured. The numbness I had felt until that point disappeared and was replaced with anger and a sense of injustice which ignited inside me. I'd been biting my tongue and the inside of my cheek so much, my mouth started to bleed, replicating the metaphorical nasty taste I'd had in my mouth for months. This was the moment. The moment to spell out very clearly the catastrophic failings Cafcass had made. The organisation's legal representative might have been able to restrain the coroner at the boys' inquests, but she could not restrain me here.

I explained in cold, hard, facts how Cafcass had taken too long to get involved in my family law proceedings. They wouldn't have had time to fill in the Section 7 report, which is produced when domestic abuse is suspected, in time for the final hearing on November 17. The Cafcass officer had also ignored my warning not to see my ex-husband alone, leaving herself in a vulnerable position. But far worse, Cafcass, as far as I was concerned, had completely failed to safeguard Jack and Paul. At this point, Pater Ward, who was interviewing me, said he would have to have a meeting with Cafcass before he could complete the Serious Case Review.

'Is there anything else you would like to add?' he asked.

'Yes,' I replied instantly. 'I want Jack and Paul named in the review.

Claire Throssell

Mr Ward stopped writing and looked up at me.

'It's not government policy I'm afraid.'

I wasn't fazed. 'It may not be,' I said. 'But I am making a formal request and giving my full permission for my sons' names to be published in the review. They are not letters, they had names, and they are my sons. They have been named by the coroner and by the media, please don't dehumanise them in the review.'

Mr Ward warned me he didn't think it would be possible but would make a note of my request. He also explained he would be in touch regarding a meeting with Cafcass. I would have to go through all this again. More trauma, more upset, but no number of meetings would bring my sons back. I was exhausted.

I then had to face the bank. HSBC had requested a meeting, but when I arrived, instead of being taken into a private room, I was sat down at a table in the middle of the bank, with people all around, and asked very bluntly how I intended to pay the £50,000 back that was outstanding on the mortgage. I was horrified and humiliated, but I guess to them I was just another account holder, and they wanted to redeem their debts. I had printed off photos of the broken, burnt-out shell of my former home. I now had to hand them over in a very public space, despite how horrifying it was just to see those images, knowing my sons had been mortally injured in that house. I had to prove I was the victim of a crime and ask the bank to find a way to support me. When I repeated what had happened, the bank manager struggled to speak as he put the photos in my file and then told me they would extend the repayments, without interest. Another meeting and another part of my soul was ripped apart, but worse was still to come.

For My Boys

On July 6, 2015, I met with Christine Banim, the national service director of Cafcass. I again explained how I felt the service had let my boys down and failed to safeguard them against their father. I had warned the organisation repeatedly he was a danger and very capable of hurting Jack and Paul. I had stated very clearly he was aggressive and narcissistic, but I hadn't been believed, heard or seen. In my opinion, they had just been ticking boxes and not really listening to how dangerous my ex-husband was. Nine days later, on July 15, I received a letter from Christine, admitting Cafcass had failed my sons, and they would say the same to the Serious Case Review. They also stated national training would take place and all the issues I had raised would be addressed. Christine ended the letter admitting nothing she could say would bring my boys back but hoped that I now felt I had been listened to and taken seriously. She assured me that in the future as an organisation, they would act on the learning I had brought to their attention. It's hard to say I was grateful for the attention they had given the case. I did hope no other child would suffer at the hands of an abusive parent, but for Jack and Paul, it was too little too late.

Although I'd had one harrowing meeting after another, there were some positives to 2015. Springvale Primary School, where both my sons had been pupils, established a Jack Sykes award in music and a Paul Sykes sportsmanship award, both of which I was asked if I would present on an annual basis. Barnsley Music Service, where Jack had been a member, also created shields in the boys' names to inspire and encourage young musicians.

Then, in September, the Serious Case Review was published and it came as the biggest hammer blow of them all. The Review concluded that the deliberate and devastating actions of my ex-husband could not have been predicted by anyone. Research suggests that such incidents are rare, and the vast majority of estranged fathers would never consider such atrocious actions, and there is no way of identifying who will do so. The police were criticised for their lack of action, as was my GP practice. Social Services were also criticised for not carrying out the Section 7 report. It was noted that although my sons' medical records were clear, if mine had been checked, it would have been spotted that on three separate occasions I had been treated for injuries consistent with domestic abuse and no questions had been asked. I had always been the boys' human shield. It should have been my life my ex-husband took. It was me he hated and despised.

The Review didn't mention any of the failings Cafcass had made and admitted to. It also failed to mention that I had warned everybody involved – the judge in the Family Court hearing, Social Services and Cafcass that my husband was a threat to the boys and capable of killing. It didn't mention that Jack and Paul died because he wanted to punish me and giving their father unsupervised contact allowed him to do just that. The Review also failed to mention my sons by name. Against all my wishes, Jack and Paul had become Child A and Child B, hidden in a report destined for a desk at Whitehall. I vowed this would be the last time my children weren't known by their names.

After everything I had been forced to endure, I knew it was time to take a stand. Everyone had failed Jack and Paul, including me, but I was not going to let David Cameron's government sweep what happened to my sons under the carpet. Their lives mattered. They mattered. It should never have to be about predicting harm;

it should be about preventing it. It was time to challenge the government's stance on domestic abuse. I knew it was going to be a challenge, but giving up was not an option

18

EARLIER IN 2015, I had written to Fylde Council asking if they would consider placing a plaque on the bandstand in Lytham St Annes, where my sons had played on all our breaks. Jack had always wanted to take his trumpet on holiday with us and play it in the bandstand, but never got the chance. I still feel guilty about this, as every time he asked, I looked at the car, packed to the rafters and promised we would take it next time. Only next time never came.

The council wrote back and explained that due to the protection orders on the bandstand, a plaque wouldn't be possible, but they offered to refurbish a bench and dedicate it to the boys. I was, once again, touched by the thoughtfulness and kindness of people I had never even met.

A date was set for September for an unveiling and the council kindly paid for me to stay in the St Ives Hotel, the same place I had stopped at with Jack and Paul. On the afternoon of the unveiling, I was walking to the council building with my mum, sister, Caz, and her husband, Ted, and noticed chairs were being set up in the bandstand, but didn't think too much of it.

When we arrived at the council building, I was introduced to the mayor. We exchanged hugs and a kiss on the cheek.

'Oooh, you have just kissed my arse,' he chuckled.

'What?' I laughed, slightly taken aback.

He explained that he had been in a fire as a child and skin for his graft had been taken from his bottom for his face. I didn't know whether to giggle or apologise, but the mayor quickly put me at ease, chuckling at his own story. He then explained that due to his own experience, the story of Jack and Paul had really touched him.

After a cup of tea and a chat, one of the council directors, Paul Walker, took my hand and said he had a surprise for me. Instinctively, my heart dropped, because all surprises over the last year had been bad ones. He led me down a corridor and everything went quiet, then Paul opened the door and in front of me was Barnsley Town Concert Band, which Jack had been a member of. I was speechless. This had all been arranged without me suspecting a thing, and once again, I was overwhelmed by how wonderful some people could be.

We were all led outside. It had been an overcast morning, but as soon as the band started playing the sun made an appearance and shone brightly on the bandstand and the musicians Jack had classed as his second family. I now realised why all the chairs had been set out. The full band had come to play in memory of Jack and Paul. It was such a special occasion and one that still holds a very special place in my heart.

Back home, the anniversary of the boys' deaths drew closer and I knew I needed to concentrate on commemorating them so I arranged a musical celebration at St John's Church. I asked Barnsley Town Concert Band to perform alongside Marsh Ladies Choir. I decorated the church with the hand and footprints the pupils of Penistone Grammar School had drawn after the boys had died, along with the written messages on them. I had kept each and every one of them in a special box.

Claire Throssell

The concert was everything I could have hoped for. It was a wonderful and fitting tribute to the boys. On the night, I paid my own personal homage to my beautiful boys. I am a flautist and decided I would play *Tears in Heaven*, accompanied by a friend, Chris, who plays the guitar. The local BBC news, Look North, came and covered the event, and a few days later Chris and I made a private recording, creating a memory that, however bittersweet, was something to treasure.

At the concert, I also launched a charity, Heads Together Barnsley Charitable Trust, with the aim of helping families in their darkest times. I wanted to give something back in recognition of what everyone had done to help me. The concert raised over £800 and I donated it to Bluebell Wood Children's Hospice, which helped me find something to smile about on what was such a difficult milestone to cope with.

In December 2015, domestic abuse charity Women's Aid got in contact via Barnsley Music Service and asked if I would be willing to meet them. I had no idea what it would involve but agreed and we set up a time for the following month. That meeting was about to change my life.

I will always remember that train journey to Sheffield to meet Alice and Sian from the charity. They sent me several reassuring messages to say they were looking forward to meeting me. I was at such a low ebb, still struggling to get through each day, so to hear someone was looking forward to seeing me made me smile. As soon as I arrived at the café, where we had arranged to meet, Alice and Sian stood up and both gave me a huge hug. I instantly warmed to them.

Over several cups of tea, I discovered the core values Women's Aid stand for aligned with my beliefs. They had conducted research to discover how many children had died as a result of unsafe child contact with a known perpetrator of domestic abuse between 2004 and 2014. It made me feel physically sick as they explained there had been 19 child homicides in that decade alone. The loss of 19 children's lives that could have been prevented. Each one of those children had been reduced to an anonymous number or a letter in a Serious Case Review, gathering dust in a file in Whitehall. Jack and Paul were amongst them. Sadly, apart from Jack and Paul, for legal reasons the children identified in Women's Aid's research cannot be named. It made me more determined than ever that children should not become an anonymous statistic after their deaths.

As I showed Alice and Sian pictures of my sons, they explained they were turning the findings of their report into a campaign. They said it would come under the title, Child First – it was perfect, summing up exactly how I felt. The charity was about to launch a petition calling on the Justice Secretary to end the presumption of contact between known perpetrators of abuse and their children. A Presumption of Contact clause had been introduced after the Children's Act 1989 became legislation to protect parent's rights over the rights of a child.

This presumption in my opinion was wrong and misguided. Every child deserves a happy childhood, a childhood without fear. But to ensure this, I knew presumption of contact had to end and be taken out of law. To me it was, and is, dangerous to assume every parent, male or female, is safe and will protect their children. Jack and Paul were and are evidence this is not always the case. Removing presumption of contact will not affect safe, responsible parents who have good relationships with their children, but it will save the lives of children, who are at risk of harm from domestic abuse.

'Will you join forces with us?' This was the question Alice and Sian posed to me.

Would I stand alongside Women's Aid and fight for the changes needed to protect children, both now and in the future? I didn't have to be asked twice. My last promise to Jack and Paul was that their deaths wouldn't be in vain. If this campaign was successful, Cafcass, Social Services and judges would have to follow better procedures. This wasn't just about Jack and Paul, though, this was about the other 17 children over the last decade who lay permanently sleeping. It was also about every child who was living scared and silent in an abusive home. Witnessing and experiencing domestic or sexual abuse is something no child should have to endure but far too many do, as a result of poor family court decisions.

Sian and Alice were giving me the opportunity to make real and impactful changes to make children's lives better, to be able to hold my head up and say 'I'm trying' when I visit where my own sons sleep. Of course, I said yes straightaway. From that moment, Women's Aid held my hand tightly and to this day have never let it fall. Alongside the community I lived in, they gave me hope, dignity and a reason to live again.

On January 16, 2016, the Child First campaign was launched. That morning, I appeared alongside Sian on BBC Breakfast, followed by the Victoria Derbyshire Show, then an interview with Radio 5 Live. My sons were no longer anonymous when it came to the law. Jack's final words 'My dad did this and he did it on purpose' had now been heard by millions of people across the UK. With Women's Aid, I asked all those watching and listening to take a stand with us, and for all the children who deserved a better, safer, future. We appealed for the public to sign the petition in order to secure a debate in parliament, to prevent another child ending up like Jack, having to reach for help in the darkness, terrified, and to say they had been hurt on purpose by one of their parents. The campaign became a living and breathing collaboration which saw thousands of people unite in the form of a signature, turning every child's voice into a roar.

The following month the Sun newspaper asked if they could feature me in an article about the campaign. Once again, I immediately said yes. I wanted as many people as possible to know about the petition. They sent a make-up artist and a photographer to take pictures. The photographer was called Paul, and we formed a wonderful rapport. He very kindly created a photographic canvas, featuring Jack's trumpet and Paul's running trainers. You can still see the imprints of Paul's feet in the trainers and Jack's fingerprints on his trumpet. It meant the world to me, especially as Jack's hands had been destroyed in the fire.

I still keep Jack's PE kit and trumpet in the boot of my car, alongside Paul's running trainers. It was where they were left after they were used for the final time, and 11 years on, I still can't take them out.

In March 2016, I moved out of Mum's house and into my own flat. A property developer, who had converted a paper mill in Penistone into apartments, offered me one of them rent free for a year, with the option to buy it afterwards. He wanted no thanks or recognition, but that wonderful, generous and kind man gave me the opportunity to start building my own future.

Through the end of 2015 and into 2016, other kind people had been tirelessly working on my old house. So many had even given up part of their Christmas holidays to work on the renovations, something I will be eternally grateful for. I will never know the exact number of people, trades people, businesses and organisations that helped rebuild the house, but their support also played a huge part in putting me back together. They made me believe in humanity and kindness again. They gave me the strength to live, a reason to fight, and the means to start again.

During the work, Ged, the Project Manager, had posted a picture of himself posing in the new bath, on Facebook, and with it, a new idea was born – a fun, risque calendar – to raise money for my charity, Heads Together Barnsley Charitable Trust. So many members of the community said they would love to be involved and the photographer from *The Sun* agreed to take all the photos – and it made me chuckle thinking about the cheeky poses they would strike!

Finally, in May 2016, the house was finished, put on the market, and sold. A mixture of emotions soared through me. I'd been scared no one would buy the house, knowing its devastating history, so I was relieved that a buyer had come forward. But there was also overwhelming sadness that this is what had become of my once family home. Although it had ended in the most awful of ways, there had been good times in that house too. I was flooded with memories of how Jack, Paul, and I had sat at the kitchen table, with glitter and paint, after going on an acorn and pinecone hunt, and made Christmas plates, or how we had spent year after year carving pumpkins, and making gingerbread houses. Memories of Jack pulling off my calf-length boots and then wearing them himself, complete with one of my gold bangles, and dancing around the kitchen. Or the time Paul put the stalks of tomatoes on the worktop and made them look like spiders just to make me jump. And like so many other families, I had used the kitchen doorframe to annually mark the boys' height, but they had been erased from history. I knew I couldn't allow myself to drown in sadness, otherwise I wouldn't be able to get up each day. So, although the marks on the kitchen door were gone, the memories lived on in my heart. And what I kept reminding myself was that the house which had ended with such harrowing sadness, would once again be filled with love and laughter.

May was hard for other reasons too. My eldest sister, Christine, lost her battle with cancer, her beautiful smile disappearing forever. She had suffered for years but had been adamant the boys should never know, as my sister was aware of how upset they would be. Since Jack and Paul had died, there had been so many times, I had wanted my life to end so I could be with them, while my sister had fought to live. I would have swapped places with her in a heartbeat. Life can be so cruel.

Somehow, despite being consumed by another wave of overwhelming grief, I found a way to get up each day. A month after the house sold and my sister had closed her eyes for the final time, the photoshoot was arranged for the calendar. We all met in the upstairs bar of a local pub, which agreed to let us use the room. We made a plan for the photos and agreed that each month would be linked to the boys in some way, with a cheeky pose from one of the volunteers. January, which was Paul's birthday, featured

Stephen Baumber, the dad of one of Paul's classmates, as well as his running shoes and last race number. For February, Ged was holding a strategically placed menu board with Ohana written on it. March, which was Jack's birthday, featured his trumpet being held by Shane Johnstone, a dad of two boys who my sons were friends with. He posed wearing my dad and Jack's dicky bow next to music sheets and a music stand. April saw David Brearley wearing a hard hat, with bricks from the old house and Mum's much-used shovel, in homage to the renovation. May was a thank you to all the volunteers who had come together to help with the house or the calendar, with one of them, Andrew Green, sitting on a bag of plaster. June included Dan Donovan wearing a Barnsley FC hat and scarf, while July pictured a planter the Gildersome brownie pack had decorated for the boys. August featured a kite which had belonged to Paul as a reminder of all the happy summer days we had shared together. September was the raciest image of all, and a nod to the driving lessons Jack had taken as a young driver at Penistone Grammar School, with just a number plate covering Connor Shiggins' modesty. October was a thank you to the senior school, with a montage of some of the tributes created by the pupils, while November commemorated the circle of love the community had created for me at the boys' final farewell and December saw Nev Shiggins, a member of the Round Table, who helped with the house, dressed up as Santa.

As I watched so many elements of my life being captured on photo, I laughed and cried in equal measure. I was so touched by the kindness so many people had shown to help me create another lasting tribute to Jack and Paul.

In July, with Women's Aid's guidance, Radio 4 programme *The*

Archers aired several episodes focussing on coercive control and domestic abuse, which received lots of positive feedback. As a result, I was invited to a reception in the garden of Clarence House by Camilla, the Duchess of Cornwall, as part of an event to raise awareness on the topic. Only, I nearly never got there after deleting the email invitation, assuming it was a scam! *Why would Camilla's secretary be contacting me?* It was only when Alice from Women's Aid got in touch to explain they had nominated me that I realised the invite was genuine.

The day itself was a gloriously sunny day. As I walked through Green Park towards Clarence House, I saw the ghost of my youngest son; a small boy whose blonde hair shone brightly in the sunlight. He was running and my mind flashed back to a moment, years earlier on the athletics track, when all the birds in the sky seemed to fly out of my son's way as he started sprinting. As the memory surrounded me, I whispered Paul's name, remembering how exhilarated he'd felt that day and how I'd smiled endlessly as I watched him race around.

As I queued at the gates of Clarence House waiting to be admitted I watched celebrities being approached for interviews and autographs, stunned I was part of the group of famous people who had been invited. We had all been warned that the Duchess of Cornwall, as she was then, wouldn't be able to stop and talk to everyone, but not only did she approach me, the woman who is now Queen asked me about Jack and Paul, and listened as I talked about my much-loved sons. She kindly offered words of comfort, mother to mother, making me feel seen, heard and supported. I no longer felt invisible.

Later that month, I was invited to the leaver's assembly at Springvale Primary School – it would have been Paul's final month there. The headteacher, Andy Platt, had planted a tree in memory of the boys. As we all gathered around, environmentally friendly balloons, inscribed with the words 'Infinity and beyond' were released. Attached to them were little parcels, which enclosed messages from Paul's classmates on biodegradable paper containing forget-me-not seeds, so the delicate blue flowers would grow wherever they landed. We were celebrating Paul but setting him free at the same time. I was incredibly touched by Andy's thoughtfulness for the tribute.

19

AFTER STARTING the Child First campaign, I had reached out to my then MP, Angela Smith, for help in relation to changing the procedures and legislation in the family courts. She was openly supportive and agreed to meet with Sian from Women's Aid, to find out how she could become more actively involved in the Child First campaign. Not only did Angela listen, but she also secured the first debate for the treatment of domestic abuse survivors in the family law courts in parliament in September 2016, by which time the petition had reached 40,000 signatures.

On the day, I was invited to sit in the public gallery of the House of Commons with representatives from Women's Aid to watch the debate, which was feeding into the much hoped for Domestic Abuse Bill. It was hard hearing Angela talk about my life and what had happened to my sons, but to hear Jack and Paul's names spoken in parliament felt like a huge step forward. Sarah Champion, the MP for Rotherham, also stood up and said: 'We will remember Jack and Paul'.

It was a bittersweet moment. I shouldn't have been there at all, but finally Jack, Paul and I were being heard at the highest level. In total, 18 MPs from across all political parties spoke and in a show of unity it was agreed the government needed to transform the family court system and ensure that perpetrators of abuse could no longer use the arena to carry on abusing women and children. At that point perpetrators of abuse were still allowed to cross examine their partners in the family court, which gave them further power.

Dr Phillip Lee, from the Ministry of Justice, pledged to work with Women's Aid to review both the Implementation of Practice Direction 12J, which states a fact-finding exercise needs to take place if there is a risk of harm to a child, and the training provided to judges, court staff and Cafcass officers. Then Jess Philips, the now- Parliamentary Under–Secretary for Safeguarding and Violence Against Women and Girls, stood up and said the debate was 'a rallying cry to all the victims in this country and their children that, down here, in this bubble, we can hear them'.

At the end of the debate, it was agreed the proposed Domestic Abuse Bill would be progressed to a second reading. I forgot where I was and through a hazy shroud of tears I shouted 'yes' and punched my fits into the air. This was democracy at its finest, and my sons were no longer papers or letters. They were Jack and Paul. Seen, heard and loved.

Around the same time, I received an email from Red Magazine informing me I had been shortlisted for a Women of the Year award. Unbeknown to me, Alice from Women's Aid had nominated me in the 'Difference Maker' category. I was stunned and it was completely unexpected – in my eyes I was just fighting to ensure my sons' deaths weren't in vain. I was invited to London for a photoshoot, but when I arrived, I was told I had actually won, I couldn't believe it! The ceremony was a humbling and uplifting experience, but as I watched so many incredible women receive their award, I definitely had Imposter Syndrome. For years I had been told repeatedly I was useless, unattractive and worthless. Abuse doesn't stay with the abuser, it stays with the victim, so it was hard to believe I was being called on stage to collect an award.

As I climbed the steps, I took a deep breath, squared my shoulders and looked directly at Prime Minister David Cameron's wife Samantha, who was in the audience. I thanked Women's Aid for nominating me and said how humbled I was to be among so many amazing women. And then I turned to the reason I was on stage. 'We should never lose hope,' I said. 'Without hope, we have nothing, and then nothing will ever change. With hope, love and a community behind me, I went from on my knees to my feet and eventually became a voice for the silenced. I have drawn strength from my boys' courage and the fact 42,000 people have signed the petition to ensure children's voices are heard. I have learnt the two things my ex-husband can never take away from me is the love and friendship people had for the boys and the love and bond I had with Jack and Paul. That bond is unbreakable wherever they are, and I will carry on building a legacy, full of love, for them.'

When I finished, the audience rose from their seats and started clapping and I walked back to my seat, humbled by the standing ovation. I was still navigating my new, raw existence but I was still standing – just.

A month later, The Pride of Barnsley awards took place. Ged, who had project-managed the house renovation, was presented with the Community Hero award. I was delighted for him; everyone needs a Ged in their lives.

At the end of the summer of 2016, I saw a post on Facebook advertising a new community choir that would be starting in October. I knew facing another anniversary would be incredibly hard, and how much joy I had found in music and singing throughout my life. As I looked at the post, the memory of the last Saturday I had spent with the boys came to me – when Paul had told me I should sing for everyone, not just for my sons.

As I stared at the Facebook post, calling for new members, Paul's words were as clear as day in my mind. It was his words that encouraged me to respond to the post. But when I got a friendly response back, welcoming me to go along to the first rehearsal, my nerves overtook me. For years I had been told how useless I was and suddenly my initial confidence dissolved.

Something must have told me not to disregard the idea, though, as I spoke to my family about it. My brother-in-law, Ted, insisted I went along, repeatedly telling me how good it would be for me, but the reality was far harder than the idea. As I drove there, a niggling voice in my head kept whispering I wouldn't be any good. The first time I pulled into the car park, I drove straight back out, deciding to go home, only to turn back in a couple of minutes later. Even when I had pulled up, it took six attempts for me to get out of the car and walk through the door of the hall. In the end, it was only the fact that someone was behind me, ushering me inside, that forced me into the first Barnsley Singers rehearsal.

By then I had convinced myself I couldn't sing anymore. When you have been told for years to *shut up* and *be quiet* or *nobody wants to hear you sing* and *what makes you think you can sing*, you do stop. But what was even harder, was that after Jack and Paul died, I had vowed I would never sing again because I had always sung with my heart and it had been smashed beyond repair.

It's always hard to open a closed door for the first time and even harder to walk through that door alone, but from the moment I stepped into the rehearsals, I never felt alone again. I found my musical voice again and from the first note I sang; I felt a sense of calm. For two hours a week, the heavy rucksack that had become my existence, was left at the door. I had forgotten that music speaks when your heart and words have frozen.

After being forced to be silent for so many years, I was grateful to find my musical voice again. I found so much strength as I stood shoulder to shoulder and sang with the other choir members. They were helping to break the chains that had been imposed upon me and a new version of me was forming.

Other people were inspiring me to keep going too. That summer, I was introduced to Joan Lawrence, whose daughter, Claudia, had vanished in March 2009. Joan had been forced to endure so much after her girl disappeared. By that point she had been without Claudia, with no answers to what had happened to her, for seven years. I couldn't imagine how she had got through but, on the day we met, Joan appeared with the biggest smile and a huge hug. Although our circumstances are very different, we had a shared pain. We were both mums who had lost the most precious things in our lives. We didn't have to say anything to know how each other was feeling. Joan's determination and hope gave me strength. The way she had carried on fighting to get answers about what had happened to Claudia, keeping her daughter's name in the public domain, with dignity and compassion, was inspiring. Since that day, we have become firm friends and Joan helps me to keep going. On anniversaries, birthdays and at Christmas, Joan, a talented artist, sends me homemade cards, which always include a heartfelt message to keep me strong. I have kept every single one of them and on those days when I feel like I am going to be overcome with grief and give in, I get them out and they spur me on to keep going.

20

FOR ANYONE who has lost a loved one, the festive season is particularly hard. Christmas was and still is one of those emotional milestones that threatens to destroy me and leave my heart in a million pieces. The Christmas of 2016, I couldn't bring myself to put up Mum's Christmas tree; a job that Jack and Paul had always loved, and instead, my cousin, Jo, came to do it. Over the years, I had collected many special baubles and ornaments. The first year after I'd married, my sisters bought us baubles to celebrate our first Christmas as a married couple. Four years later, I bought two special ones in memory of my dad, because the boys had never met him but knew all about him. Then over the years Jack and Paul made decorations at school, all of which took pride of place on the tree. I would smile as I listened to the boys explain how they had made them in class and would compare each other's creations. The baubles had been lost, like so many other precious possessions, in the fire but my ex-husband hadn't managed to rob me of my memories, which I hope will stay with me forever.

The Christmas period is full of them, from choosing my sons' presents and secretly hiding them to making festive plates, baking, wrapping and writing cards. But all of those once-loved traditions had been taken away from me, so in the years after Jack and Paul were murdered, I had to survive on my memories, each one swirling through my mind like delicate snowflakes, soft, unique and beautiful.

Not all of the memories are happy ones – when you are in an abusive relationship, the level of threat is always high. You simply concentrate on surviving what should be special days but which all too often left my heart racing for all the wrong reasons. It really was a game of survival.

So the mixture of happy and devastating memories, along with the fact my boys were gone, meant getting through Christmas and New Year was physically and mentally draining. It took all the strength I could summon to muster a smile, be sociable and attend events in the lead up to the day itself, when all I could hear was a deafening internal scream. To survive the festive period, I went back to Lytham St Annes, our happy place, and on Christmas Day, I walked on the beach the boys and I had played on so often and wrote their names in the sand. With each footstep I took and each time I scrolled Jack and Paul onto the beach, I felt like I was preserving my sons' memories. Over the years, Mum, Jack, Paul and I, made marks in the sand, and although the sea washes them away, the memories remain.

For five years, I went back to that beach. I found the sea calming, the surf helping to relieve the overwhelming sadness I felt. I could watch it for hours and the sound of the waves tumbling into one another gave me a rare feeling of peace.

And 2017 brought me a new reason to keep fighting. Women's Aid had managed to secure a date to deliver the Child First petition to 10 Downing Street. On January 23 I waited at Penistone train station, my stomach in knots. My nerves and anxiety were getting the better of me and I was terrified the train wouldn't arrive and

Claire Throssell

I would miss my connection to London. I had a photograph of Jack and Paul in my bag, which a friend had framed for me the year after I lost the boys. Not only was it a source of comfort and strength, the picture of Jack, smiling proudly in his band uniform, and Paul also in his band uniform, from when he used to play the cornet, has been used to show the world who my sons are. It's a constant reminder to those in power that Jack and Paul were children, and not simply letters in an official report. That particular day, I wore the same dress I had for my children's final farewell. It just felt apt. And on my feet I wore purple pumps, to represent the colour of domestic abuse.

It was a momentous day and I didn't want to let anyone down, especially Jack and Paul. I checked my bag at least a dozen times, making sure I had the photo, as well as my passport and driving license, which I would need for security checks. I knew they were in there, but my demons of past abuse were threatening to swallow me whole. I gave myself a good talking to, took a deep breath and lifted my head, doing my best to ignore the inner voice which was telling me I wasn't strong enough.

It took five years of therapy for me to realise that the inner voice that speaks your fears, past experiences and insecurities, is lying to you. On that trip to London, I was only two years into counselling, so I was still battling against all my insecurities, but I knew, despite how low my self-esteem was, how little self confidence I had, that I had to take myself from zero and become my own hero. I had to take myself to London, walk down the street where so much power was homed, and tell the government they were repeatedly failing children. It was those thoughts that enabled me to stand up and make the journey to London.

When I arrived, the sun was shining and its bright rays lit up the city all day, which also gave me strength, as I thought about how children could light up the world if they were given the love and nurture they needed. Alongside Women's Aid, I wanted to pay tribute to all the children in the charity's report who had been lost at the hands of an abusive parent. Their lives and futures had been brutally taken away from them, through no fault of their own, but due to the failings of those who should have protected them.

Before we handed the petition in, I walked with the representatives from Women's Aid to Parliament Square. Alice, from the charity, had brought a teddy for every child lost and we placed them gently on the pavement in a neat row. Parliament Square was busy and noisy, but as soon as we started to lay the teddy bears down, passers by stopped and stood silently. On impulse I put Jack and Paul's photo by the railings in the middle of the teddy bears. As I looked round, I realised people were getting their phones out and taking photos. And then I realised the media were also there, and respectfully started capturing images.

'Can you stand with the teddies?' one photographer, very politely, asked.

I agreed, and as I stood there, amongst the love we had created, holding Jack and Paul's photo, I fleetingly became a living memorial, not just to my sons, but for all those children who had been so needlessly, and cruelly, lost.

Then it was time to go to 10 Downing Street and at the gates Polly Neate, the then CEO of Women's Aid, and MPs Jess Phillips and Peter Kyle met us. Alongside Alice and Lucy from Women's Aid, and fellow abuse survivor and warrior, Zoe Dronfield, we passed through security. We had been instructed to walk up the right-hand side and wait for a police officer to signal to let us get to the famous door. The press must remain on the left-hand side, behind barriers. I focussed on putting one foot in front of the other, until I got to the steps and the most famous black door in the world. I took the biggest breath I could and lifted the polished door knocker. It was much heavier than I had imagined, so as I pulled it down, I ended up knocking on the door rather loudly. I then did it twice more. There was a pause which seemed to take forever, but was only a few seconds, and then the door was opened, and I was faced by a rather official looking man, as Larry the cat shot out.

The petition was in a big, bright, orange box, and a clear message had been embossed onto the side. It read: '42,372 say: Safe Child Contact Saves Lives'. I handed the man the petition, and he formally accepted it, paused for photos then closed the door. I felt ok. I had achieved a fundamental and potentially life-saving task, but as I put the photo of Jack and Paul by the door, and we stepped away to allow the photographers to catch the moment, the tears came. Jack and Paul had gone from being two anonymous letters in a Serious Case Review, to their names and lives being recognised by parliament. They had been noted and recorded in its history and now the image of their beautiful faces was by the most photographed door in the world.

Suddenly, an all too familiar void opened up inside me. This was not a victory or a win, it was bittersweet and painful. The tears were now pouring down my face and wouldn't stop. Jess Phillips pulled me into the tightest of hugs, while everyone else used their bodies to shield me from the view of the country's media. I caught the empathetic glances of the police officers who kindly nodded their heads in respect and I felt touched by their kind smiles.

For My Boys

When I pulled myself back together, we all turned to face the waiting photographers and once again I knew I was doing all I could to keep children safe and ensure my sons' deaths hadn't been in vain. As I stood on the steps of 10 Downing Street, Larry the cat strolled over to me and nudged my leg with his head. I bent down to stroke him, and there he was posing alongside me for photos.

Not long after handing in the petition, I received an invitation from Women's Aid to meet with Camilla, the Duchess of Cornwall, at their Bristol office. A small group of domestic abuse survivors had been asked to go and talk to the future Queen about the Child First campaign and I felt honoured and privileged to be asked.

On February 14, I sat around a table with other survivors and the Duchess and I talked about Jack and Paul. I wasn't sure what to expect, but Camilla made me feel heard, seen and supported, which meant so much, as this is the complete opposite to how survivors feel when they are trapped in an abusive relationship. The Duchess was genuinely pleased with how the Child First campaign was progressing and the number of signatures it had garnered. Whether you are a royalist or not, it means a lot that such an important member of our national institution was taking an interest.

Later that same year also saw the first documentary about the boys being filmed for a crime series called Britain's Darkest Taboos. It was important for me not to hold anything back, even though I was acutely aware the sheer nature of what I had to say would be upsetting for the documentary crew and for the audience that would eventually watch the show. It was my chance to publicly call my ex-husband what he really was – a murderer. It didn't state this on his death certificate, nor did it say on my sons' that they had been murdered, but that was the brutal and painful truth. Although it hurt to re-live the trauma Jack, Paul and I had suffered, I knew it was important for their stories to be heard.

On June 21, during the Queen's Speech to parliament, Her Majesty confirmed that a draft Domestic Abuse Bill, landmark legislation, would be brought in to better protect victims experiencing and suffering the effects of domestic abuse and violence, including children. The Queen also confirmed that the Courts Bill would be re-introduced with measures to prevent abusers directly cross-examining victims. The Bill should have succeeded two years earlier but had been sidetracked due to the May 2015 general election. If an MP really understood how terrifying and intimidating it was to be quizzed by the very person who had left you physically and emotionally shattered, in what should be a safe space, I'm sure it would have been passed years earlier.

As summer slipped into autumn, despite assurances from Theresa May – who had become PM the previous year – that the Ministry of Justice were looking into the implications of the antiquated guidelines, nothing had been done.

On November 22 of the same year, Women's Aid invited me to a parliamentary reception in Speaker of the House John Bercow's chambers. As I walked through the halls of parliament, the hairs on my arms raised and I had goosebumps. From the photos of the past Speakers to the images of the bed that the then Queen sleeps in the night before parliament is opened, it was all so full of grandeur. And now Jack and Paul's names, as well as their faces – as I had their photo with me – were going to be part of this history. I was determined no child would ever be dismissed again or their lives discounted.

For My Boys

I was the second person to speak in the official reception. In the moments before I stood up, I fixed the images of my two beautiful boys in my mind, but as I took to my feet, I was representing every child who had been lost or hurt at the hands of an abusive parent. I spoke for the silent. I spoke for the scared. I spoke for the lost. And I spoke from the heart.

'The last thing Paul, Jack and I said to one another was that we loved each other to infinity and beyond,' I started. 'It's that love my sons took with them as they left this world and it's also the love they left behind. It's that love that gives me the strength today to stand here and say that children, as well as any victim of domestic abuse and violence, deserve better. One of our basic rights as human beings is to live free. Free of fear. Free of oppression and risk of harm. Nobody should have to live their lives feeling invisible, isolated and in fear of anything happening to them, their children or their family.'

I held up the photo of my boys and looked into the eyes of the MPs in front of me.

'This is not Child A and this is not Child B,' I added. 'This is Jack and Paul. Jack's voice was never heard, apart from by a firefighter, a police officer and a doctor. Jack was critically injured but he was desperately trying to tell as many people as he could the truth of what happened, and he lost his life believing he had saved his brother's. It's every parent's worst nightmare not to be there for your children when they need you the most. I had shielded and protected my sons from their father, as much as I could, all their lives. I truly believed the family court would shield and protect them too, but I was wrong. I went through the humiliating and barbaric process of trying to protect everyone but ultimately, I protected no one.'

I took a deep breath.

'I hope Jack and Paul can somehow forgive me. I hope all children can forgive us all.'

Another deep breath.

'It's time for things to change, especially the dangerous culture and practice within the family courts of contact at any cost. Children deserve to have a voice, a childhood and safer, brighter futures. They deserve a better world to live in. I made a promise to my boys that no more children would die at the hands of an abusive parent, but I haven't been able to keep that promise, because Jack and Paul have not been the last children to die at the hands of a parent who is a perpetrator of domestic abuse.'

With a final intake of breath, I finished with: 'When I visit where Jack and Paul sleep, I put my hand on the stone and whisper "I'm trying". Maybe one day I will rest my hand, head and heart there and whisper, "I've done it."'

When I looked up tears were flowing down John Bercow's cheeks. He slowly walked over to me, openly crying, took my hand and pulled me into a tight embrace. As he hugged me tightly, I felt a sob coming up through his chest and as it vibrated through me, I thought of Jack and Paul, and how I would never stop fighting for them.

Afterwards, as I stood in the darkness on the Westminster terrace, watching the lights and the stars reflect on the river, I thought about my sons again. We had come to London for my 40th birthday and celebrated on a river cruise. I never envisaged on a returning visit I would be fighting to protect other children, who like Jack and Paul, had lost their lives. Suddenly the terrace went cold. Despite the pain that sliced through me like a blade, I was determined to stay strong and refused to be broken.

For My Boys

At the end of 2017, I took part in a particularly hard-hitting report for the BBC around domestic abuse and the devastating consequences it had on survivors. I talked in detail about the emotional harm that is caused and how survivors carry this with them for the rest of their lives. We are all human beings with hearts, with lives that deserve to be lived, free of oppression and fear. I wanted to really stress the point that the government needed to do more to protect victims, which includes children, both boys and girls, as well as adults, against the tyranny and hurt that is all too often bestowed upon them. Nobody should be meaningless in this world, but far too many victims and survivors must constantly look over their shoulder, as they are stalked and harassed by their abuser. While they carefully navigate a life that has been damaged beyond repair, perpetrators of domestic and sexual abuse are frequently free to walk without fear, challenge or consequence. For victims and survivors there are very few places where they are safe. I highlighted the urgent need for action by the government against domestic abuse and violence. But, to this day, they still aren't doing enough for those who are most in need.

It isn't just the victims or survivors who are affected and scarred by abusive perpetrators, it's family members too. All of them are at risk of being on the receiving end of post-separation abuse hell. Whether it be through text messages, malicious lies or intimidation. I lost count of the number of times my ex-husband hurled abuse at my mum, shouting in her face and accusing her of siding with me. And after Jack and Paul died, my whole family grieved, their hearts torn apart by the devastating loss we had all suffered. The trauma we had all suffered was like a stone being plunged into still water. The pain ran deep and rippled outwards, to family and friends, to Jack and Paul's school pals, their teachers, and to everyone who was touched by their beautiful smiles.

Statistics have revealed domestic abuse costs the UK £66 billion a year, which is bad enough, but the impact on a family member is impossible to calculate. The grief of losing a child to an abuser suffocates you, prevents you from breathing and ends your life as you knew it. Your path forward is blocked, your vision permanently tainted and the internal agony cripples you. It makes you hate the world, encourages you to end your own life and prevents you from feeling love. It is an all-consuming life sentence – if you survive at all. I chose to live my sentence by honouring the courage Jack showed at the end of his life by telling the firefighter who rescued him, and therefore the world, what his dad had done. I directed the love I had for my children into making a difference in their names. Hate can't make children's lives a better place, only love and hope can.

On January 9, 2018, Paul should have turned 13. It is supposed to be a milestone birthday; becoming a teenager, dipping his 'foots' as Paul referred to his feet, into the first waves of adult water. On what should have been his special day, my mind inevitably drifted. When my sons were alive, I would reminisce about their younger years, memories of blowing out candles and ripping open birthday presents. Instead, on what should have been Paul's special birthday, I thought about how his life was cut short far too soon. My heart ached as I also realised by the time Paul had turned five, he had lived more than half his life, which is unbearably cruel. I had always bought balloons on my sons' birthdays, but this year I bought flower bulbs and a climbing rose, called Paul, and planted them next to where he and Jack sleep.

For My Boys

March proved to be a pivotal month, not just for me but for the Child First campaign too. On the 8th, International Women's Day, I was invited to a reception at 10 Downing Street for the launch of PM Theresa May's flagship Domestic Abuse policy. I was understandably nervous, but my attention was distracted when I woke up to a blanket of snow. The journey to the train station was certainly eventful, and then when I was in the taxi from Kings Cross to No 10, I was told off for giving my teeth a quick clean. Well, I didn't want to talk to Theresa May with stale breath!

Anyway, I got to Downing Street in the nick of time and met staff from Women's Aid. Once again, we went through security and walked down that famous street. I was asked to speak to the media, which I didn't mind, but as I stepped up to the door of No 10, my confidence plummeted. I hadn't realised everyone else had been ushered inside, so I had to go through the front door alone. As required, I handed over my phone and walked up the stairs, but my nerves suddenly got the better of me; they felt like a mountain. I had to dig deep and push my ex-husband's voice – telling me I wasn't worthy of being here – out of my mind.

Mustering every ounce of courage I had, I took a deep breath, pulled my shoulders back and held my head high. I can't explain why, but in that moment the image of Hugh Grant, dancing across the landing in *Love Actually*, came into my mind and made me smile. Then I felt the imprints of Jack and Paul's hands in my own, and the mountain disappeared as I climbed the stairs. I looked at the portraits on the walls of former Prime Ministers and reminded myself that I was here to speak for the lost generations of children. I wasn't going to let them down.

Claire Throssell

Halfway through the reception, someone approached to tell me I had been invited to a private reception with Theresa May. I was stunned, it was the last thing I had been expecting but I was directed into a private room. A minute or so later, Theresa came in and invited me to talk about my sons. She listened intently, visibly moved, as I told her all about them, and why the Child First campaign was so important.

I was so proud of myself for holding it together while I spoke, but when Theresa moved onto the next person, I felt my legs wobble, as the enormity of what I had just done sank in. After I left the room, I watched the Prime Minister stand on a dais and deliver her speech to a packed audience. She began by saying she had decided to spend International Women's Day with survivors of domestic abuse and violence. It made me think about the choices we have in life. As a victim of domestic abuse, trapped in a volatile relationship, you don't have any choices, and certainly not around where you spend your time or who you spend it with. What makes it even worse is the fact you often spend every second of your waking day flinching, holding your breath, watching every word that you say and constantly guarding your children. There are no choices when it comes to domestic abuse.

The Prime Minister went on to say that it wasn't just her government who had let down victims and survivors of domestic abuse, it was decades of previous governments that had failed. She was right. They absolutely had. No one had stood up to make the country a better place for those impacted by abuse. But Theresa May announced as part of her Domestic Abuse policy she was going to create a Domestic Abuse Commissioner to provide public leadership on all elements. The person who took up the role would also play a key role in overseeing and monitoring the provision of domestic abuse services in England and Wales.

The second important moment of March 8th came when Theresa May announced she was pushing for a new Domestic Abuse Bill and a three-month consultation had been launched. I left Downing Street feeling hopeful. This came just a few months after the government had launched an urgent review of the damage being caused by perpetrators being allowed to cross-examine their victims in family courts and mandatory training for judges around domestic abuse.

The following month, a second documentary aired as part of Judge Rinder's Crime Stories. Mum and I had been filmed for the show a year earlier. I was so glad Mum had been given the chance to talk about what she'd endured, but it was hard listening to her explain how tough it was watching her own daughter suffer. For so long she had felt powerless. All I could do was remind Mum that her constant love and support had helped me through the hardest years of my life.

I have been filmed for several documentaries over the years and I don't find them easy for many reasons. Emotionally, they take their toll as I have to relive what happened to my lovely boys, but I know talking about them also helps others and addresses the failings in the system. Another element I find hard is around the fact I have crippling insecurities about how I look. When you are told for years that you are ugly and unattractive, you believe it. And when all your confidence, self-worth and everything that defined you has been trampled on, you begin to believe you belong under someone's shoe. I stopped looking in mirrors a long time ago, mainly because I no longer recognised the person staring back at me, and I'm terrified of what I will see. There are still no mirrors in my apartment and there never will be. I'm scared of the image I will see staring back at me. Mental scars last a lifetime.

In so many ways it can be easier to talk to film crews than family, as they don't get as upset. Little things, like explaining how certain phrases are really upsetting, can offend family members. I had to kindly ask my Mum to stop saying 'I'll let you be mother' instead of just asking me to pour the tea, as the words struck me like a knife. I will never be a mother again. And although all the film crews I have dealt with have had an emotional reaction to my life story and what happened to Jack and Paul, they aren't embedded in the pain and grief that surrounds our family.

It also means I keep my sons' names alive and hopefully stop other children being murdered. If I make a difference to just one person's life or encourage someone to talk about domestic abuse, then it means the voices of my sons have been heard, seen and made an impression. It means their handprints and their footprints are embedded in people's hearts and souls. A legacy of love, a legacy of change, a legacy to last always.

That spring, I was invited to The Royal Armouries in Leeds for the Yorkshire Woman of Achievement celebration, after being shortlisted for an award. On the day, all the nominees were greeted with a champagne reception and it was humbling to be surrounded by so many lovely people, who all worked so hard to help others. I couldn't have been more shocked and surprised when my name was called out as the overall winner of the 2018 Woman of Achievement and the Jane Tomlinson Award for Courage. I have never seen myself as brave or strong. I was, and still am, just a grieving mum who wants to make a difference.

At that point, everything still felt so raw, and although it was a huge honour to win two awards, I did feel overwhelmed by the amount of people, most of them strangers, wanting to congratulate me. People were kissing my arms as I passed them and pulling me in for hugs. I knew they were just being kind, but old habits die hard, and I felt dirty. Just like I had, when I was being abused, I went home and scrubbed myself in the shower. I hated the fact that my ex-husband had done this to me, especially as this was such a special occasion.

I was humbled and proud of the awards I had been given, though. I hung the framed certificate of the Overall Yorkshire Woman of Achievement on the wall. On the days when I still struggle to get up off the floor and I can't see past the next hour, it reminds me of how far I have come, it helps me out of the darkness and gives me the strength to get up. The Jane Tomlinson Award for Courage certificate hangs at the side of the front door to remind me that nothing out in the world can ever be as hard to navigate as the days I held my lovely boys in my arms as they died. Whenever I leave my apartment, I look at that certificate, pull my shoulders back, stand tall and face the world with a smile.

In April 2018, Michelle Rawlins wrote a piece for the Guardian on myself and my ongoing campaigning. I had taken part in many interviews by then but for this piece I reflected on how difficult it was when Jack was in hospital, his whole body wrapped in bandages. I couldn't hold his hand or take him in my arms and hug him. The only way I could communicate with him was with my voice, by talking and reading to him.

For a couple of years before the fire, Jack had lost interest in reading, until he discovered David Walliams' books, which he devoured. And, as I've mentioned before, as he lay in his hospital bed, I decided to read Jack his favourite books. Michelle wrote about this in her Guardian article and after it was published, she received an email from David Walliams' PA. He had seen the piece and wanted to invite me and a guest to the *Britain's Got Talent* semi-final. I was so touched. In the years since my sons had died, I had seen the best and the worst of people, and this token of kindness brought on a cascade of tears. My counsellor, Angie, had worked miracles in helping me process everything I felt, thought and experienced. I had managed to put so many feelings into little boxes in my mind, but this box called joy, which lives in our hearts, had remained tightly locked. Going to *Britain's Got Talent* allowed me to open that box.

On the day of the live show, David came to see me before the show began. He was warm and friendly, genuinely touched by what had happened to Jack and Paul. During the break, he invited me and my friend, Helen, over to his stage chair.

'Whatever you do, don't touch the red button,' he warned. 'It will cause chaos.'

I couldn't help but think about how amused Jack and Paul would have been. They would have been egging me on to hit the button and would have been doubled over with laughter at the havoc I could have caused.

At the end of the show, another trickle of joy seeped out from that normally sealed box in my heart as Alfie Boe took to the stage. Singing and music had always meant so much to me and being able to hear his glorious voice, only metres from where I was sitting, was simply sublime. That night we were in the same hotel as the contestants. It was a night of music, friendship and kindness.

It reminded me that sometimes in life, no matter how devastating the world feels, you have to take a moment and allow yourself to be lit up by small tokens of happiness, to help combat the hardest and darkest of days.

As spring turned to summer, Victoria Atkins MP, who was the parliamentary under-secretary of state for women, requested a meeting with me. What should have been 30 minutes became an hour. I spoke about the importance of keeping victims and survivors of abuse, along with their children, safe in the family home. I explained how I had no choice but to take Jack and Paul away from their home, while my ex-husband was able to carry on living there in comfort, despite being the perpetrator.

At the same time, I was still working closely with Women's Aid and pushing for guidelines around the family court to be included in the proposed Domestic Abuse Bill, in particular access to special measures for survivors and victims of abuse in court, including screens, giving evidence via video, and separate waiting areas and entrances. By then, we had succeeded in pushing through the ban on cross examination by perpetrators of abuse towards victims, but we wanted this extended to all parties in the family courts. We also wanted the act to end the presumption of children's contact with parents, when abuse had occurred. I was also campaigning to prohibit unsupervised contact between abusive parents and their children. This alone would have saved Jack and Paul's lives. The ongoing consultation was called 'Transforming The Response to Domestic Abuse'. If successful, the Domestic Abuse Bill would be landmark legislation for generations to come.

On July 18, a week after my meeting with Victoria Atkins, Jess Phillips secured a debate in parliament regarding domestic abuse victims and the family courts. During the debate both Jess Phillips and Angela Smith spoke about Jack and Paul in their speeches which I was eternally grateful for. Once again, the debate had cross party support, in recognising the urgent need for a Domestic Abuse Bill as soon as possible. I was delighted when the motion was passed to move forward with the Bill.

That September I was invited back to a Remembrance Day ceremony at Bluebell Wood, where I'd received counselling. I was asked if I would like to be part of the 'Bluebell Choir' as it was affectionately known. Not only was I delighted to be asked, as music had become my escapism, it was a privilege to be part of something so special. I played *Somewhere Over The Rainbow* on my flute, which had been performed at the boy's final farewell. Afterwards, I stood alongside dozens of other parents who had lost children, holding onto a photo of Jack and Paul as their names were read out. The Hospice gave every parent a pebble with their late children's names on. Those pebbles still sit on my windowsill at home, but every year Mum and I go back to Bluebell Wood to hear Jack and Paul's names remembered.

In 2018, I also became an ambassador for the Independent Domestic Abuse Service (IDAS), a fantastic organisation who support victims and survivors of domestic abuse in North and South Yorkshire. I began collaborating with them on several initiatives to improve the response to domestic abuse. I became actively involved in the Speak Up campaign across the two counties, calling on GPs to be more proactive when they suspect patients are victims of domestic abuse.

Fear and isolation are a perpetrator's biggest weapon and IDAS can take away both. Nobody should have to suffer abuse alone, like I did, which is why I'm proud to be an IDAS Champion and Ambassador. If you are a domestic abuse victim or survivor, I see you, I hear you. And I believe you, because Jack, Paul and I have paid the ultimate price because we weren't.

Women's Aid invited me to speak at their annual conference in January 2019. I challenged Cafcass over their working practice and procedures in regard to presumption of contact. This presumption had cost my children their lives and a chance of a future. On the train on my way home, I couldn't help but think that despite all the hard work, campaigning and lobbying from all the domestic abuse sectors, charities and organisations, we had yet to see any real or lasting change.

21

EVERY YEAR, the months between October and March are the hardest to navigate. From mid-October, it's an onslaught of one painful day after another, days that simply have to be endured in the best way I can. There's the anniversary of the boys' deaths, my dad's death, the boys' final farewell, Christmas, New Year, and all our birthdays. These are the months where I have to dig deep and look harder for something good in every day. There are still days when I sit with my duvet wrapped around me, watching the sunrise, or sunset, just to find something beautiful in every day, particularly in the winter months when the sky puts on a spectacular display of colours. It's almost as if nature is making up for the lack of colour on the ground and on the trees.

Many people remember the events, but understandably they forget there are two anniversaries, October 22 and 27, because Jack and Paul fell eternally to sleep five days apart. Every year, I put on an event to remember my sons, in-between those dates. On the first anniversary, we had a joint concert with Barnsley Town Band and Marsh Ladies Choir, donating all the proceeds to Bluebell Wood Hospice. On other years I've organised a ceilidh and harvest festivals. Since Covid, I commemorate the boys by recording a beautiful piece of music at the local Carriage House Studio. Some of the songs I've sung have included *Somewhere Over The Rainbow*, *Wherever You Are*, *As I Sit In Heaven* and *I Will Pray For*

For My Boys

You. Each piece holds a special place in my heart and takes me back to the moments when I used to sing the boys to sleep.

November is equally as hard. The 8th is the anniversary of losing my dad, and the 14th was the boys' final farewell. Then Christmas always seems to start as soon as the final embers of Bonfire Night are extinguished. Paul's birthday falls in January and Jack's in March. My birthday is in February, and every year I am here, I feel tremendous guilt that I have lived to see another year, when my sons' lives were so cruelly cut short. No matter how many times someone tells you 'Your children wouldn't want you to be sad, alone or angry' it doesn't help. That box of joy that lives within our hearts and souls has had parts of its contents removed and even if you manage to fill the box with something new, it's not the same and can never replace what's gone forever. All we can do is hold on tight to the joy and love that was once nestled in our hearts and cherish the memories that our children were forced to leave behind.

In the early years after the boys were taken, it still felt wrong to smile, laugh freely or simply enjoy any aspect of life. It felt wrong to be alive, as I carried on navigating through grief. I was existing behind internal walls I had built to protect me from any further trauma or pain. The only thing I could enjoy, without feeling tidal waves of guilt, was playing my piano and flute and singing. It reminded me of the boys, singing them to sleep and helping Jack with his trumpet practice. Music increasingly became my safe space, where I could temporarily escape and express how I felt. It became a positive outlet to channel everything I was feeling and get it out of my mind, heart and soul.

But in between music, there were and still are times, when life feels unbearably lonely. Even when I walk into a room and it is full of people and an abundance of love, it can feel as though I am alone in the world. It's like riding an ocean of tears, battling through every emotion that ebbs and flows with the tides.

Then, as spring 2019 slipped into summer, everything started happening at once. Nature turned the heat up when it came to the weather and at Women's Aid we were turning the heat up on the government. On June 4, the Victoria Derbyshire show broadcast an hour-long special programme on the workings of the family courts. I was invited on to the show to talk about my experience. I knew most people have no understanding of what happens in closed courts or the devastation they cause. Unlike magistrates, crown or coroner's courts, the public or journalists are not allowed into the hearings. I appreciate that children have to be protected, as do victims of abuse, but as in criminal courts, reporting restrictions could be set.

When you imagine a court, most people think of benches, judges in wigs and gowns and a dock, but family courts are not like this. The hearings take place in rooms where tables have been pushed together, and chairs placed around them. The fact that you are often just an arm's length from the person who abused you is terrifying. Their very presence in such close proximity can revert a domestic abuse survivor back to the moment when they had been stripped of all dignity, their confidence and self-esteem on the floor. Add to this the fact that many of those victims and survivors cannot afford legal representation and must walk into that room alone.

Ironically, as you enter a court building you are scanned for weapons, but the biggest weapon is the perpetrator who sits opposite you. Their boring eyes, their smug facial expressions, their cocky mannerisms, all on display to intimidate, frighten and attack you.

Every time I attended a family court hearing, fighting to keep my sons safe, I was petrified. And a perpetrator of abuse knows this. My ex-husband physically lunged at me as I waited outside the family court, hurled one derogatory and humiliating insult at me after another, each cleverly acting as a weapon to damage the tiny amount of resolve and self-respect I had mustered. I was lucky enough to have a solicitor to help protect me, but imagine all those thousands of victims who have to sit four seats away from their abuser, frightened, alone and vulnerable. They don't even get the protection of a screen to shield them from the glares, smirks and terrifying body language they once again become a victim to.

As I sat in the Victoria Derbyshire studio, I relived the harrowing experience I had endured in the family court, but I knew we were still a lifetime away from forcing the government to make any meaningful changes. Travelling to London the day before, a sudden feeling of helplessness engulfed me and there were a few seconds when I wanted to step off the platform and into the path of an incoming express train. It would be easy, my mind whispered. It would be quick. Over in seconds. But then I saw my sons' faces, and remembered the promises I had made. I had come too far to give up and it was then my body refused to succumb to the demons in my mind.

With every moment of darkness, there will always be some light. The same month, the third annual fun run, in Jack and Paul's name, took place. It was part of the Lord Mayor's Parade, a long-standing community event in the small town my sons had spent their short lives in. The whole morning was filled with colour, laughter and new memories being created for those taking part.

Forgetting was never something I could do and everyday moments most parents wouldn't give a second thought, brought the boys back to me in full technicolour. For instance, there are lots of films I couldn't watch after the boys died, including *Despicable Me* and *How To Train Your Dragon*. Movies that we had watched as a three, snuggled up on the couch, wrapped in blankets and drinking hot chocolate. The thought of seeing those childhood films without Jack and Paul was too much to bear, but on June 19, *Toy Story 4* was released. Just seeing the adverts tore me apart. *Toy Story* had always been one of the boys' favourite films and it's where our expression 'love you to infinity and beyond' came from. They never used the affectionate phrase with anyone but me, as our special way of saying goodbye to one another.

When the latest instalment of the film was advertised, a memory of paying for me, Mum, Jack and Paul, to watch *Toy Story 3* at the cinema in 3D, came flooding back.

We had all laughed at the sight of one another wearing enormous 3D glasses. Mum captured the scene on camera, a permanent record of that innocent moment. But as soon as the film started, Paul got freaked out by the special effects, and nearly fell off his seat. He was so discombobulated, I ended up paying for us all to watch it in 2D.

Then another memory flashed. We had been on holiday in Great Yarmouth, and walking down a pretty street, decorated with bunting. Paul spotted Woody and Buzz Lightyear toys in a shop window and ran towards them.

'Please can I have them,' he begged. 'I'll use my holiday pennies and paper.'

How could I have refused? I still smile at his unique phrase for holiday money.

The year after, when we returned to Great Yarmouth, Paul used his 'holiday pennies and paper' to buy a toy Jesse and Bullseye. Jack was never into teddies, but he understood the special messages we had created, due to the film, and would often play *You've Got A Friend In Me* and *When She Loved Me* on his trumpet. I can still picture him now, losing himself in the music just like I do, happy in the moment. But if I do see Jack again one day, I will be having a few words, as I have since found a few scratches and dints in his trumpet that I never knew about!

It's fair to say the release of *Toy Story 4*, just a few months before the fifth anniversary of my sons' deaths, hit me hard. Not only had the chance to watch the film, which I have no doubt we would have all loved, been taken away from us, but it was a cruel reminder that Paul's teddies had been destroyed in the house fire. Precious memories stolen away. I couldn't even hold them close and take in the smell of my son. Thank goodness, I have the memories that are permanently etched into my mind. Their words permanently encased in my heart.

22

I WAS invited to parliament for the first reading of the new Domestic Abuse Bill on July 25, 2019. I was delighted but the date made me wince – it was the same day I had got married 21 years earlier. But this wasn't a time to dwell on that fateful day so I pushed that to the back of my mind and prepared myself for what should be a momentous day, that could go on to save the lives of countless women and children. Finally, changes would be made, all the fighting, lobbying and baring of my soul would be worth it.

But as ever, life and the world are never straightforward and with peaks come troughs. On July 24, the day before we were due to go to parliament, Theresa May resigned as Prime Minister and in that same moment, I assumed everything we had worked for at Women's Aid and IDAS had come crashing down. All those debates and building relationships in government were irrelevant. I dropped to the floor in my apartment and with my back against the wall, my arms wrapped around my knees, I choked back the tears. I didn't blame Theresa May, she'd coped with a lot, I blamed the wider politics that were at play.

Unexpectedly however, I was told we could still go to parliament. So, I got up the next day, and yet again pulled on my big girl pants. I entered the House of Commons not knowing what to expect but bracing myself for the worst. To my astonishment, the Bill progressed for its second and final reading.

I couldn't believe my ears. As we got outside, still unsure I had understood everything correctly, I touched Angela Smith MP's arm.

'Has it really progressed?' I asked tentatively.

'Yes,' she smiled, putting her arm around my shoulders. 'It really has.'

Determined to keep up the momentum, in conjunction with Women's Aid, the following month we wrote a letter to the Justice Secretary, Robert Buckland, to request a meeting with him to discuss the problematic issues concerning the family courts. We received a response and a date for October 29, two days after Jack's anniversary, but in securing this meeting, I felt like we were being proactive, and I was one step closer to ensuring children who were affected by domestic abuse would have a brighter future.

But then came another potential hurdle. Boris Johnson attempted to prorogue parliament from September 9 until October 14, which would effectively prevent any debates being heard, select committees from sitting and legislation being passed. This would mean the next reading of the Domestic Abuse Bill wouldn't happen. Thankfully, Johnson's motion was challenged by all opposition parties and the UK Supreme Court ruled the prorogation of parliament was unlawful and it was once again sitting the next day.

The relief I felt was palpable. I was in Italy when I heard the news – it had been on my bucket list to see an opera in the home of where some of the finest productions had been written. But when I boarded the plane alone, I was a bag of nerves. I had never done anything so adventurous before, and certainly not alone. I had plucked up the courage to go, knowing it was another step to rebuilding my life. Music had always been a source of happiness, and after losing the boys, therapy too. As I walked the streets of Verona, I absorbed the sights, the beautiful vibrant greenery of the vineyards, and took in the aromas of fresh lemons and leather. Autumn had already arrived and on seeing puddles, I splashed in them and joyfully kicked up fallen leaves, knowing that's exactly what Jack and Paul would have done.

The city was full of music and as I entered the amphitheatre, the history of the spectacular surroundings, where gladiators had fought and chariots raced, left me with goosebumps. I sat down on my cushion, the residual heat of the day emanating through the stone onto my legs, and I thought about how far I'd come in just five years. There I was, illuminated by stars and candlelight, hearing the most phenomenal of voices soaring to the music of Bizet, bringing to life the opera *Carmen*.

After I returned home, I once again travelled to London and on October 2, I sat down on those famous green seats in the House of Commons to hear the second and final reading of the Domestic Abuse Bill 2017-2019. Theresa May, who had committed so much to the Bill, made her maiden speech as a backbencher as part of the debate. Rosie Duffield MP also spoke out for the first time about her own personal experience of domestic abuse, leaving the packed house so silent you could have heard a pin drop. As I listened to Rosie share in that room what she had endured, I was in awe of her strength, dignity and bravery, knowing the courage it takes to tell the world you have been a victim of domestic abuse.

Tucked in the shadows of the chamber, watching, I held my breath as I waited for Victoria Atkins to bring this monumental and historic day to a conclusion. As the bill was passed through to the House of Lords, I couldn't see for tears. If the Supreme Court had not deemed Boris Johnson unlawful in attempting to prorogue parliament, if MPs hadn't challenged his decision, this day would not have come. But the moment, despite how much I had fought for it and desperately wanted it, still felt bittersweet. The only reason I was part of the truly monumental occasion was because my beautiful sons had been murdered, and that awful feeling of emptiness threatened to engulf me once again, all the confidence I had momentarily found in Italy, now swept away.

Another stumbling block – and a big one – did come our way just over one week later, when parliament was prorogued from October 8 to 14, and a General Election was called on December 12th 2019. Everything came to a standstill, and we would now have to put the Domestic Abuse Bill before a new government. It was another mountain to climb, but whenever I'm down, it's the promise I made to Jack and Paul as they died that forces me back up again. The meeting Women's Aid and I had secured with Robert Buckland MP was still permitted to go ahead. On the day, I channelled all my emotions into the changes that I knew were needed. I would do everything I could to honour my sons' memories. The problems victims of abuse face in the family courts had to be addressed and I was determined not to let the Child First campaign be forgotten. Robert Buckland listened as Lucy, from Women's Aid, and I explained why children must be put at the heart of legislation. I held my photo of Jack and Paul, told him my story, and explained why children must be protected.

Lucy and I left the meeting feeling we had done all that we could to try and ensure victims of abuse would have more protection in the future, but it still felt like a blow to the heart on November 6 when Boris Johnson dissolved parliament. All legislation was put on hold and the progress we had made on the Domestic Abuse Bill was lost. All that time, effort, hope and tears was now in a state of limbo. Theresa May's flagship domestic abuse policy was now lying in tatters around her feet along with thousands of children's futures.

New Year's Eve of 2019 felt hard. I didn't know if I had enough strength, hope or love left inside me to carry on. For over five years I had been desperately trying to create a legacy for Jack and Paul, fighting for children's lives, hoping to create a better and safer future for those who were affected by abuse. The only way I justified my existence was by making a difference to others but after parliament had been prorogued, it felt like I wasn't able to achieve my mission. I'd always found a way to pick myself up, dust myself off and carry on, but whether it was the time of year, or I was just exhausted, I found it hard to see a way forward.

In the end, I reminded myself the Child First petition was still live and people were still signing it. I told myself I just had to hang on and take strength from the love I had for my sons. I recalled the words a good friend, Emily, used to say to me. 'On the days that you want to give up and join the boys, it's their hands pressing on your heart to keep it beating, and their hands lifting your chin and pulling your shoulders back.' It was Emily's words that helped pull me through the start of a new decade.

In the dreary and dark days of February we put pressure on the newly elected Conservative government in relation to the Domestic Abuse Bill. We secured a meeting with Dan Jarvis MP, who had supported the Bill. But the week before the meeting I tripped outside and hurt my ankle. I managed to get up and hobble on it, but as the days passed, the excruciating pain increased.

Mum insisted we should go to hospital. Initially, I refused. Hospitals had nothing but bad memories for me, and the thought of stepping inside one ever again, made me incredibly anxious. But eventually, my ankle swollen and throbbing, I reluctantly relented. As we went through the hospital doors, the memories of holding both my sons in my arms as they took his last breath floored me.

In a state of shock, I sat down and waited for my name to be called. When I finally saw a doctor, he asked: 'That looks badly broken. How many minutes or hours ago did you do it?'

'A week ago,' I confessed.

'Why on earth haven't you had it checked out? And how on earth have you managed to walk on it?'

Before I could stop myself, the words were tumbling from my lips.

'Because I would rather endure this pain, then face the raw, unbearable pain in my heart and mind that walking into this hospital brings.'

The doctor nodded empathetically. I was taken for an X–ray and then wheeled into a cubicle. Suddenly, I began to feel lightheaded. A nurse was by my side. My blood pressure had dropped, and only later did I realise that the visit to the hospital had triggered an attack of post-traumatic stress disorder (PTSD). I was given a mild sedative as Mum held my hand. At some stage a temporary plaster was put on my broken ankle and then I was given the crushing news I would have to return a week later to have a second cast put on. It took all the courage I could muster to get through those hospital visits, and the nights which followed were filled with the harrowing images of Jack and Paul's final moments. The plaster cast I had been told I had to wear for six weeks also meant I couldn't go and see the boys in their final resting place, so instead, I lit a candle for them of an evening and made sure it constantly shone brightly.

On March 3, 2020, the newly-titled Domestic Abuse Bill 2019-2021 was reintroduced to parliament for its first reading at the House of Commons. Thankfully, it once again received cross party support and was progressed to a second reading. The relief I felt was enormous. The Bill hadn't fallen or been lost, instead due to the unexpected hiatus it had been strengthened. There was now a Domestic Abuse Commissioner, Nicole Jacobs, and refuges were awarded more funding. Non-molestation orders Domestic Abuse Protection Orders (DAPO) were given more power and made more readily available. There was also a push to end cross-examination by perpetrators of domestic abuse in family courts. My hope had been restored despite the turbulent political landscape and a government which had no clear manifesto or policy to tackle domestic abuse.

Then the Covid–19 pandemic ripped across the world and lockdown happened. I don't think any of us will forget being told by Boris Johnson we had to stay at home. I formed a bubble with mum and we stayed at her house. The end of March also marked what should have been Jack's 18th birthday. Between the pandemic and the heavy cast on my ankle, with strict instructions to keep it elevated as much as possible, I was restricted on what I could do to mark what should have been my eldest son's special day. All I could do was light a candle and remember the special moments we had shared together.

As you would expect my mood dropped, but just when things

began to feel all-consuming again, music, once more, saved me. The choir I attended began rehearsals and singing lessons on Zoom and it was such a boost. I also took part in Opera North's 'Couch to Chorus' and signed up for Gareth Malone's *The Great British Home Choir*. Every week, we would learn a new song, practice it every day, then record ourselves for a subsequent CD, dressed in a branded T-shirt. It became a comforting ritual to hit the notes, but it was quite the task singing to the piano track, from memory, on one device through headphones, and recording myself using another device.

I can look back and laugh now, but on more than one occasion, Mum would tell me off for swearing after it took me three attempts on 'recording days'. Then I would tell her off for adding her 'ums and arghs' to my recording. But despite our amusing bickering, it got us through lockdown. Mum's favourite saying about weathering the weather together is so true, as lockdown proved – when people come together and form an umbrella, you can take shelter from life's storms.

Despite the country being in a state of turmoil, by some miracle the Domestic Abuse Bill was heard for its second reading on April 28 and as I watched it live on TV, I hardly dared to breathe. Four years of campaigning rested on the next few hours. Justice Secretary Robert Buckland reflected on the courage of MPs who had bravely shared their own experiences of abuse in the past. He explained for so many the sounds and sights witnessed in our own homes, often as children, haunt them for years.

Then he said: 'I have heard no more harrowing account recently than that of Claire Throssell, whom I had the privilege to meet last October. Claire's young sons, Jack and Paul, were killed at the hands of her abusive partner. No one can imagine the pain and suffering that she has had to endure, but we owe her a debt of gratitude for giving such a powerful voice to survivors of domestic abuse.'

I closed my eyes as a torrent of tears ran down my face. The Justice Secretary had done what the coroner at my sons' inquests could not. He put on the record, to be kept for all time, that Jack and Paul were murdered by their own dad. The words Jack had said to the firefighters had finally been heard in parliament, in the beating heart of democracy itself, the House of Commons.

The Domestic Abuse Bill has four aims. Firstly, to raise awareness of the crime. Secondly, to protect and support victims and their children. Thirdly, to transform the response of criminal, civil and family justice systems. And lastly, to improve performance across all national and local agencies. A clear definition of domestic abuse had also been agreed on, defining it as violent, sexual, controlling or coercive behaviour, alongside psychological and economic abuse. As part of the Bill, Domestic Abuse Protection Orders (DAPOS) were introduced, bringing together the most effective elements of non-molestation orders, restraining orders and domestic violence protection orders. In theory, if the order is broken a perpetrator can be imprisoned for five years.

The Bill also stated that special measures will automatically be available for victims of domestic abuse in family courts. This could mean a victim or survivor could be permitted to give evidence from behind a screen or via video link and could be allocated a separate waiting area in the courts. All this was a direct result of the Child First campaign. Another win for the campaign was the ruling that perpetrators could no longer cross-examine their victims in civil and family courts. Never had there been a time when this Bill and protection for victims and survivors felt more necessary. As Covid took its toll on the country, domestic abuse escalated. In the first three weeks of lockdown alone, 16 women and children were murdered.

In June 2020, the Ministry of Justice published the Harm Panel Report and the Domestic Abuse Commissioner, Nicole Jacobs, assessed the potential for harm to children and parents in the family courts. The report recognised the family courts were putting children at risk and made a number of recommendations, some of which were also being addressed in the Domestic Abuse Bill. One of the points included the fact that presumption of contact was putting children in danger.

On July 3, 2020, the Domestic Abuse Bill was passed through for its third and final reading. I cried with sheer relief when I heard the news. By then the Government had amended the Bill to include that children could and should be recognised as victims of domestic abuse in their own right, if they see, hear or experience it under the now newly-formed definition of abuse. The Bill was now in the hands of the Lords and all I could do was continue to wait and to hope.

That September I was invited back to a virtual event at Bluebell Wood for their Remembrance Day ceremony. Every parent was sent a sunflower-themed notepad, candle and bunting, as well as a packet of sunflower seeds. The bunting brightened up the room and made me smile so much we kept it up for three years. Mum and I sat together on the couch watching on a screen and as Jack and Paul's names were read out, Mum squeezed my hand. Picking up the sunflower notepad, she said: 'Put this to good use. Make it count and write a book in it.' I could never have known then that less than five years later, I would be doing exactly that, putting pen to paper, and allowing words and memories to flow to write this book.

The sunflower seeds were also a poignant reminder of the boys. Mum had bought seeds every year, when they were alive, for them to plant. Without fail, Jack and Paul would argue over whose sunflower was the tallest, but we just laughed at how competitive they were. As the new seeds grew the following year, I would have given anything to hear my sons' competitive banter about which sunflower had won.

23

ON DECEMBER 31, 2020, it was announced in the New Year's Honour's List that I had received an MBE for services to children experiencing domestic abuse. I didn't accept the medal for me, I accepted it for Jack and Paul and the promise I'd made for them as they slipped from this world to the next.

But the high I was feeling soon came crashing down. Paul's birthday arrived and I was once again shrouded by an overwhelming cloud of pain and grief that suffocated me. A throbbing in my chest left me gasping for breath and in agony so Mum rang 101 and I was admitted to hospital. We were in another Covid lockdown and no visitors were allowed but I didn't mind. Strong painkillers helped shut my mind and body down, but there are no tablets to ease the cruel feeling of loss. I was allowed home four days later and I felt detached and disconnected from everyone, but I was still standing. As always, Mum and music were there for me. Mum was unfalteringly supportive, and I attended online choir and singing sessions, which supplied the escapism I needed.

I told myself I had to carry on. I couldn't give up now. I had watched as The Domestic Abuse Act had been read and debated in the House of Lords which had voted against any changes to the current legislation around presumption of contact, covered by The Children's Act 2004. I was crushed. The Lords knew about the Child First campaign, as well as the shocking figures which made the fight necessary. Between 2004 and 2014, 19 children had been murdered due to unsafe, court ordered visitation to parents who were known perpetrators of domestic abuse. Independent research also revealed that in the 20 years between 1994 and 2004, 29 children, that we know of, were murdered due to unsafe contact with parents who were known perpetrators of domestic abuse. Yet, astonishingly, the Lords had made the decision that there was nothing wrong with the dangerous and fatal culture of contact at any cost. They had decided a debate was not needed around the issue of unsafe contact and as a result, the abolition of presumption of contact was not included in the Domestic Abuse Act. Since that decision, every year more children have been murdered, abused and neglected at the hands of parents. Every single one of those deaths and cruelties was preventable and could have been stopped if only changes had been made to the legislation and the legal framework,

The Children's Act 2004 was an amendment act replacing the 1989 Children's Act and came into place after an inquiry into Victoria Climbie's death. Or, to put it more accurately, Victoria Climbie's murder. This was the devastating death of an eight-year-old little girl that shocked the nation after she was tortured and killed by her great aunt and great aunt's boyfriend. The case lifted the lid on the failings of organisations who had a duty to care and to protect vulnerable children. Victoria's death led to a public inquiry and major changes in child protection policies, but not enough lessons had been learnt and children were still dying.

When I visited Schindler's Factory and Museum in Krakow, Poland, there was a quote on the wall by the Spanish-American philosopher, George Santayana. It read: 'Those who do not remember the past are condemned to repeat it'. Never a truer word said. Between 1994 and 2015, 48 children had been murdered at the hands of their parent or guardian; add to that the 19 more children who lost their lives in the same way in the nine years up to 2024. That's 67 children who have been murdered over a 30-year period, yet presumption of contact was not addressed and not included in the Domestic Abuse Act 2021. This seemed utterly nonsensical to me.

My reaction was palpable – I wanted to scream. Scream at the Lords who hadn't felt presumption of contact should be addressed and scream at the one person who had taken away my children from me. But he wasn't here and he would never have to pay for what he had done. When Jack and Paul had been overwhelmed with how their father was treating them, or me, I would take a couple of cushions outside and give them both a bamboo cane each.

'Take it out on the cushions,' I would tell them.

As the news from the House of Lords sank in, I took a cushion and put it in front of my face, but the rage I felt burning inside me didn't ease. I took myself up to the nearby stone quarry and screamed into the abyss. It was loud. It was inhuman. It was guttural and I didn't like the sound of it in my own ears. In all honesty, it was probably the silent scream that had been raging like a volcano inside me for years, and after seven long years, had finally erupted.

Then came the tears. It's not often I cry for myself, but that day, I sobbed and sobbed. I wept for lives that can never be and an existence that has to be lived alone. The wild beauty of the quarry called to the temporary wildness within me and then everything went silent. Wild has never been my personality, I'm not easily angered and I don't easily hate.

It would have been easy to give up at that stage. I allowed myself three days at the bottom of that very dark pit, then I slowly climbed a ladder and resurfaced. Don't get me wrong, I still occasionally trip over the rubble and detritus of my life, which constantly circles my feet, but I refused to let the dust it kicks up blind me.

I had to believe there was still hope. Women's Aid were still by my side, tightly holding my hand, and the Child First petition was still live. Love and a strong dose of stubbornness kept me going. Children deserved better, Jack and Paul had deserved better. I would not stop fighting.

On April 29, 2021, the Domestic Abuse Act, a huge and long-awaited piece of landmark legislation, received Royal Assent and became law. It was much needed, and I was happy progress had finally been made but presumption of contact had to be addressed. I was determined to keep my promise to Jack and Paul. I would be their voice to the end. I had also become the voice of thousands of other women and children who had been silenced, scared or alone. IDAS and Women's Aid hadn't given up and neither would I. I just needed to keep reminding myself to keep my head up and keep my eyes to the sky. I'd always told Jack and Paul the sky and the stars had no limits and neither did they. The only limits you have are the ones you put in front of yourselves, and if they ever needed help, they could use my shoulders to climb on and reach it.

I had to follow my own sage advice now. A dream spoken or just whispered aloud becomes a possibility and with hard work, grit and some teamwork, could become a reality. No matter how old we are, how broken we feel, we should never be scared to have a dream. The world needs hopers and dreamers to keep us evolving and improving, to create a better place for us all. Every debate I sat in, every debate I watched on TV, every meeting I attended felt like a step closer to achieving that dream. I wasn't going to let it slip away now.

Over the years I have had many messages of love and support from all over the world. Complete strangers took time out of their own days to get in touch to tell me they were thinking of me. Their kindness left me in tears. It's these messages about Jack and Paul, that have given me renewed hope. I always try to message every single person back who contacted me to say thank you. Others told me of their own harrowing experience of domestic abuse or of losing a child. One told me she realised the same thing was happening to her; she walked out of the marital home the next day, with her children, and told me I had saved four lives. Some explained how domestic abuse laws had been changed in their own countries. The latest I know of is in Sweden. On January 1, 2025, in the Parental Code, legislation around parental contact was amended ensuring the wellbeing of a child takes precedence over the rights of a parent, if there's suspicion of violence or risk to a child.

In July of 2021, my niece got married at a beautiful hotel in Settle, North Yorkshire. It was another bittersweet moment. It was a wonderful occasion, Mum had written a poem which she read out and my niece had asked me to play the piano at the start and end of the ceremony. I was proud to play for them and it meant the world to be asked, but I couldn't help thinking that there were two faces missing.

Towards the end of the evening a familiar melancholy came over me. Mum had gone up to our room and I was sitting taking in the last rays of the day's sun. Jack and Paul had always loved weddings, getting dressed up, looking smart and seeing everybody. I never had to worry about their behaviour, they were always angels. Since losing them, I'd always struggled in a room full of people celebrating life, there's always a slight detachment. I'm glad people are enjoying themselves, but I knew I could never reach that level of happiness again. It's exhausting living with the loneliness of grief. It's like looking through a window of life; you see it, feel it and hear it, but you feel like a spectator not a participant. It's no longer easy to just open a door and join in, and opening doors alone for the first time is always the hardest. A smile is sometimes the heaviest burden to carry.

Two months later, on September 24, a short documentary about the boys and how the community had rallied together to help me premiered at our local cinema, the Penistone Paramount. The documentary had been created by a young, local film director, Saul Tyler, with the aim of shining a light on domestic abuse and the Child First campaign. The cinema was packed as people came together to watch the viewing. Yet again, I was moved by the community's support.

I was invited back to the Proud of Barnsley Awards that year. The event had grown since I'd received my award, but the emotion, pride and uplifting feeling was still there. Barnsley is often described as one of the most deprived areas of the country and maybe it is financially and economically less prosperous than other towns, but its sense of friendliness, warmth, resilience and enormous spirit shines through. At the end of the evening, to my complete surprise, a video started playing of Jack and Paul and my sister, Caz, instinctively took hold of my hand. I wasn't sure what was happening, but it soon became clear, when I was called onto the stage. As I was presented with a Special Recognition Award for all the work I was doing to ensure children's voices were heard, confetti cannons exploded. I was so touched that my own town was announcing they were proud of me. It was yet another reminder to keep going, to simply be me, and never stop elevating my son's voices, memories and love.

After a quiet Christmas and New Year, I was told my MBE investiture would finally happen on January 25, 2022 at Windsor Castle. So, on Paul's birthday on January 9, I went to visit my sons at their final resting place to tell them all about my Royal occasion. The only problem with going to the boys' grave, where they sleep with my dad, is that I never want to leave. Every time I stand up to come away, a tearing pain courses through me but it helps knowing their ashes are always with me, in the form of a tattoo and the ring I never take off.

When I chose the wording for their gravestone, I wanted it to resemble the love and closeness we had always shared. It reads: *Our arms entwined, all love enfolded, to infinity and beyond.* I know, in my heart, the boys went from my arms into my dad's, and he would have held them tightly, as he had held me in life. But on the days when the wind is howling and the rain is falling so hard it stings your eyes, it's very hard to leave my sons. Instead, it takes all my strength to stop myself from digging them up and bringing Jack and Paul home.

I asked my sister, Caz, to come to Windsor with me and after we checked into our hotel, we decided to go for a walk. I was so taken by Windsor, it was such a beautiful place, the skyline is dominated by the castle and its walls. By the time we headed back to settle down for the night, the castle was illuminated against the night sky and our hotel had strings of fairy lights strung around the building. Everything looked so quaint and pretty.

As we walked back to the hotel, memories of the time I took Jack and Paul to Legoland as part of my 40th birthday celebrations came unbidden. It had rained all day, but the boys had a ball, driving around the car track. Jack had just passed his cycling proficiency, or bike ability as it is now known, at school. On the car track at Legoland, when he got to a junction, he put his arm out to indicate he was turning. I had smiled, thinking Jack had obviously listened to his instructor. But that innocent, and lovely, moment was destroyed a second later by the vile and brutal words of my ex-husband.

'He's such a fucking wuss and you have made him that way,' he scowled.

The words had cut me in two. Yet again, he had managed to destroy what should have been a special occasion. I refused to let him ruin it for the boys, though so I fought back the tears, locked away the hurt and painted a smile on my face.

When I woke up the next morning, despite how momentous the occasion was, I didn't feel nervous at all. I wasn't sure how I was feeling. It was nice to be dressed up and have my sister with me, who looked beautiful, but I think I was probably feeling a bit numb.

The town was bristling with activity and as we approached the castle, the police officers and guards couldn't have been more friendly and helpful, checking our documents and passes. Every royal aide we passed greeted us with smiles and congratulated us, which felt lovely. Then we reached the magnificent quadrangle. I don't think a single blade of grass was out of place, it really is the grandest doormat in England.

Suddenly, the feeling of being elated started to vanish. I knew I should be beaming, but inside those old demons, that had left my self-confidence in tatters, were edging their way towards the front of my mind. *Was I really worthy enough to be here?* My ex-husband would have told me I was kidding myself. I began whispering, hiding my own voice. As we walked towards St George's Chapel, I turned to Caz.

'Why are we whispering? I asked, finding my voice. It was as though the reason I had been invited to this magnificent setting came back to me. I had as much right to be here as anyone else. Taking a deep breath, I slipped my hand into Caz's, walked through the impressive doors of the historic castle and the entrance took my breath away. Once inside, we were directed towards a staircase. So mesmerised by the ornate ceiling, I walked straight into a soldier of the Household Cavalry, who was on guard. It was only then I realised two of them were positioned on every stair of the staircase. I quickly apologised, silently blaming my dad, who had always been fascinated by church and cathedral ceilings. Another memory came. During a family holiday to Cornwall, it had started to rain, and we had all run into Truro Cathedral to take shelter. After a minute or so, I couldn't see my dad but eventually found him laying on the floor looking up at the ceiling, because he thought a design wasn't running at the angle it should have been. Anyway, the Household Cavalry soldier put his arm around me to stop me falling, but apart from that, in true style of the regiment, he barely flinched.

Claire Throssell

The accidental bump brought me back to the moment and made me focus on why I was at Windsor. At the top of the staircase, I was asked what honour I was receiving, before being directed to the Red Room. The crimson drawing room is a semi-state room that was used regularly by the late Queen Elizabeth for private events and was used to film that famous scene of her taking tea with Paddington Bear. The room had also been partially destroyed by a fire in 1992, but luckily all the oil paintings had been rescued before the blaze took hold.

We were directed to the very expensive, ornate French chairs to sit on and suddenly, I felt overwhelmed again. As Caz chatted to people around us, I felt myself withdraw. It was the irony of being in a room that had once been destroyed by fire. My mind retreated to October 2014 and all the roads I had travelled to get to this point. I tried to focus on the reason I was here as opposed to what had happened to my lovely boys.

Then before I knew it, I was standing in front of Prince William. He reached out to touch my arm and his warm smile instantly relaxed me. After asking whereabouts in Yorkshire I was from, we talked about the Child First campaign.

'Cherish every moment with your children,' I said. 'And protect their childhoods.'

'I will,' he promised, giving my arm a gentle rub. One parent offering comfort to another and a thoughtful gesture, which meant so much.

The fact he mentioned Jack and Paul by name meant the world. After eight years working to ensure my precious boys never became anonymous letters on a piece of paper. MPs, Prime Ministers and now the future King of England had said my sons' names.

For My Boys

After Prince William had pinned my MBE onto my dress, as protocol demanded, I managed to curtsy and walk away without any mishaps. Afterwards we had some professional photos taken for Mum, which she had insisted on. When we got home to Yorkshire, I poured Mum a Baileys and gave her my MBE to hold as I thanked her for holding me together for the last eight years.

The following month, on February 26, 2022, I turned 50. I wasn't looking forward to it. Not because I'm vain, far from it, but simply because I would be entering another decade of my life that the boys would never see or share with me. On my 30th birthday, I had been eight months pregnant with Jack, and on my 40th birthday I had taken the boys to see *Robot Wars*, before a trip to London, and tickets to see *The Lion King* in the West End. I had always loved sharing my birthday with the boys, but now as what should have been a special day drew closer, my birthday felt like another ordeal to endure. This, combined with the fact I felt so guilty about living to see another birthday when my sons would never get the chance meant I struggled in the days and weeks leading up to the occasion.

But as always, I picked myself up and got through the day. Then, in March, Barnsley Sixth Form asked me to speak at their crime and justice week. I was delighted as I am passionate about educating people about domestic abuse to try to make a difference. I firmly believe if you can educate young people then it could help change attitudes. I also hope it will empower young people to know their own self-worth when it comes to relationships and the choices they make about who they let into their lives. It's crucial that they know the difference between good and toxic relationships. It feels like they are the generation who will challenge and call out abusive language and behaviour. So, I was more than happy to speak to the sixth form students, talking to nearly 200 young people. I hoped it would have a ripple effect and they would talk to friends and family, so the pool of knowledge would grow. The age group most at risk and vulnerable to life's dangers are people between 11 and 16. Why? Because they are the tweens and teens. Not young children but not adults either. They are frequently easily led and lack the life skills and self-awareness to be able to protect themselves in difficult or dangerous situations. Education, empowerment and open communication are the key to helping keep children safe.

The sessions I delivered were a safe space to validate and process information and feelings. Lots of children and young people grow up not realising they live in an abusive home. It's only when they go out into the wider world or start going to friend's houses that they often begin to realise their house is different, but they don't know why. That's where educating them about domestic abuse becomes vital, so they don't continue the behaviour they've seen all their lives and replicate that when engaging in intimate relationships. With education, we can stop the cycle from carrying on ruining lives.

24

EVERY YEAR Women's Aid holds an event for survivors and ambassadors to come together for the day. It's a day I always look forward to, when I can spend time with women who, like me, have experienced abuse. We all understand what each other has been through, we believe each other, see each other and support each other. No amount of money can equal how much that is worth. There's nothing more empowering than women supporting other women, uniting to help make a difference.

It was at one of these events that I met Mel B, the former Spice Girl, who has spoken about being a survivor of domestic abuse. Melanie became a patron of Women's Aid in November 2018, on what was the International Day for the Elimination of Violence against Women. At the event I attended, Melanie was very open and honest, dispelling the myth that domestic abuse only happens to a certain cluster of people. Her bravery highlighted that domestic abuse could and does happen to anyone, regardless of status, and went on to help change the perceptions on the topic. Her openness means a lot to survivors, it makes us feel like it isn't just us. I am so grateful for the support Melanie has shown me and other survivors. Her voice has told the story of so many and helped keep domestic abuse in the public eye.

But despite high-profile voices speaking out and laws being changed, not enough was being done to protect victims and survivors. February 2023 marked six years since the Ministry of Justice first committed to banning perpetrators of domestic abuse from cross examining their victims in the family and civil courts. But that same year, research and testimonies revealed victims and survivors were still being humiliated, bullied, harassed and retraumatised in the family and civil courts. Why? Because, quite nonsensically, the ban only applies to new cases from 2022 onwards. Family Court cases can take years before a final hearing is reached, so anyone already involved in court proceedings which started before 2022 had to continue to endure the barbaric and unjust process of cross examination, allowing perpetrators to inflict more emotional harm, fear, power and control over their victims in front of a judge in a court of law.

To add to this, the Ministry of Justice set the fees that solicitors and barristers can charge for their work in family law proceedings at a rate which is not competitive. Consequently, many solicitors and barristers don't sign up to Legal Aid schemes. The grim reality is more and more victims of domestic abuse face the prospect of representing themselves in court and fighting their abusive ex-partner alone, or they simply don't leave their abuser, as the road ahead is too overwhelming.

It was with this in mind that I added my voice to that of Women's Aid, along with other domestic abuse organisations, who were calling on the government and the Ministry of Justice to review the legal fees for cross examination and ensure that the ban applies to all cases. We asked for effective monitoring systems of implementation and regular reviews to check how it was working. The Domestic Abuse Act has the power to deliver significant, wide-reaching, reform, but time and time again delays implementing that power and legislation meant family courts were still failing to protect adults and children experiencing domestic abuse. People like me. Children like Jack and Paul.

We sent a letter to the then Justice Secretary, Dominic Raab, who was also the deputy Prime Minister, but due to the Hokey Cokey of government, it wasn't long before he was out – resigning in 2023 – and Alex Chalk had taken over the position. While ministers swapped positions at a rate of knots, women and children were dying. After Theresa May, not one of her successors, including Boris Johnson, Liz Truss or Rishi Sunak, championed her Domestic Abuse policy. Not one of those rapidly formed governments went on to protect victims and survivors of abuse, whether they be women, children or men. Their inaction meant they failed to safeguard future generations, failed to end domestic abuse and violence against all.

Language around domestic abuse is crucial. Although we have the Violence Against Women and Girls (VAWG) strategy, domestic abuse does include boys too and when you examine the gender divide between the 19 children that were killed between 2004 and 2014, the split was 50/50. The only part of Jack's body that wasn't injured were his legs and feet. Paul was poisoned with fumes and his whole body overcome with smoke inhalation. Prior to their deaths, both had suffered harm mentally and emotionally, as well as physically at the hands of their father. I strongly feel the language has to change from Violence Against Women and Girls (VAWG) to Violence Against Women and Children (VAWC), because boys suffer all types of abuse too. Generally, children do not willingly disclose that they are being or have been abused. And they certainly don't see themselves as recognised or represented in the VAWG strategy. Language is so important, especially when it comes to domestic abuse, as it is often invisible to everyone except the victims or survivors. In the current climate, I really believe the language should be 'Violence Against All'.

By the start of 2023, the Child First petition had reached 54,000 signatures and needed 100,000 to be considered for debate a second time. I was hoping by 2024, the 10th anniversary of their deaths, I would be able to do something meaningful to light up their memories, and I was determined to keep my promise to Jack and Paul and repeal the presumption of contact guidelines.

I asked Women's Aid if they would update the Child First report and find out how many more children had been killed due to unsafe contact since Jack and Paul had been murdered. I wanted to fight on, to shake off all the setbacks, and to ignore the mocking voice in my head telling me I would fail. I would silently scream back that I would only fail if I never tried at all.

I have lost so many people in my life who I love and there were times when I had been driven to the point where I felt like I had lost everything, including myself. But over the many years of campaigning, I have also been blessed to meet and connect with some amazing people and organisations. In 2023, I spoke at the Nottinghamshire Women's Aid Annual General Meeting. As soon as I entered the building, the calmness, safety and empathy was visceral. I could not just feel it, I could see it. Every space was colourful and positive affirmations and powerful messages of hope had been printed onto the walls, offering strength to carry on, letting anyone who came into the building know that they are not alone. They had been created by domestic abuse survivors, including children. I was blown away by their warmth and dedication to make women's and children's lives safer. The organisation provides help, support and advice and they are a refuge, a safe space, and a welcome relief to all those affected by domestic abuse.

I was soon to discover they would offer me the same form of refuge. They welcomed me into their organisation, providing me with a safe space to talk and a comforting shoulder to lean on. They didn't just take me into their hearts, they took Jack and Paul too. They stood by my side, campaigned alongside me, calling on the government to remove presumption of contact. The Child First campaign is now as much a part of their organisation as it is me. They had banners made and their support gave me, and still does, renewed hope and strength.

I gave another talk at Barnsley College and some of Paul's closest friends attended. It was hard and upsetting for them to hear about what Paul, Jack and I had gone through. In the aftermath of Paul's death, his classmates at school created a memory book full of notes written about Paul, they all described him as fast, funny, caring, kind and a good friend. What really stuck out to me is not one person described Paul as sad, but as they listened to the harrowing circumstances in which he died, they felt sad. As young adults, they now heard about how a huge part of his life had been hidden behind closed doors. This is why I'm so passionate about educating young people. If we can make them aware of the dangers, we can help to keep them safe and give them a chance of a brighter future.

As had become the pattern, every time I had reason to feel hopeful, something would happen. Around this time, the government, in particular the Ministry of Justice announced they wanted to introduce mandatory mediation before proceedings could begin in the civil and family courts. I don't deny that in some cases mediation is a sensible and financially better option for couples who separate amicably, and the balance of power between them is equal and mutually respectful. However, when it comes to abusive relationships where there is an imbalance of power, mediation is not fair, helpful or safe. It becomes a new tool, a new stick for perpetrators to use to intimidate, control and bully their victim to get what they want, or feel they deserve or are entitled to. I know from my own experience of mediation how difficult it becomes when abuse is part of the equation. And mediation cannot resolve disputed child contact.

When I was informed I would have to attend mediation before applying for a divorce, my husband immediately tried to take control. I had found a mediator in Barnsley, but he tried to force me to go to one in Leeds, despite it being much further away for both of us. I objected, stating it was an unreasonable demand, which was thankfully accepted. The irony was he said he would feel intimidated attending mediation in Barnsley, despite the fact he had left me a shell of my former self. The reality was he just wanted to control the situation, and show he had that power.

So, when the government announced they wanted mediation to become mandatory, I once again added my voice to Women's Aid's opposition to the move. Wherever domestic abuse or violence is known or suspected to have occurred, mediation would be unsafe, traumatic, and unregulated. Mediators are not domestic abuse specialists, they can't make decisions or rulings around parental rights or visitation regarding children. An application to a court would have to be made regardless, so it seemed ludicrous that the legal system would be putting power in the hands of perpetrators and giving them another way to bully, scare and harass their victims, without a judge or barrister to protect them. For any victim or survivor of domestic abuse, facing their perpetrator is one of the hardest things they will have to endure. It can reduce them to a quivering wreck, destroy any confidence they may have started to build and re-trigger them.

In the lead up to the mediation I was told I had to attend, I felt physically sick and overwhelmingly anxious. I barely slept a wink and the demons in my head, which my husband had caused, told me he would get whatever he demanded, as I was worthless. In a bid to empower myself, I spent a long time pulling together all the financial information I needed, requested by the mediator. This was hard as a lot of the information was still in the family home, which my husband denied me access to. It all added to the stress and worry of the situation. With the support of my family and friends, I mustered up all the courage I could and turned up for the appointment, only to discover my husband hadn't arrived, and from that point onwards he refused to engage with the process. In many ways, I was one of the lucky ones at this stage, as the divorce was allowed to proceed, but for so many others they are forced to face their attacker, who refuses to compromise in any shape or form, lie or intimidate their former, and often very frightened, partner.

Something had to change. In 2023, Lord Christopher Bellamy KC was parliamentary undersecretary of state in the Ministry of Justice. I asked Lucy at Women's Aid to request a meeting with him regarding presumption of contact, mandatory mediation and legal aid provision. It took a few weeks but eventually the Ministry of Justice agreed we could have a meeting with Lord Bellamy and a date was set. Once again, Lucy and Sophie from Women's Aid and I were meeting a minister of the judiciary to try and push for the repeal of presumption of contact within family law and to consider more carefully the impact mandatory mediation would have on people trying to escape domestic abuse. No one should ever have to defend themselves in a court of law and be cross-examined by their attacker simply because they can't afford a legal representative and can't access Legal Aid. When I went to court and faced my ex-husband, I was verbally abused with both a solicitor and barrister present, which was frightening and humiliating enough, but imagine not having that level of protection. If I had been forced to stand there alone, as so many survivors of domestic abuse are, and been faced with the barrage of abuse I had encountered, as well as trying to protect and advocate for my sons, it would have completely broken me.

As I spoke to Lord Bellamy, I recalled the emotion, worry, stress and fear I felt during the Family Court hearings. What was even more worrying was that Lord Bellamy had incorrectly presumed my ex-husband was medically insane and severely mentally disturbed. I explained very clearly he was not medically insane, he was a perpetrator of domestic abuse, driven by an all-consuming hatred of me. 'He murdered our sons to punish me,' I stated, holding my photograph of Jack and Paul so their faces were very visible, refusing to let him diminish the raw facts of the matter.

After our meeting was over, Lucy, Sophie and I had a further conversation with one of Lord Bellamy's aides. We reiterated all the points we had made, emphasising that although the government were saying if victims could prove they had experienced domestic abuse, mandatory mediation wouldn't apply, this wasn't good enough. Once again, the onus would be on the victim or survivor to prove they are suffering or have been abused. They were being forced to retell and relive their trauma, just to avoid mediation. How is that healing, believing and supporting victims and survivors? In any other crime the onus is on the police to prove a crime has been committed and by who. Domestic abuse is a crime, but over and over again, it's always the victims and survivors, including myself, Jack and Paul, that have to prove what we have been subjected to. And it often feels like no one is listening and even worse, every time you are ignored or dismissed by the very people that should be helping you, it breaks another part of you.

Thankfully, mediation didn't become mandatory and at the time of writing this book in the autumn of 2025, it still hasn't. Hopefully, it never will be as the consequences will just cause more pain and trauma.

25

DESPITE HOW difficult it was to constantly battle against the government, I always tried to remember the reason for it. In September 2023, Mum and I went to Norfolk on holiday and as we walked along the beach, we bathed not just in the sunshine, but in the memories of years long gone, when we spent endless days crabbing, building sandcastles, playing crazy golf, laughing and enjoying picnics. Lovely images of afternoon tea in quaint cafes, when Jack accidentally squirted us all with jam from his doughnut. Memories like those that kept me putting one foot in front of the other, determined to do my best for other children who were at risk from an abusive parent.

A few months later, as another year came in, I knew I had a lot to face. There were the 10th anniversaries of the boys' deaths which I was determined wouldn't be shrouded in sadness, but instead full of love, memories and music. I began planning and asked the band Jack had played in if they would be willing to put on a joint concert with Barnsley Singers, where I was a member, to celebrate the boys' lives. They both agreed, which I was so grateful for.

But 2024 did end up being a very emotional year. Mum's health began to deteriorate, including her eyesight and it was heartbreaking to watch this once feisty, strong and stubbornly independent woman deteriorate as I cared for her. That New Year's Eve, Mum had made a huge effort to stay awake until midnight, after months of going to bed between eight and nine o'clock. Together, we crossed arms, sang *Auld Lang Syne* and raised a glass like we always did for those who were in our memories and hearts, including my dad, my sister Christine, and of course Jack and Paul.

Despite how exhausted Mum was feeling, as ever she was there supporting me, holding my hand and sharing the pain. After she finally went to bed, I had one more drink as I looked out of the window watching as the dark, indigo sky erupted into a kaleidoscope of colour from the fireworks which were embracing the new year. I was amazed, but not particularly impressed, that I was still standing and breathing nearly ten years after my sons had that opportunity stolen from them. The feelings of guilt, yearning to be with them, missing their presence, never lessens with time but I knew by then it was more about learning to co-exist with the grief, to be able to carry on without them. Some days are easier than others and there are always milestone dates that feel much harder.

As a parent, losing your child is the wrong order of things, and those feelings of loss and heartache never go away, because you can't turn the clock back or bring your children back. It's impossible to truly fix a grieving parent because we are broken in such a way that even a smell, a memory, or an occasion, will trigger us and break us all over again.

People mean well and try their hardest to say the right thing and I'm grateful to every single person who has ever supported me. But there is one thing you should never say to a grieving parent and that is 'time is a great healer', because in our case it really isn't and never will be. Instead, time merely serves as a reminder of how long it's been without the people we love and the things they never got to do and see. Time may physically age us but changes nothing.

There is no time limit to people's grief and another hard thing to hear, no matter how well-intentioned, is that loved ones wouldn't want you to be upset or devastated that they aren't here anymore. I assure you; we know that, but it doesn't take the pain of the loss away or stop us struggling to live without them. Grief is the biggest price we pay for love. We would have loved our precious children forever and will therefore grieve forever.

However, it's also true that spending time with people makes difficult days easier. It brings comfort, smiles and laughter, especially when they talk about your lost loved ones and actually say their names. The biggest comfort I get from people is when they say Jack and Paul's names, even if they never knew them. I don't expect my sons to be talked about all the time. I know there are thousands of other things going on in the world, but it really does mean so much when Jack and Paul aren't invisible. When they are spoken about their memories live on, in the hearts and souls of others, as well as mine.

I am very conscious that I don't sound like the world revolves around me, that it moves on, forever changing and evolving. The one thing that never stands still is time. I've been in far too many hospital rooms, and watched as Jack and Paul took their last breath, and the hands on the clock keep on ticking. Before and after the people most precious to me lived and slipped away, the hands on the clocks on those grey, soulless walls never stopped and never changed, even if my life did. But being around people who love me, like me, understand and support me, gives me a space to be myself. They are the umbrellas to my storm, the temporary respite to my pain. I am very lucky to have people to sing with, people to laugh with, cry with and fight alongside.

There are people who alongside me, look at the world and help me make a difference.

Without all my friends, life would be an even bigger battle, and as 2024 arrived I was grateful to them all. Mum was already poorly but the day before what should have been Paul's 19th birthday, Mum opened the car door awkwardly and cut her shin open, resulting in a trip to Barnsley A&E. Hospitals are always my biggest trigger and where I find myself unable to function the most. No coping strategy works and every visit causes me untold pain. A&E is right next to resuscitation where my ex-husband was brought to on the night he killed our children. The medics were duty-bound to try and save his life, and I understand that, but just being so close to that specific location, leaves me in a complete mess.

As soon as I walk into a hospital, a barrage of memories and feelings hit me, but mainly the sense of powerlessness and lack of control. And the sheer force of it doesn't give me time to withstand the onslaught, to regulate myself quickly enough to function and not fall to pieces. It's a trauma that I have accepted won't go away and will be forced to re-live both in reality and in sleep. When the boys died, I was with them, and those harrowing moments will never escape me.

Occasionally, I wonder who else was present when my ex-husband died. Initially, I didn't care that he had died. Grieving for Jack and Paul meant I had no emotions left to spare, but in the run up to the inquest I was furious my ex-husband, the man who had murdered our precious children, had died, because I wanted him to stand trial for what he had done and face the consequences. Mum, however, had a different train of thought. She believed if he had lived, in some way or another, he would never have let me be. She believed even from prison he would have found a way to contact me, to gloat and mock me. Mum firmly believed only my ex-husband's death set me free, but no matter which way I look at it, the reality is he gave me a life sentence when he murdered Jack and Paul.

This all meant taking Mum to hospital was hard. I had to find a way to swallow down my fears, blink away the flashbacks and keep myself composed, Mum needed me and I couldn't let her down. It was a nasty cut and required stitches, but Mum's skin was so fragile and thin, doctors had to use special dressings and bind it tight, so it could heal from the inside. Unfortunately, Mum's leg didn't heal properly and ended up ulcerating, so I moved back into her house to care for her.

Things weren't all bad, though and we got some good news in the form of the Child First petition reaching 100,000 signatures. Women's Aid were equally delighted and, keen to support me marking Jack and Paul's 10th anniversary, they began the process to initiate handing in the petition again at 10 Downing Street. They also secured funding to ascertain how many more children had been murdered due to unsafe contact with a known domestic or sexually abusive parent. This report would show how many children had died in the last 30 years.

In the spring of 2024, I also received another boost, this time from Nottinghamshire Women's Aid. Ever since handing in the Child First petition the first time, and walking through Parliament Square many times since, I have dreamt of having a statue made to honour Jack and Paul's memory, with a plaque worded in such a way that it embodies and remembers all the children murdered. All the children who governments, Cafcass and Social

Services would rather forget. So, I was chuffed to bits when they told me they would raise funds for a statue, a permanent, powerful and poignant memorial, depicting love, hope and sanctuary, to be erected. Initially, I wanted the statue to be in London, a reminder to all the governments that had let all those lost children down. But I gradually came to see my dream isn't about politicians being forced to walk past a memorial every day, and although that would be great, I know it would never happen. Instead, it's about giving strength, hope and belief to everyone who looks at it and to everyone who needs it.

The statue will stand outside the Farr Centre, the home of Nottinghamshire Women's Aid, to act as a point of reassurance to everyone who walks through the door. To every single person who is experiencing domestic abuse, knowing that once they take those first steps into the centre, they are a little closer to a better, safer, life. The sculptor is a good friend of mine, who I met through choir. This in itself means so much, because even after everything that has happened, I hang onto hope, humanity, friendship and love, because without those things, I really would have nothing left to live for.

Sadly, in April of 2024, Mum's health deteriorated rapidly and she became completely housebound. It was around this time, during filming for another documentary, I slipped and dislocated my thumb in two places. The doctor at A&E initially put my thumb in a splint, so I could carry on caring for Mum and finish filming the documentary, but after a week I needed a cast to help it repair properly. It was certainly a challenge helping Mum, changing her surgical stocking and remaking beds with only one working hand. Not that I minded, I wanted to look after Mum, like she had cared for me for the last ten years.

The following month Mum was admitted to hospital for a week. I was worried sick and then to make matters worse while she was in hospital I fell again, this time landing on my face. I cut my eyebrow open, bruised my eye and most of my face. One of my eyes was purple and three quarters shut. I now had a purple cast and a purple face. Don't get me wrong, purple is my favourite colour, but I didn't want to wear it on my face. Coincidentally, the eyebrow I cut open was the same one and in the exact same place that Jack had hurt himself years earlier at school. He had been walking towards a door when it was pushed open by pupils on the other side and caught him in the face. The difference being people praised Jack for being a trooper for carrying on despite the mishap, while I got some strange glances for how I looked. It gave me an insight to how abuse victims must feel, when they are left with visible injuries.

Those scars and bruises are deliberate acts by a perpetrator to indicate ownership or given as a warning. Wherever I went with my bruised face onlookers appeared shocked and I very quickly became very self-conscious. Strangers would either stare or completely avoid eye contact. Not one person was comfortable looking at my face, nobody made a joke, but nor did anyone ask if I was okay or how it happened. I felt incredibly uneasy and began pre-warning people about what had happened.

I tried to imagine how hard it must feel for those who had been physically assaulted by a partner and how often they must have made up stories about what had happened to them. We know that for many they are inadvertently protecting their attacker, who could be standing next to them smiling, as charming as ever. There were many times my ex-husband would verbally attack me to ensure whatever we were doing next was ruined. I would try and pretend that everything was okay to avoid a scene and any further repercussions. Jack and Paul could always tell though and stayed close, letting me know they were there for me. Even if they did go off and play or talk to friends and relatives, they would always come back, lean against me and say 'Don't worry, Mum. We love you'. These are words that I really miss hearing now, but I do feel blessed that my boys never shied away from being affectionate.

When Mum came home, I knew she didn't have long left, but I did everything I could to keep her with us a little longer. Despite how poorly Mum was, we tried to make the best of life. The Jack and Paul fun run went ahead, and I was invited to sing alongside Barnsley Youth Choir as they celebrated their 15th anniversary. I sang a verse of *Hallelujah* solo. The words have always resonated with me and I sang them from the heart. The words explain how my ex took my name in vain and how he broke me. To set those words free and allow them to soar, for me, there's nothing more powerful. Mum had heard me sing it solo many times and knew the words as well as I did because she helped me learn them. And although she never said it, I knew the words meant a lot to Mum too. She asked me to make it her ringtone on her mobile phone, which is what it will now remain forever.

Preparations were also well under way for the boys' 10th anniversary concert. That summer I visited Wentworth Church, where it was arranged, to discuss the plans. As soon as I stepped into the huge stone building, memories of Jack stood on the step playing his trumpet flashed before me. I saw and heard my eldest son playing brightly and clearly as the sun came shining in through the stained-glass window. That precious memory warmed me, warmer than the heat from any sun.

I devoted the next four months to caring for Mum. That summer she was so weak she barely made it downstairs so, instead I sat with her upstairs watching the Olympics and Wimbledon. Her sight started to go too, which was heartbreaking. Mum would ask me to sing to her and as soon as I did, she relaxed. 'It soothes me,' she told me.

Then in September, Mum was admitted back into hospital again and one afternoon she asked me to lie next to her. It was the most innocent of requests, but harrowing images flashed before me of the night Paul slipped away. After Paul had died, Mum and I were led to a side room and told to rest while Jack was in theatre. In the same way, Mum and I lay next to one another. Physically we were touching but neither of us could emotionally reach one another, each of us consumed with grief and fear, unable to offer any comfort apart from one another's presence. Now, nearly ten years on, I blinked back the tears, took a deep breath and lay down next to Mum. She took my hand and asked me to sing her favourite songs from the choir.

From the very first concert I had attended with Barnsley Singers Mum had supported me. She would tell the whole choir how uplifted and joyful she felt after the concerts, especially when they started up again following Covid.

'What songs would you like me to sing, Mum? I asked, as I lay next to her fragile body.

Squeezing my hand, she listed them. *Somewhere Only We Know* by Keane, *Chasing Cars* by Snow Patrol, *Shine* by Take That, *The Seal Lullaby* by Eric Whittaker, *Hallelujah* by Leonard Cohen and a relatively new piece which we had performed called *Ukuthula'* a Zulu song which incorporates peace, redemption, praise, faith, victory or comfort. Mum had heard Barnsley Youth Choir perform the last song and she had adored it. When I finished singing it, Mum squeezed my hand a little harder.

Then she said: 'When I die you mustn't stop singing. I've spent the last ten years of my life helping you sing and making sure you live. You must carry on now. One day victory will come.'

I held her hand and just nodded. Although I didn't want to hear it, I knew Mum was telling me she was dying. After I left the hospital that night, I sat in my car and cried and cried. On September 14, I received a phone call to say Mum was unresponsive. I immediately called Caz and we drove to the hospital. When I arrived the doctor who had rung me was waiting for us. He had the same look in his eyes that I had seen before, and I understood all too well what it meant. Another resuscitation room, but this time it was calm. There wasn't an army of medics desperately fighting to try and save a young life. Instead, this was a time of thanks, love, comfort and solace to a much-loved mum in the last hours of her life. By that time Mum could no longer talk or respond, but she knew Caz and I were there and held our hands when we took hers. I sat on one side and Caz on the other. We gathered as a family to wrap mum tightly in our love as she fell into sleeping for the last time. Mum's colour and breathing changed. Suddenly I felt my dad's presence and began to sing *Ukuthula*. It came naturally because I wished Mum comfort and had faith that she would see Dad, Jack, Paul and our sister, Chris. Redemption for all the times she had stood by me, and peace, because all her grief and pain had finally gone. Mum's life was complete, and she slipped away peacefully, surrounded by music, her family and love.

Claire Throssell

The rest of September went by in a haze as I endeavoured to come to terms with the loss of Mum and tried to prepare for the 10th anniversary of the boys' passing. IDAS were keen to support me and suggested holding a vigil outside Barnsley Town Hall, while Women's Aid arranged for an online one too. The concert was set for October 12, and the vigils were arranged for ten days later. In the middle would be Mum's final farewell on October 18 and I had arranged to record songs for Jack and Paul on September 30.

I had to make the decision to carry on. It would have been so easy to cancel everything and retreat, but I knew I couldn't. And then, as if someone knew I needed a boost, an email landed less than a week after Mum passed, offering me the opportunity to take part in an Opera North project, which involved performing at Leeds Grand theatre. I knew then, more than ever, I had to be brave. By accepting such a unique opportunity, I would be able to honour my mum and carry on the joy the way she had always encouraged me to, in the form of singing and music. I had to do it.

Mum had spent the last years of her life making sure I was still standing, gently reminding me of my focus when I was falling apart and continually doubting myself. She had poured all her strength and resilience into me. I knew I couldn't let her down now and waste all that support she had given me. My voice had been taken away from me by my ex-husband. I couldn't and wouldn't let it happen again. I told myself I would be honouring Mum's loss by carrying on, as opposed to allowing everything to come crashing down around me. I had to push on. I had to exist.

I went ahead with recording my songs for Jack and Paul with

For My Boys

Rob at Carriage House Studio. It had become an annual tradition and I see the recordings as an everlasting tribute to Jack and Paul, a permanent gift of love. Rob has a way of taking your music and creating something special. In 2024, I recorded *I Will Pray For You*, which the boys sang together in the school choir and *Somewhere Over The Rainbow*. When the boys were little, I would often sing that song to them to bring them comfort if they were upset or couldn't sleep. I wish I could say it brought me the same comfort, but sadly it didn't. In many ways it just reminded me of what I had lost. But it still meant a lot to me, so I recorded it a cappella style, a feeling of nostalgia mixed with hopes of better days to come.

After the day of recording it was all action getting ready for the anniversary concert. Alongside the town band and the choir's musical directors, we had carefully chosen the music. The combination was a mixture of uplifting, mixed with a personal account of mine and the boys' lives. I was determined it shouldn't be a morbid and sad affair. I couldn't have faced it if it was full of sadness so, I filled the church with colourful flowers, and the handprints and footprints that Penistone Grammar School students had created and dedicated to the boys ten years earlier.

On the night itself, a montage of pictures of the boys throughout their lives were projected onto a big screen and just seeing their faces smiling back at me spurred me on. I was overwhelmed with how many people came to support the event. The church was full, as 200 friends and family filled the pews.

As I stood on stage and looked around at everyone who had turned up, my heart swelled at the scores of familiar faces who had come along to pay their respects to Jack and Paul. The feeling of love and emotional support was palpable. It was as though I had been swathed, once again, in the arms of a community who had kept me going for ten years.

The music and songs we had chosen filled me with joy and each piece had a personal connection. *Shine* by Take That had always been a favourite of Jack's and he loved to play it on his trumpet. Paul had always adored *Roar* by Katy Perry, he would listen to it on his mp3 player as he stepped out to compete on the running track – it helped him get into the zone and block out everything around him. As I belted out the words, I could feel my youngest son by my side, see his bright smile and feel his determined spirit. Then as we sang Keane's *Somewhere Only We Know*, I remembered how Jack, Paul and I would snuggle under their comfort blankets; our little safe space where no one could hurt us.

Part way through the concert, Luke announced there was a piece he, another musical director, Natalie, and James, the musical director for Barnsley Town Concert Band were going to perform. Luke, who has become a close friend, looked at me and smiled, announcing: 'Claire doesn't know anything about this.'

As soon as he explained they were going to perform *Bring Him Home* from *Les Miserable*s, a shiver ran through me. In 2013, when Jack was only 11, he had stood tall in his band uniform and delivered a hauntingly beautiful rendition of the same piece. He had been so nervous and in the lead up to the performance, we had watched Colm Wilkinson and Alfie Boe sing it over and over again. On the day itself, Jack captured the essence of the piece perfectly, and now over a decade later, Luke, James and Natalie, knowing how much it would mean to me, had brought Jack home, completing the piece that was missing from the evening.

As Luke sang, accompanied by Natalie, and James played the

For My Boys

trumpet, members of the audience held hands and tears rolled down their cheeks. I closed my eyes, and suddenly I couldn't hear James, I could only hear Jack. It was perfect. An incredible act of friendship, that had helped bring the boys into the room, into everyone's hearts, ensuring Jack's music lived on through others. Jack and Paul were only boys, children. Peter Pans forever. For an entire evening, we celebrated their short lives, remembered how they lived, not how they died, and gave them everything they were and adored – rainbows, joy and love. It was a night I will always remember.

I had decided to donate the proceeds from the ticket sales to Nottinghamshire Women's Aid, who had helped me so much over the years and we managed to raise just short of £2,000.

Then, six days later came Mum's final farewell. It was a bright, sunny day and we gathered at Mum's house, one last time as a family, before a service at our Barnsley Crematorium. As we arrived 'Ukuthula' was playing and just like at the boys' anniversary event, we had a montage of photos running through the ceremony. But this time, instead of feeling joy as I watched the pictures of Mum with her children, grandchildren and great-grandchildren, pain smashed into my chest, with the realisation of what could never be again. A huge void of loneliness opened as I said my last goodbyes and it hit me that not only had I lost my children, but I had also now lost both of my parents too.

Somehow, I managed to pull myself together for the candlelit vigil which was held outside Barnsley Town Hall at 6pm on the evening of the 10th anniversary of the fire. IDAS had provided candles, as well as heart-shaped cards for people to write messages on. Representatives from IDAS, the council and Women's Aid made heartfelt speeches, remembering Jack and Paul. As I looked out across the crowds, my eyes filled with tears, and my heart and soul with warmth as I took in how many people had turned out to pack the gardens in front of the Town Hall.

As I stood up to speak, a hush descended across the town centre and suddenly a lump formed in my throat and I couldn't speak. I swallowed and then emotionally reached out to all the people in front of me. I drew on their strength and found my voice, finally able to recount all my favourite memories of the boys.

'Paul earned himself the nickname of Danger Mouse,' I explained. 'He once completed a breakfall over a line of seven children and cleared them all. On another occasion, when he was competing in the long jump, he got his spike stuck in the plate, so his shoe got left behind and he ended up somersaulting into the sand instead.' I smiled as I recounted the time both boys were fighting and Jack got tangled in the curtain, causing the pole to come crashing down.

As the night grew dark and the stars and candles flickered against the sky, we had a moment of silence, and images of my lovely boys appearing in my mind. Then we started to sing *Somewhere Over The Rainbow*, shoulder to shoulder, in unison of body and spirit. People across the country and world joined the vigil online, all of them shining a light on Jack and Paul. It was a wonderful moment but one which simultaneously highlighted all that was wrong with domestic abuse.

On November 4, I travelled back to London and my first stop was a visit to the Women's Aid office, where I was presented with a hardback copy of the Child First campaign, which held the names of all 105,000 signatures. To see the physical, and very tangible, result of the years of hard work, tears and campaigning, against a backdrop of political uncertainty and self-doubt, was overwhelming. My name had also been inscribed in purple ink, the colour of domestic abuse. It's the little things that mean so much.

After many hugs, tea and cake, we went back to 10 Downing Street, to hand in the petition for the second time. I had brought one of my teddies from our last visit. When I had taken him out of my suitcase, a white feather was stuck to his fur, right next to where his heart would have been. We walked through Parliament Square, and I momentarily placed the teddy and a photo of the boys in exactly the same spot I had done years earlier. Then I placed them under the statue of the suffragette, Millicent Fawcett, holding the banner that proclaims 'courage calls to courage everywhere'.

With my friends and allies, we once again passed through security and walked down one of the most famous streets in the world. This time I was accompanied by Mandy and Lucy from Nottinghamshire Women's Aid and Sarah Hill from IDAS, alongside Isabelle and Sophie from Women's Aid. For the second time I banged on the front door. A second time I had been forced to challenge the government over the protection of children who were living, and dying, as they experienced domestic abuse. Yet again, I handed in the petition, which was graciously accepted.

We then headed to a reception in the House of Lords. I felt great comfort and gained confidence in the fact I wasn't walking alone. On the other side of the gates a small army of incredible women, all survivors themselves, were waiting. We were all determined to, once again, get this message across to the government and the new justice secretary Shabana Mahmood. No child should have to die knowing it's at the hands of a parent

– someone who should protect and love them the most, when people in authority and society can prevent it. Safeguarding and protecting children, along with anyone who is suffering abuse, is everyone's business. We should no longer accept the responses that authorities give after the death of a child. Stating harm could not be predicted is not good enough. Lessons need to be learnt, but people will not learn without comprehensive training, accountability and legislation that's fit for purpose.

The reception in the House of Lords was kindly sponsored and held by Baroness Ayesha Hazarika MBE. She is passionate about the life-changing reforms which are needed in the family justice system and therefore added her voice to ours. I was invited to make a speech, but I did roll my eyes as I realised I was literally blending into the very red room, wearing my red dress. Regardless, I stood on stage, surrounded by my formidable team of allies, and spoke words I knew would echo through the House of Lords, if not literally in sound, but in meaning. I named Jack and Paul in the Baroness's presence, and as I did so I saw her very emotional and visceral reaction. My words prompted her to later speak in the Chambers to try and push through the much-needed reform.

26

A FEW days after Mum had passed away, I had made the decision to sign up to one of Opera North's lifelong learning opportunities, following her advice that I should never stop singing. I had already fulfilled one of my greatest dreams to go to Italy and watch an opera in an open-air arena, but I never thought it would be possible to sing a number of choruses from some of the greatest operas ever written and perform them live on stage at Leeds Grand Theatre. I enjoyed every part of the project. As always it felt good to sing and express myself through music. There was one aria, *The Evening Prayer* from the opera *Hansel & Gretel*, that reduced me to tears and cut so hard it physically hurt. '*Where each child lays down its head, angels gather around the bed. Two will stand above me, at my feet two love me.*' It took me back to the moment, when Jack was lying in his hospital bed, fighting for his life. Paul and my dad were already up above, while Mum and I sat touching his legs and feet.

On the night of the Opera North concert, I stood on the stage looking out into the theatre, I knew my music coach would be in the audience. I wanted to do him proud and I also wanted to remember every single second of this once-in-a-lifetime opportunity. If I could commit these precious minutes to memory, I knew they would be there for darker days when life feels impossible. The beauty of the day becoming a beautiful memory tomorrow. So, I took a deep breath, thought of my wonderful boys and sang my heart out.

I do feel very lucky that I have received so much support.

A couple of years earlier, during an event at the grammar school Jack had attended, as part of a remembrance service for former pupils who had fallen during wartime, I met Dr Marie Tidball, who at the time of writing this book, was the Labour MP for my hometown, Penistone, and Stocksbridge. On that icy cold day, we bonded over a cup of tea but more than that, Marie was empathetic and understanding. She was there as I laid a wreath for Jack and Paul under a tree and promised me she would do everything she could to try and help me repeal the presumption of contact from legislation. Marie, a proud Yorkshire lass, full of compassion, was true to her word. In October 2024, the two of us met with Alex Davies-Jones, the Parliamentary Under-Secretary of State for Victims. We discussed the issue of catastrophic harm that presumption of contact causes for children, and ultimately results in many of them dying, including Jack and Paul.

Three months later, a couple of weeks into the new year, Marie invited me to give evidence at a select education committee in relation to the Children's and School's Bill, which is set to be introduced after the death of ten-year-old Sara Sharif, who was cruelly murdered by her father, Urfan Sharif, and her stepmother, Beinash Batool, in August 2023. I was nervous giving evidence, wondering what I could bring to the table and I didn't want to let Marie down, but my past insecurities were raising their head again. I have 20 years of school governance, 15 years of being a safeguarding governor and I have a Level 3 Diploma in Supporting Specialist Learning and Development, let alone my own lived experience of abuse, but I still felt nervous – added to when my train to London was late, and I had to race to get to Westminster on time. In a way though, things going wrong did me a favour because when I reached the committee room with just minutes to spare, my face resembling a ripened tomato, I didn't have time to think about my nerves and doubts.

I did wince though, as I walked into the room as it was named after Margaret Thatcher, who was far from loved in the Yorkshire community I am from. But I had travelled hundreds of miles to talk, so after I was positioned behind the microphone, I took a deep breath, sat tall and let my voice be heard. I explained the importance of children being heard, that their thoughts and opinions mattered and they must be protected. I was one of many witnesses who had been called to talk, including the CEO of Barnardo's and the CEO of the NSPCC. Between us, we did everything we could to elevate the voices of children in the limited time we had.

That night I stayed in London, as Marie had secured a debate around repealing the presumption of contact guidelines in parliament for the next day. As always, I had taken the boys' photo with me. Before putting it in my suitcase, I had traced Jack and Paul's faces with my fingers and drawn on their love. If it was down to me, I would have photographs of every child that had been let down by social care on every page of a document that discussed children's safety. I turned up to parliament the next day and this time I didn't resemble a ripened tomato, but I still had those old familiar nerves in my chest. I didn't want to raise my expectations too high, in case they were knocked back down, but I did want to stay positive and strong.

This time, as it was a parliamentary debate, I wasn't talking, but I was allowed to sit in the room, observe and listen. The first thing I saw was a huge clock that dominated the room, followed by the number of important people who were entering, including the Minister of State for Courts and Legal Services in the Ministry of Justice, Sarah Sackman. It was heartening to see so many MPs from different political parties uniting against presumption of contact. I sat on the front row, cradling Jack and Paul's picture and listened to Marie's powerful speech opening the debate. Their faces were in the room and the Minister, along with all the MPs couldn't ignore the images of my beautiful boys. They weren't just a number or a letter in a stack of review papers. They were real people, whose lives had been lost forever. I sat through MPs raising issues connected to domestic abuse. They peeled away layers of the monstrous onion and sliced it to the grim reality at the core. Women died. Children died. But still the Ministry of Justice would not commit to a date to make an announcement on the findings of the review around presumption of contact or the Harm Report. Instead, all that came was a generic response that they would reveal their findings in the spring.

After the debate finished, several MPs came and shook my hand and took the time to speak to me, including Sarah Sackman. I really appreciated the support everyone showed towards me, it felt as though they had really listened and were kind as they paid tribute to Jack and Paul.

After I left, I walked past a young, homeless man at the top of the stairs to a tube station. I made eye contact and smiled, something I have always done, believing if I can make one person smile, then it might brighten their day. As well as my tattoo being visible, I was wearing a top with the word 'Believe' printed on it, and as I got halfway down the stairs, I heard the man's voice ring out. *'Believe Jack and Paul'*. I stopped, turned around and went back to the man.

For My Boys

This was a man who believed the world had given up on him, and so he had given up on himself. I stood and talked to him as trains and people went by. I explained that so many people had given up on Jack and Paul, but now there were so many who believed in me enough to want to help bring about change. I gently encouraged the young man to go to a homeless charity and ask for help. There is always someone in the world who is ready to help and believe. He didn't ask for any money, and I didn't give him any. Instead, I tried to give him hope and a reason to try and find a better life.

February 2025 was a difficult month, as Mum's birthday is on the fourth and it was a very tough reality check that I had no reason to prepare the living room with banners and surprises, in the same way there was no one to do that for me on the 26th. It was hard not hearing Mum's voice on my birthday, no phone call with her singing happy birthday down the line.

But I'm a great believer that around every corner is something that will pick you up again and on February 28, I was invited to be part of a panel of incredible women speaking at the launch of Lindsey Burrow's book, Take Care, in memory of her former English rugby league and Leeds Rhino husband, Rob, who had lost his battle with Motor Neurone Disease. I've said it before but there's nothing more empowering than women supporting women, lifting each other's spirits, adjusting our crowns and encouraging each other forward. Reminding us to keep strong and believe in ourselves and each other.

In March, Marie Tidball held a parliamentary drop-in session that was open to all MPs to discuss presumption of contact. It was well attended and had cross-party support. Not only are more survivors and victims of abuse going to their MPs, but they are being listened to and those MPs are raising their concerns at Westminster. Marie explained they are asking what is going to be done to protect children. I have done everything I can to make the government listen. I have taken my sons' photo to parliament, I have delivered a petition with over 110,000 signatures, but so far Keir Starmer has done nothing. My question to the Labour government is 'what do you want your legacy to be?'

In June 2025, a new report was published revealing how many children have been murdered in the last nine years. Another 19 children have died at the hands of perpetrators of domestic abuse. In all but one case, the killer was a man and 15 were killed by their own father. Out of the 19, the youngest was just three weeks old and the oldest was 11. In a 30-year period 67 children have been murdered. 67 lives taken away. 67 reports, giving those children a correlating letter of the alphabet, sat in a file in Whitehall. These reports don't tell you their name, what they were like as children or who is grieving the biggest loss now they have been robbed of a life. Jack and Paul are amongst those files and the 67 silent voices, but I have refused to allow my sons' voices to be silenced. And when you think the House of Lords could have repealed presumption of contact in 2021, yet they didn't, and now more children have died.

Not one of those 67 children should have died, 68 if you include Sara Sharif, who was murdered by her father and stepmother. They have all been failed by one government after another. And most of them are reduced to numbers or letters in government files. But each one of those children was a real person, entitled to a happy and full life, free from pain.

Presumption of contact is still prevalent as I write this book.

It still hasn't been removed from legislation and family law. I ask this government, do you want to be known as the latest governing power, following a long line of governments, who continue to fail to protect children? Children who are known to be at risk of harm from abusive parents. Or does Keir Starmer and his government want to be known as the party who gave all victims of abuse brighter, safer, futures, free of harm and oppression?

I have faced up to my failings. I still feel agonising guilt that I didn't do enough to protect Jack and Paul, that I didn't leave my ex-husband sooner, that I allowed the access visits to happen. I live with those heartbreaking consequences every single day, but no government has ever admitted their failings when it comes to legislation that results in children's deaths. That must and has to change. On December 5, 2024, as Women's Aid turned 50, I was lucky enough to meet Queen Camilla for the fourth time at the celebratory event. I will never forget her powerful speech and unshakable belief that one day, maybe not in her lifetime, but eventually domestic abuse will no longer exist.

I hope she is right but for that to happen we must educate and empower young people as well as society as a whole. We have to keep working hard to ensure domestic abuse stops hiding in plain sight. Maybe it won't happen in my lifetime, but it could, with the right support, end within the lifespans of Jack and Paul's friends. It would be the most perfect legacy to my sons if it did. There are six awards in Jack and Paul's names, which encourage children to try hard, never give up and try to be the best version of themselves. These are the morals we need to keep on instilling in children and young people, so they can grow up into good adults. I can only imagine what Jack and Paul would be like today, as men. I hope they would have turned out to be good men. All I can do is catch glimpses of what they might have been like, through seeing their friends.

I have written about 29 years of my life and subsequent existence, and I have written about my boys' entire lives – just nine and 12 years. This book is a truthful, honest and most of all loving testimony to Jack and Paul. As the English painter and poet, David Harkins, said: 'You can shed tears that he is gone, or smile because he has lived'. MP's, ministers and Lords have heard my sons' names said in parliament, seen their photos, and heard me speak. I have carried Jack and Paul's photo to every conference and training event I have spoken at and cradled their image, just like I cradled my sons as babies. I held their photo when I entered the House of Commons, and the House of Lords and knocked on the door of 10 Downing Street. I was never going to let the government cover up their failings by turning Jack and Paul into letters on paper, gathering dust in Whitehall. They are the only two children out of the 67 who have been named. From the moment they both died, I have made it my mission for their names and voices to be heard.

The pain of not seeing my beautiful sons is something that will never go away. It is a grief and love that will haunt me forever – to infinity and beyond. Those words that were once enveloped in love, now have a much more heartbreaking meaning. My legacy to Jack and Paul is still unfinished. I promised my sons as they died in my arms that I would do whatever I could to stop another child suffering in the way they had. I will never stop campaigning and fighting until laws are changed so children are protected. I will not allow Jack and Paul's deaths to be in vain.

Acknowledgements

FIRSTLY I need to pay tribute to my mum who spent the last ten years of her life ensuring and encouraging me to breathe, fight and sing again. Without her unique brand of tough love, resilience and spirit I wouldn't be alive today. Loving thanks also to my family especially my sister Caz who has picked up where Mum left off. Ohana – family where no one gets left behind or forgotten.

Over the last decade I have met some amazing people who I believe came into my life for a reason and were sent by either Jack and Paul or my dad. Some have remained in my life and become friends but all of them have made a positive impact on me that I will always be grateful for, now and always. To all my friends who have been a continual shining light through my darkest times and good times both past and present thank you for always being there and there is a popular saying that if you have been friends for more than 14 years you aren't just friends – you are family.

Music has always played a huge role in my life and is a huge part of who I am. It's a constant presence that brought me joy and peace until it was taken away by Sykes and I was silenced. When I lost Jack and Paul I vowed that I would never sing again. Thanks to Luke Mather and Rob Cooper plus the Barnsley Singers Community Choir I have rediscovered singing and music along with a part of me that had been lost for a long time. I will never let anyone tell me not to sing ever again.

To the Penistone Community, Penistone Round Table and 41 Club, Women's Aid and IDAS there aren't enough words to say how much you have kept me standing. You extended your hand to me, held it tight and haven't let go to this day. It's thanks to you all that I still believe in humanity and love. Love that, wrapped up with the boys' love, gives me the strength and hope to fight for brighter safer futures for others. I am blessed to live in such a amazing community and was even more blessed to be Jack and Paul's mum.

To Michelle and all the team at Mirror Books and Northbank Talent Management thank you for believing in me and allowing me to create a lasting testimony for Jack, Paul and all the children who's childhoods are forever lost to domestic abuse. Michelle, the notebooks and post it notes of doom – purple of course will always be a reminder of the journey we took creating this book alongside a lasting friendship. To infinity and beyond.

Saying Goodbye
By Claire Throssell

Saying goodbye is the hardest thing to do

Because all we want is to stay with you

To share your laughter and wipe away your tears

Listen to your worries and soothe all your fears

Saying goodbye…for now something is ended

And you're broken inside, never to be mended

Time moves forward as it always will

But the moment we lose you, time remains still

We say goodbye to life as it used to be

Just living day by day, holding back our tears to see

But see you we do, in rainbows and the stars that shine up above

For the things we never say goodbye to are memories and love

Sleep peacefully now, wrapped tight in our love, forever a part of our soul

May we one day be united again and then become whole

So when you stand under a sky full of stars and all you feel is pain

Close your eyes, hold tight to the memories and suddenly they will be near us again

Because their love for us is wrapped tight around our hearts and gives us strength within

Goodbye…the hardest word to say or hear but love binds always our hearts as one, helping us love, cry and laugh - their light throughout darkness enduring